The Price of Fire

The Price of Fire
Resource Wars and Social Movements in Bolivia

Benjamin Dangl

AK Press
Edinburgh, Oakland, West Virginia

The Price of Fire: Resource Wars and Social Movements in Bolivia
© 2007 Benjamin Dangl
ISBN 978-1-904859-33-8

Library of Congress Control Number: 2006924196

AK Press
674-A 23rd Street
Oakland, CA 94612
USA
www.akpress.org
akpress@akpress.org

AK Press
PO Box 12766
Edinburgh, EH8 9YE
Scotland
www.akuk.com
ak@akedin.demon.co.uk

The above addresses would be delighted to provide you with the latest AK Press distribution catalog, which features the several thousand books, pamphlets, zines, audio and video products, and stylish apparel published and/or distributed by AK Press. Alternatively, visit our website for the complete catalog, latest news, and secure ordering.

Printed in Canada on acid free, recycled paper with union labor.

Maps used courtesy of the Central Intelligence Agency (really), www.CIA.gov.

Front cover photo by Noah Friedman-Rodovsky (noahfr@gmail.com)
Back cover photo by Jeremy Bigwood (http://jeremybigwood.net)
Cover by Chris Wright (www.seldomwright.com)
Interior design and layout by ZB

Contents

MAP OF BOLIVIA

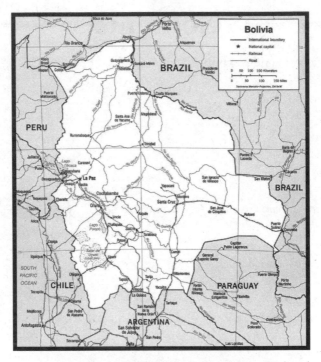

MAP OF SOUTH AMERICA

Author's Note and Acknowledgements

While crossing into Bolivia from Peru for the first time, I ran into a series of protests and road blockades. Angry Bolivian grandmothers with coca leaves in their cheeks tossed grapefruit-sized rocks at our bus windows as I cowered confusedly under my seat. Shortly after that encounter, I arrived in Argentina during the 2001–2002 financial crash. Unemployed workers took over factories, street assemblies between neighbors emerged and the country went through five presidents in two weeks. My small-town, North American brain was dizzied and inspired. I began writing news articles and interviewing people like the women who had tossed rocks at my bus window. This curiosity and note-taking led to *The Price of Fire*, a product of five years of traveling back and forth from the empire to the south, many late night conversations and street protests, press conferences and bus rides.

Yet these pages are the result of more than curiosity. While writing articles from Bolivia during the bloody 2003 Gas War, I was shocked at the lack of attention the conflict received in the English-based media. The more I wrote about Bolivia, and the less big media outlets covered the country, the more I thought about bringing my articles together into a book. *The Price of Fire* is an attempt to counter this lack of information, and ample misinformation, as Bolivia has now entered the international media spotlight.

In writing this book, I wanted to document the regional clash of corporate and people's power, and offer an analytical tool for those interested in a country where Latin America's most powerful social movements have risen up to resist and change destructive economic policies. By spreading information about these inspiring struggles, I hope the book can contribute to a revolution in your home town.

Besides these motives for writing *The Price of Fire*, I agree with author George Orwell, who wrote, "One would never undertake such a thing [write a book] if one were not driven on by some demon whom one can neither resist nor understand. For all one knows that demon is simply the same instinct that makes a baby squall for attention."[1] This demon and others drove me across the continent and back on numerous occasions. During those travels I met countless people who patiently answered questions coming from a bearded gringo with a notepad. I am indebted to those who explained some of the intricacies of this complex

1

region and am grateful to the authors and activists who served as com-
passes throughout the writing process. I also need to thank many people
without whose guidance and support this book would never have been
written.

Thanks to my grandparents, Doc and Betty Summers, for their
example, confidence and enthusiasm from the start. Much love to my
mother and first editor, Suzanne Summers, who is largely to blame for
any lack of grammatical mistakes in this book, and to my father, Jon
Dangl, whose hereditary sense of humor and street wisdom has led me
into and out of all kinds of trouble. Thanks to both my grandparents and
parents for encouraging me to march to the beat of my own typing, and
accepting the collect calls afterward.

Thanks to Nick Alicino, my rebel high school English teacher, who
invited me and many others into the adventure of writing. Robert Rock-
man painstakingly went over each sentence in the novel I wrote in college. His lessons made the writing of this book much easier. Thanks to
Melanie Nicholson, my Spanish teacher, who might not be surprised to
hear that one of her worst students is still in South America. Lucas Palero, a walking history book and natural teacher. The seeds of this book
were first sown during conversations in his family's kitchen.

Rafi Rom not only saved my life during one humid Philadelphian
summer, he saved this book from many shortcomings by editing drafts
and offering the crucial, honest advice of a good friend and careful reader. Mark Engler, Fred Fuentes, Wes Enzinna and Susan Spronk applied
their expertise on Bolivian and Latin American issues through helpful
editorial comments on complicated chapters. Renate Lunn and Mi-
cheál Ó Tuathail helped with interview transcriptions and translations.
Thanks also to Marielle Cauthin for reminding me to get back to work
on the book and to Luis Gonzalez for pulling me away from it.

Thanks to Pablo Gandolfo, a travel companion in Bolivian jungles
and Uruguayan bars, and to Abraham Bojórquez for his music and stories. I am grateful to Leonilda Zurita for opening her home and coca
growing community to me, and to Julio Mamani, who spent many af-
ternoons in El Alto discussing the social fabric and politics of his city.
Carlos Arze unwearyingly deconstructed the labyrinth of the Bolivian
gas industry for me, while Raul Prada illuminated many issues, from the
constituent assembly to the history of capitalism in the Andes. Thanks to
Kathryn Ledebur, whose vast knowledge, advice and clear analysis have
been a wonderful resource from the beginning.

Tom, Meg and Eli Howard have been enthusiastic supporters of this book project, offering their friendship, great food and reasons to leave the computer screen when I needed it the most. Many thanks to Thomas Becker, Nick Buxton, Dana and Charle-Pan Dawson, Matt Dineen, Graham Forward, Carl Irving, the Palero family, Kuky Pardo, Justus Rosenburg, Woody Shaw, Jim Shultz, Peter Sourian, Jason Tockman and Veronica Villarroel for their past and present help and camaraderie. Thanks to the following people and organizations for sharing their stories and analysis and opening some doors for me: Carlos Crespo, Noah Friedman, Claudia Lopez, Pablo Mamani, George Ann Potter, Mark Weisbrot and Raúl Zibechi, *Mujeres Creando*, *Teatro Trono*, and the Bolivia Solidarity Network (BoliviaSolidarity.org).

The great folks at AK Press helped develop this project, get it off the ground and running. Charles Weigl provided good-humored help at crucial stages and Zach Blue has been an excellent editor throughout what has sometimes been a daunting and complicated project. His straightforward advice and insightful editing made this a much better book.

Thanks to Cyril Mychalejko, Jason Wallach, April Howard, and Patricia Simon at *Upside Down World* for picking up the slack while I dug into the research and writing of *The Price of Fire*, and for making the online magazine what it is today. *Toward Freedom* publisher, Robin Lloyd, board members Nat Winthrop, Gerald Colby, Scott Harris, Joy Hopkins, Carol Liu, Anna Manzo, Jay Moore and former editor, Greg Guma, have been very helpful. I am indebted to them for the space and encouragement they provided.

Finally, thanks to April Howard, *mi compañera* and *enamorada*, who helped me make it through that first road blockade in Bolivia and many others. From the initial book outline and each stage of writing, to the cover design, her advice has been essential and refreshing. Her editorial prowess, bountiful knowledge of history, unique analysis and emotional support made writing this book not only possible, but enjoyable.

Though I am grateful for all the help from the people listed here, any weaknesses or mistakes in the book are solely my responsibility.

(Endnotes)

1 George Orwell, *A Collection of Essays by George Orwell* (New York: Harcourt, 1953), p. 316.

Introduction

I t was supposed to be a day of celebration for the Virgin of Rosario, the patron saint of miners. Yet events in Huanuni, Bolivia delayed the festival interminably. In place of the celebration, the archbishop presided over a mass for 16 people killed in a two-day conflict between miners over access to tin deposits. As an uneasy peace returned to the town, a nearby soccer field turned battlefield was still carved up by craters from dynamite explosions and stained red with the blood of miners.[1] The desperation that led the miners of Huanuni to turn their sticks of dynamite into weapons is the product of economic policies that have pitted the poor against the poor, leading Bolivian Vice President Alvaro García Linera to describe Huanuni's tin as "something that should have been a blessing for the country [and] has been turned into a curse."[2]

The clash in Huanuni in October 2006 was but one of many resource conflicts, which continue to ravage Latin America. In the last six years, new struggles and protest movements have emerged in Bolivia over what I have called the "price of fire," access to basic elements of survival—gas, water, land, coca, employment, and other resources. While national and international business and political elites have worked to open Bolivian markets and sell public services to the lowest bidder, the majority of citizens have found that the price of fire has risen beyond their means. In the face of unresponsive government ministers and corporate executives, excluded sectors have often decided to take matters into their own hands. This book looks at these struggles, in which everyday people have risen up against the privatization of survival.

The trajectory of the book uncovers the larger story of a region in revolt, beginning with indigenous uprisings against Spanish rule, focusing in on social movements in the last six years and ending with reports from the first year of the administration of indigenous president Evo Morales. The following chapters view Latin America through the lens of Bolivian protest movements, traveling beyond the landlocked country's borders to make comparisons between similar resource struggles. These narratives also document the recent transition of Latin American leftist movements from the streets into the political office.

Bolivia has been a longtime lab rat for neoliberalism, an economic system that promised increased freedoms, better standards of living and economic prosperity, but in many cases resulted in increased poverty and weakened public services. When the system failed and people resisted, governments applied these policies through the barrel of a gun.

Popular social movements emerged in response to this economic and military violence, leading neoliberalism to dig its own grave in Latin America. *The Price of Fire* tells the story of the successful movements that developed in the wake of these failed military and economic models.

The first chapter is designed to create a political, social and economic context through which the reader can see Bolivian and Latin American resource conflicts as a continuation of past clashes. This includes not only an introduction to the history of Bolivian indigenous, mining, and farmer movements, but also a primer on neoliberal economic policies and imperial strategies in Washington's "backyard."

Bolivian *cocaleros* (coca farmers) organized unions to defend their right to grow coca leaves and resist the military repression of the US War on Drugs. In the second chapter, I address the failures of US-funded anti-coca policies and military activities in Bolivia, and present a history of how one of the country's most powerful social movements grew in the face of repression, transformed itself into a political party and put *cocalero* Evo Morales into the presidential palace.

Though Bolivian social movements have always been strong in the face of corporate robbery, the Cochabamba Water War in 2000 brought international attention to Bolivia from the "anti-globalization" activist community. The residents of Cochabamba rose up when the multinational Bechtel Corporation bought their public and communal water systems. In a classic example of the failure of the privatization of a basic resource, the company's rate hikes and exclusive water rights sparked a revolt that continues to rock the country's social and political landscape. In chapter three I discuss the disastrous effects of corporate control of water, as well as the lasting impacts the 2000 uprising had on Bolivia and the limited success of the subsequently public-controlled water system.

Much of Latin American economics in the last 50 years has been dictated by the forceful advice of financial institutions such as the International Monetary Fund (IMF) and the World Bank. In 2003, Bolivian police took up arms against a government that wanted to slash their pay in an IMF-backed income tax increase. In chapter four, I look at this conflict through the eyes of a soldier turned hip-hop artist and a policeman involved in the street battles, while linking the crisis to Argentina's IMF-inspired crash just two years earlier. Both conflicts exhibit the disparity between what IMF officials advocate and how these policies play out on the ground.

Governments and economies that favor corporations and wealthy elites have created such an unequal distribution of wealth in Latin

America that many people are left without the means to survive.[3] In many cases, the much-needed jobs, land or public space are unoccupied, but off limits. This situation has given rise to social movements which have occupied, defended, and put to use these spaces in order to support themselves, their families, and their communities. In chapter five, I describe common threads between struggles over land in Bolivia, Paraguay, and Brazil and the occupation of factories and businesses by unemployed Argentine workers. I also tell the story of former detainees taking over a jail in Venezuela and transforming it into a community radio station. Each of these occupations was based on the slogan "occupy, resist, produce," a strategy which typifies the larger people's struggle against corporate exploitation and neoliberal displacement.

The history of Latin America has been one of expropriation. Governments and companies first in Europe, and then in the United States, saw these countries as a source of free raw material and open markets for manufactured goods. Resources, and with them workers' rights and public services, have been squashed in a post-colonial free for all. In chapter six, I discuss how Bolivians want their gas reserves used for national development, and how Venezuela has used oil profits for social change. The history of Bolivian gas industrialization and nationalization offers insights into ongoing conflicts over the resource. Though the current nationalization process in Venezuela could be applied to Bolivia, policies in both countries have their faults. Here, I explain how one of the countries with the most wealth in its subsoil can be one of the poorest above ground, and how Bolivians tried to change this resource curse through the Gas War, a popular uprising in 2003 that reversed corporate policies and ousted a president.

Better worlds—some that have lasted, some no more than euphoric glimpses—have been forged by Bolivian community organizations and mobilizations where people created their own infrastructure and banded together to demand necessary changes. In Bolivia, where state rule exerts a historically weak hegemony over the country, power is decidedly in the hands of the people. In the city of El Alto, the indigenous and union roots of rural and mining migrants have created a country within a country. These neighborhood organizations have filled the void of the state to build and maintain public infrastructure, make political and economic decisions, and represent residents. In chapter seven, I discuss the history of this self-made city, its capacity for mobilization and how these grassroots strengths were put to use in the 2003 Gas War.

Next to the social organizations and unions, political artistic movements have flowered in Bolivia, creating change in their own way. Chapter eight looks at three social organizations that do more than protest and lobby government officials. *Teatro Trono*, in El Alto, is a theater troupe of homeless and at-risk children that uses the stage to grapple with difficult social issues and to transform the lives of young actors. The feminist-anarchist group, *Mujeres Creando*, seeks to change the world without taking power, and fights against gender inequality and *machismo* in Bolivia. A growing hip-hop movement in Bolivia is using lyrics in Spanish as well as Quechua and Aymara, the languages of the two largest indigenous groups in Bolivia, as "instruments of struggle." These three groups have collectively built their paradises outside the realm of state and corporate power, widening the capacity for broader social change in Bolivia.

While social movements can oust governments and corporations, they also take their toll on stability and transitions between political leaders. Chapter nine deals with the tightrope walk of Bolivian President Carlos Mesa over a country in turmoil. Conflicts regarding water and gas nationalization re-emerged during his time in office, leading the country once again into a national uprising. In this chapter, I also look at other worker and political gains and challenges in Argentina and Uruguay, where along with Bolivia, people-powered movements gained momentum both in the street and the government palace.

At Evo Morales' traditional inauguration in the ancient Aymaran ruins of Tiwanaku in January 2006, hope was enough to carry the day. Morales, a self-described anti-imperialist, promised radical changes for his impoverished nation, pledging to nationalize gas reserves, expand legal coca markets, redistribute land to poor farmers and organize an assembly to rewrite the country's constitution. While social movements dance with Morales to the music of globalization, the chains of previous neoliberal policies and right-wing governments still hold the country down.

At the time of this writing, Morales' campaign promises are in jeopardy and many wonder if his administration has done all it can to formalize and protect the victories forged in street mobilizations. My analysis of the dynamic Bolivian social movements that have emerged in the past few decades illustrates how organized citizens paved the way to the Morales victory. In the last chapter, the lens widens to include Morales' first several months in office and his place in the current leftist shift sweeping the continent.

This book is a people's account of re-colonization and resistance, with dispatches from the streets, coca farms, mines, and government palaces. It is based on interviews with activists, factory workers, hip-hop artists, Evo Morales, street vendors, policemen, right-wing business owners, and community radio producers. The similarities and differences between the people, movements, and conflicts discussed here have much to teach. They present a range of creative strategies for resisting global neoliberalism in urban and rural settings. They also manifest an affirmation that these struggles are not isolated events, but part of the battle for vital resources in an ever more populated and corporate world.

At best, this book is but one representation of a vast and complex region. My aim is to make complicated issues more accessible and give a human face to the looting and struggles of a continent. Within that goal and scope, there are many important issues and inspiring Latin American movements that time and narrative do not permit me to discuss in the depth they deserve, or at all. I hope, however, that the accounts presented here will be of use to students and workers, activists and academics, travelers and homebodies, and and any combination. In that light, this book provides a colorful introduction to Latin American social movements and resource conflicts, with a focus on Bolivia, as well as new perspectives and insights for experts and longtime observers of a region where corporate globalization has met its match.

Benjamin Dangl
Cochabamba, Bolivia
November 7, 2006

(Endnotes)

1 "Los sectores mineros de Huanuni declaran una tregua," Especiales/Guerra del estaño. La Razón (October 7, 2006). Also "Bolivia deploys 700 police to quell deadly miners' conflict," The Associated Press (October 5, 2006).

2 For more information on this conflict, see April Howard and Benjamin Dangl, "Tin War in Bolivia: Conflict Between Miners Leaves 17 Dead," Upside Down World (October 11, 2006), http://upsidedownworld.org/main/content/view/455/1/.

3 Nearly half of the people living in Latin America and the Caribbean are poor, and nearly 20 percent live in extreme poverty. For more information, see Latin America & the Caribbean, United Nations Population Fund, http://www.unfpa.org/latinamerica/.

Chapter One

Revolution in Reverse

Young miners push a cart of tin ore out of a Cerro
Rico mine in Potosí.

Photo Credit: Benjamin Dangl

"Campesino! Your poverty shall no longer feed the master!"

—Tupak Amaru[1]

The rooster on the side of the road to Potosí did not budge when the bus roared past, its windows rattling with cumbia music. Propaganda from recent elections faded on most of the poor, rural homes. As we neared our destination, a snowstorm of garbage filled the air. Through the colorful debris I saw families picking through trash and a sign welcoming us to the city. Towering over its short buildings and church steeples was *Cerro Rico*, or Rich Hill, the source of the silver that powered Europe's capitalist empire. Like the city that grew out of its riches, the mountain is now a bruised, gutted husk of what it once was. As the bus rolled into town, graffiti on one building announced, "Here there is no president."

Potosí is an example of the looting of Latin America at its worst. Once one of the wealthiest cities in the world, it is now one of the poorest. Its troubles began on a cold night in 1545 when a llama herder camping near Cerro Rico found a vein of almost pure silver. The news of the discovery traveled quickly to the Spanish. They flocked to the city, transforming it into a booming mining town almost overnight. To extract the silver, they forced Bolivian men to work in the mines in horrible conditions for months on end. Residents of the city say the silver taken from Cerro Rico could have built a bridge all the way to Spain. Others say such a bridge could be made out of bones: an estimated eight million people died in the bowels of the mountain.[2]

The slave labor and the ease with which the silver could be extracted transformed Potosí into one of the wealthiest and largest cities of its time. As the Uruguayan author Eduardo Galeano writes, the Spanish living in the silver city were showered with the opulent wealth that Bolivian slaves dug out of the ground. Bull fights and parties were regular occurrences. Gambling houses and dance halls sprouted up and silver-clad horses walked the streets. The "sinful," extravagant lifestyles led by many Spanish in Potosí motivated them to donate handsomely to the Catholic Church in exchange for their own salvation. As a result, at the peak of the silver mines' production, ornate churches nearly outnumbered homes in the city. When the silver ran out, the party was over. The city fell into ruin. One church was transformed into a movie theater, a whorehouse, and eventually a storage area for charity food. An old resident of the city told Galeano that Potosí is "the city which has given most to the world and has the least."[3]

The exploitation of Cerro Rico was a sign of things to come. After the Spanish pillaged and enslaved most of Latin America, the English and North Americans arrived, marking their new territory not with flags, but with company logos, factories, and coups d'états. As time went on, the exploitation that began with Potosí continued in the form of neoliberal economics. For five hundred years, wealth in Europe and the United States depended on poverty in Latin America. As social movements rose up against this systematic looting, they were met with gunfire and torture chambers.[4]

Hundreds of years after the boom and bust of Potosí, I walked its dusty streets. The wealth of the city was gone. The parties and bull fights had ended. Instead of silver-clad horses and gambling houses, there were beggars and moldy churches. In this ghost town, even the living seemed haunted. A young boy used an empty soda bottle as a soccer ball while a drunken man limped past, stopping in front of a brick wall to rant about his wife's infidelity. Handicapped men stumbled over a cobblestone plaza. I asked an old woman selling coca leaves if the men were ex-miners. "We're all from the mines," she said.

Down the street, I listened in a 500-year-old church steeple as Geraldine Poveda, a young student with a head full of Potosí's history, told stories of headless miners flying through the city, ancient balconies full of gold coins, and howling prostitutes in stone towers. "I live in a very old house. There are ghosts in the street all the time," she said. "Just a few years ago, a young girl was chased until dawn by black slaves, horses, and Spanish royalty in 17th century clothing." I looked up to the red mountain that had cursed the city with its own wealth. Although likely the result of an un-mined mineral, the color looked more like the dried blood of Bolivian miners.

Outside the church was a government building with a lady of justice statue perched on the roof. Her scales flailed wildly in the wind, the sound of clanking metal echoed across the cold plaza. To survive, many *Potosínos* had migrated elsewhere. Others, like their ancestors, went back into the mines. Thousands still work in the tunnels of Cerro Rico, searching for what silver, tin, and zinc is left. Though some technology has improved, dozens die each year from accidents and lung disease. At a market below the mountain, vendors sell coca, dynamite, and other mining equipment. A local drink, which happens to be 98 proof, is a popular item in the stores. "Miners drink a lot because they know they

won't live long," Roberto Mendez, an ex-miner, told me through a tooth-
less smile.

Inside the mines of Cerro Rico, dynamite explosions rattled the
walls intermittently, raining down dust and rocks. While I breathed in
the dank, toxic air, miners chipped away at the walls with the same style
of tools that had been used for centuries. Outside the entrance, two children hunched over wheelbarrows. The expression on ten year old Ha-
cunda Copa's face hinted at his misery. Whereas older workers had solid
helmets, all this boy could afford was a cracked one, with a hole in the
back. Copa said he had to work to help feed his younger brothers. His
father had died in the mines and his mother washed clothes for a living.
"I have to work, otherwise my younger brothers can't eat," he said.[5]

Later that same day I sat in an empty park chewing coca leaves.
The only sound I heard was the rattle of soda bottles being delivered to
a nearby store. In the middle of the park stood a broken fountain with a
question mark messily spray painted onto its base. This question mark
begs many answers, answers that have their beginnings in Bolivia's
countless stories of popular resistance against exploitation of labor and
natural resources. Although the legacy of pain and looting lives on in Potosí, other regions of Bolivia still carry on centuries-old struggles. One
of the greatest stories of resistance to colonialism in Bolivia is that of the
1781 siege of the city of La Paz, led by indigenous rebel Tupak Katari.

Like many other eighteenth century workers in the *altiplano*, a
high, flat arid region in the Andes, Julian Apaza sold coca and wove
clothing for a living. Through his work-related travels, he developed
ties with people in the region that would later aid him in insurrections
against the Spanish. He took on the name Tupak Katari in homage to
two other contemporary dissidents in whose footsteps he followed. One
of them was Tomás Katari, a direct descendent of Incan royalty who
tried to regain his leadership position through legal means. In 1778, he
walked all the way to Buenos Aires, Argentina from Potosí to speak with
the Viceroy of Spain about the injustices the Andean indigenous faced
under Spanish colonialism.[6] The elite ruled Bolivia with an iron fist,
forcing indigenous people into slavery in mines and large farms, taking
their land and coercing them into paying exorbitant taxes.[7] Tomás Katari
fought to abolish such colonial repression and replace Spanish authorities with indigenous leaders.[8]

Tupac Amaru, from which Julian Apaza took the first part of his
rebel name, was also a descendent of Incan emperors. He was literate
and had connections in high places in Andean society, which he uti-

lized for subversive activities. In the famous revolt of Tinta, a community which had been depopulated due to forced slavery in Cerro Rico,
Tupac Amaru condemned local Spanish leaders to death and issued
a decree that abolished slavery and taxes to Spain. His battle cry was,
"*Campesino*! Your poverty shall no longer feed the master!"[9] Amaru
and his colleagues were captured after he led a siege of Cuzco, Peru in
March, 1780.[10] Amaru's Spanish captors intended to quarter him, but
his body wouldn't break easily. When the soldiers finally dismembered
him, they sent different parts of his body around the region to intimidate supporters.[11]

In response to such brutality, revolts broke out across the Andes
against Spanish rule. Large rebel militias, armed with rocks and clubs,
succeeded in overpowering the Spanish occasionally, but were quickly
suppressed with firepower. In response to regional uprisings, the Spanish living in La Paz constructed a wall around their valley city of 30,000.
The wall did not stop Julian Apaza—a.k.a Tupak Katari—and his wife,
Bartolina Sisa, from leading a siege of the city in March, 1781. They
launched rocks from high plains above La Paz—now the city of El Alto,
burned down buildings, and blocked all routes in and out of the city.
This first siege of La Paz lasted 109 days. From their base in El Alto, Katari and Sisa mocked colonial masters by taking on Spanish names, eating with silver utensils and dressing in their oppressors' fancy clothes. At
night the indigenous army sang, danced, and raised a celebratory ruckus
in order to keep the Spanish below from sleeping.[12]

For the Spanish, these sleepless nights were torture. Worse still
was their diet. La Paz residents, cut off from standard food supplies,
were forced to eat dead rats, dogs, and mules. Many subsequently died
from infections and malnutrition. Still, the indigenous army's cunning
and persistence was no match for the Spanish reinforcements, which arrived in the city and temporarily ended the siege. Sisa was captured after
being betrayed by close allies.[13]

Though some rebels fled when the Spanish troops arrived, others
remained to prepare for a second siege, which began on a cold day in
early August, 1781.[14] Besides slinging rocks, building road blockades,
and burning down homes, the indigenous rebels built a conduit to redirect water from the mountains into the city. The tactic worked. A witness to the event wrote that around 15,000 La Paz residents were killed
in the subsequent inundation. Throughout the second siege, Tupak
Katari tried to free Sisa, but failed. The Spanish made an example of her,
as they had of Tupac Amaru. After they tortured, raped, whipped, and

dragged her by horses on the ground, they hung and decapitated her, then displayed her head in various towns to frighten her followers into submission.[15] On October 17th, Spanish troops regrouped and attacked Katari's forces, breaking the siege. The indigenous army continued to resist, but Katari was overtaken by the Spanish and, like his predecessor, quartered. Before his death he promised, "I will come back, and I will be millions."[16]

Spanish fears of a successful insurrection were well-founded. The spirit of Katari returned again and again in the form of miners, farmers, indigenous people, and workers who revolted against similar exploitation.[17] Like Katari and Sisa, they were violently crushed. Though the rebellions in Katari's time would serve as an example for generations of oppressed people to come, the goals of his movement would not be realized for decades. Bolivia was the first South American country to rebel against Spanish rule, and, in 1825, the last to win independence. When Bolivia's first constitution was drafted in 1826 by Simon Bolívar, he stated that the country would "be known as an independent nation."[18] Constitutional rights went unenforced, however, and many inequalities persisted. Katari's demands were echoed among workers in the Revolution of 1952, and 50 years later among citizens protesting neoliberal policies.[19] El Alto served as a launching point for these future struggles.

Popular ferment among workers and farmers paved the way to the 1952 Revolution. Throughout the 1940s, rural peasant farmers called *campesinos*, in tandem with the miners, coordinated national strikes, boycotts, and protests demanding access to education, land, and better salaries and working conditions. Common at the time were the non-violent *huelgas de brazos caidos*—fallen arm strikes—organized in the middle of a harvest time in response to forced labor without pay. Through these actions, which stopped the transportation of products and work in fields, pacts were formed between urban workers and *campesinos*. In 1940, there were 43 such strikes in large farms within the department of Oruro alone, many of which were met with repression from land owners, police and military forces.[20]

Throughout 1947, the smallest sign that any kind of worker organization was being formed was a cause for bloodshed.[21] Different police and military outposts were established in the *altiplano* and other areas with frequent indigenous uprisings. A slogan at this time among Quechuas and Aymaras illustrated their courage and creative resistance:

"You have weapons and planes, but we will invade the cities from under-ground."[22]

Campesinos, workers, and miners united in their demands and in 1952, their revolutionary fervor was carefully channeled into the National Revolutionary Movement (MNR) party.[23] The MNR was a product of camaraderie in the trenches of the Chaco War in the 1930s, and was led by students and veterans from the elite classes. Though many believed in its cause, the MNR would never be the true vehicle of change. In September of 1949, Siles Zuazo, a leader in the party, organized a revolt against the government in all major Bolivian cities. Government forces crushed the rebellion—made up entirely of armed citizens—in two months. In spite of this loss, the MNR continued to gain support, particularly among labor organizations. The party ran Victor Paz Estenssoro as their candidate for change in 1951. He won a clear victory, but the army intervened, placing General Hugo Ballivian in Estenssoro's rightful place. The MNR knew that taking power by force was their only option.[24]

On the night of April 10th, 1952, the army, with Ballivian at the helm, called for all lights to be put out in La Paz in order to disorient the armed MNR rebels poised to attack. However, a full moon lit the terrain, providing the rebels a problem-free descent into the city from El Alto. MNR forces quickly trapped the army by blocking key routes to and within the city. Uprisings against the illegitimate military government flared up around the country. In some cases, police and military joined the rebels or surrendered.[25] After three days of bloodshed had left over 600 dead, the MNR took control of the government.[26] Decades later, even after a significant weakening of the MNR platform, the arrival of miners in La Paz from other areas of the country still struck fear in the hearts of the elite and right-wing politicians. With their helmets and sticks of dynamite, the miners continued to serve as a powerful symbol of rebellion.[27]

Estenssoro arrived in the El Alto airport from exile in Buenos Aires, Argentina, on April 15th, 1952. He exited the plane, met by a crowd of 7,000 people waving placards that read "Nationalization of the mines," "Agrarian Reform," and "Welcome, father of the poor." The crowd was so large that it took Estenssoro thirty minutes to walk half a block to the presidential palace. The first words of his first presidential speech were in Aymara, the language most of the audience spoke: "*Jacca t'anta uth-jani*," he promised—"There will be a lot of bread."[28]

Three days after Estenssoro assumed power, the recently founded Bolivian Workers' Center (COB) demanded that the MNR nationalize the country's mines without payment to owners, redistribute land to poor farmers, grant citizens universal suffrage, and formalize the armed worker and *campesino* militias as a replacement for the military. Such demands coming from the COB and other worker and farmer movements pushed the MNR to make radical changes, though Bolivians have never seen the full enactment of those demands.[29]

On July 21ˢᵗ, 1952, the government established the right to vote for all Bolivians over the age of 21, bringing 80 percent of the formerly ignored indigenous population into the electorate. In spite of this hopeful move, democracy was not truly established. Yet rights were gained nonetheless, and gained in the way that Bolivians have often found most successful: through pressuring powerful institutions from below, and with the tools at hand. *Campesinos* and rural workers' unions, using their weapons from the Revolution, applied their own systems of justice through militias, took over land, reorganized systems of production and often superceded the power of local political authorities.[30] Every one of these changes was proposed, enacted and enforced at the grassroots level: once in power, the leaders of the MNR were unwilling to jeopardize their own supremacy.

Due to pressure from their base of labor organizations and miners, the MNR signed a decree that nationalized the country's mines on October 31ˢᵗ, 1952. An enormous crowd of miners gathered at the event to celebrate the signing with cheers, dynamite explosions and gunshots into the air. The festivities raged for days. The worker-run Bolivian Mining Corporation (COMIBOL) took over the operation of 163 mines and 29,000 workers formerly controlled by the three 'mining baron' families: Patiño, Hochschild and Aramayo.[31] In spite of the COB's demands not to pay the owners a cent, the families were given $27 million to 'buy back' Bolivia's underground wealth.

When she was a young girl, Domitila Barrios de Chungara, a woman from a mining family, heard a story from her father, a radical miner during the Revolution of 1952. He explained the anger he felt about the payment to the mine owners through a story about a doll. "Suppose that I bought you a beautiful doll or one of those puppets that can walk and talk," he told her. Then the doll is stolen by a man who makes it work a lot. "But one day, after so much fighting, you grab [the man] and hit him hard and take the doll away from him." After so long, the doll is dirty, broken and weak. "[S]hould you pay him for the way the doll has aged? Don't you see you shouldn't? It's the same with the 'tin barons' who've gotten rich with our mine."[32]

Meanwhile, pressure continued from below to radicalize the MNR government. Poor, armed *campesinos* in various parts of the country occupied land and pressured the government to break up large farms and expropriate and redistribute land.[33] In August of 1953, the MNR passed the Agrarian Reform Law to meet these demands and appease protesting grassroots organizations, but that didn't mean that they were planning to enforce it. On a national level, the land reform only affected 28.5 percent of large landowners. As time went on, right-wing elements within the MNR co-opted and weakened the social movements that had brought it to power, pushing these radical labor and agrarian groups— particularly the COB—out of the political sphere.[34]

The momentum existed in the Revolution of 1952 to put power into the hands of the poor majority of the country. This did not happen. Instead, according to Barrios de Chungara, the "new bourgeoisie" in power began "undoing the revolution" despite the fact that the revolution was made by the working poor. "Everything's been betrayed because we left the power in the hands of greedy people," she said, explaining that most changes were enacted simply to help a new batch of people get richer.[35]

On May 14th, 1953, Estenssoro applied policies pushed by the World Bank and International Monetary Fund (IMF), leading to inflation that tripled the cost of living in Bolivia. Though international financial institutions' policies at that time did not include the privatization of state-owned enterprises, which would later cause conflicts over gas and water, they still favored the interests of corporate and political elites and paved the way for the use of Bolivia, among other Latin American countries, as a laboratory for economic policies designed in Washington and corporate board rooms.[36]

At the start of his third term, a military junta overthrew Estenssoro's government, marking the beginning of military rule which continued off and on until 1982. Though major changes were enacted in the areas of voting, education, land reform, and the mining industry, the 1952 Revolution's dream would soon turn into a dictatorial nightmare as Latin America entered the Cold War.[37]

Throughout Latin American history, those in power have used repression to sustain a system of exploitation that keeps labor cheap, land in the hands of a few and natural resources open for colonial and corporate looting. The region is currently recovering from dictatorships and destructive economic policies introduced during the Cold War. Before looking at Bolivia at the turn of the 21st century, it is important to understand the recent history from which the region is emerging. In many ways, current social movements are a result of state repression and failed economic policies.[38]

Once most Latin American nations gained independence from their Spanish masters in the first quarter of the 19th century, overseas empires vetted for power in the region. While Latin American nationalists prepared to gain control over their own resources and industries, foreign businesses stepped in line to make sure that Latin America's wealth would never stay on the continent. By the beginning of the 20th century, Washington and US corporations had taken the strongest foothold in Latin America. Control over the region was sealed after the US victory against Spain in the 1898 Cuban-Spanish war. Though the US had promised Cuban revolutionaries it would leave after the country gained its freedom from Spain, when the Spanish were kicked out, the US stayed on, enjoying the benefits of owning another country. The logos of Coca-Cola, Nestle, Ford, and the United Fruit Company were the flags of the new colonizers. In this form of re-colonization, Washington used military regimes to usher in new economic policies, which facilitated US corporate exploitation.[39]

Latin American workers, farmers, students, and families resisted this corporate colonialism, demanding better wages, working conditions, distribution of land, health care, and education. Though this movement brought socialist governments to office in Nicaragua and Chile, radical groups in Argentina, Bolivia, Uruguay, and elsewhere were repressed before taking power. These groups fought to "nationalize" industries by making the state the owner, and redirect profits to social programs and services. Meanwhile, violence, torture, and death began to accompany the application of right-wing economic policies. Governments backed by international corporate interests used military and police to clear the way for the neoliberal revolution in reverse, favoring "privatization" of industries and resources by putting them into corporate hands.

The Cold War offered the US government a continued pretext to back a number of Latin American dictators who cracked down on civil liberties in order to reshape the region into an entity easier to economically manipulate, exploit, and dominate. Regardless of which policy or politician Latin Americans voted for, the destiny of their nation was often controlled from offices in Washington.

Hope in Guatemala was met with indirect gunfire from Washington. That hope was embodied by Jacabo Arbenz, the Guatemalan president who legalized the country's communist party, gave more rights to labor unions, and took unused land from the United Fruit Company and redistributed it to poor farmers. Before he came to power, 2.2 percent of the landowners in the country owned 70 percent of Guatemalan land.[40] In 1954, the CIA (Central Intelligence Agency), which had been created just a few years earlier, conducted its first covert operation in Latin America. Agents took control of the Guatemalan media, broke down the country's economy, trained mercenaries, organized bombings, and spread destructive rumors and fear throughout the country. The psychological warfare was effective: the CIA frightened the population into submission and the military was too frightened to defend the president. Arbenz was overthrown and a military junta close to Washington's interests was put in his place. This coup model was later applied in other Latin American countries. Che Guevara—who, alongside Fidel Castro, led the 1959 Cuban Revolution—was in Guatemala at the time as part of his tour of South America, and witnessed covert US tactics firsthand from the refuge of the Argentine embassy.[41]

The Cuban Revolution in 1959 overthrew the US-friendly Batista government, initiated socialist changes throughout the country and sparked fear in the hearts of Washington politicians and business leaders who believed such tendencies could spread to other Latin American countries, threatening US corporate interests. These elite powers interpreted any country's desire for self-determination and self-sufficiency as "anti-Americanism."[42] To prevent a socialist expansion, crackdowns increased on the region's leftist organizations, unions, and student groups.[43] As Latin American countries became more nationalistic, the US government became more adept at muscling its way into presidential palaces in the region.

In the mid-1960s the Business Group for Latin America was organized to influence Washington's Latin American policies and support election campaigns among politicians who were friendly to their interests. Its members included thirty-seven corporations such as US Steel, United Fruit, Ford, Anaconda Copper, and Chase Manhattan Bank. The group's activities were led by David Rockefeller, whose family had been acquiring massive amounts of land in the region since the 19th century. Rockefeller worked as the group's connection to the White House to help open up the region to business. When their overt tactics did not do the job, the Business Group for Latin America worked alongside the CIA to create coups against populist governments in Brazil in 1964 and Chile in 1973, which sought to seize international corporate property in their countries. Major companies operating in the region such as Ford, Coca-Cola, Mercedes-Benz, and Del Monte have been accused of collaborating with death squads in Central America and crushing labor unions.[44] The Ford Motor Company provided military dictatorships in Argentina with the infamous green falcons that were used to kidnap suspected dissidents, and offered its manufacturing plant near Buenos Aires as a base for imprisoning and torturing victims of the dictatorship.[45]

The economic model pushed by the Washington and US companies has changed names and philosophies over the years, but has always enforced the same belief: that Latin America should be a cheap source of raw materials and labor, and a forced market for US goods. In the 1980s, the policies that enforced those beliefs came together under the umbrella of "neoliberalism." Neoliberalism's objectives were the deregulation of the economy and the attraction of foreign investors. Across Latin America, trade barriers were removed, labor and environmental laws were loosened, tax breaks were given to foreign companies, and public telephones, water systems, railroads and electricity were "privatized" and sold to supposedly less corrupt and more efficient multinational corporations. Spending on education, health care, and public transportation was slashed.

Proponents of neoliberalism contend that government participation in the economy (state owned businesses), or regulation of the economy (taxes that favor internally produced goods) prevent full economic growth. Neoliberal economists touted competitive capitalism as the only way to ensure the development of a free society. By limiting the authority of the government, and putting economic power into the hands of the market, neoliberal policy makers hoped to guarantee more individual freedoms.[46] Throughout the 1960s and beyond, nascent neoliberal economists used Latin America as their laboratory. In recent years, Latin Americans have lived the results. Instead of creating promised jobs, economic mobility and expanded freedoms, neoliberalism increasingly concentrated wealth in the hands of a few and bolstered global capitalism.

While open markets paved the way for a flood of US goods, the wages and working conditions of Latin Americans worsened and local businesses were destroyed in the face of powerful foreign companies. Puppet governments encouraged exportation of raw materials for cheap prices. Without strict labor laws, workers were hired and fired with ease. National businesses struggled to compete with cheaper imported prod-

ucts. The privatization of water, electric, and everything from garbage
collection to postal services resulted in a rise in the cost of living. Money
was taken from the government and sent to the coffers of foreign companies. In the US, corporate leaders pitched the idea that by opening up
and "freeing" their economies, two nations could healthily compete and
benefit from new markets and products. However, under neoliberal rule,
the strong (US and European companies) survived, and the weak were
destroyed.[47]

When neoliberal policies have to be implemented and maintained
with force, it is a sure sign that they have failed. Leaders in Washington
were unwilling to let go of their policies, and were increasingly willing to
lend a covert hand in enforcing them.[48] In 1975, George Bush Sr., then
director of the CIA, worked with Secretary of State Henry Kissinger to
develop Plan Condor, an operation designed to suppress and dominate
the region's leftist movements and governments.[49] The Plan involved
assassination teams and support for dictators that were warm to Washington's interests.[50] Many hopeful Latin American movements and governments were targeted.

One movement against corporate exploitation occurred in 1979,
led by an army of young guerrillas who called themselves Sandinistas in
homage to Nicaraguan freedom fighter Ernesto Sandino.[51] The Sandinistas took over the government of the corrupt Somoza regime. The Somoza family, which had run Nicaragua for decades, crushing any opposition
to their power, owned nearly all the land and industries in the country.
After their victory, the Sandinistas enacted radical changes, redistributed land, made health care and education widely accessible and created
a society with more opportunities for the country's downtrodden. Need-
less to say, in the midst of the Cold War, the socialist Sandinistas were
not warmly welcomed by Washington. The Reagan administration organized and funded a counterinsurgency army called the Contras to fight
the Sandinistas. This US-backed group wreaked havoc upon the people
of Nicaragua for nearly a decade.

Twelve years after the end of the Sandinista government, I visited
Nicaragua, my head full of images and stories of the revolution. When I
arrived in what is now one of the poorest countries in the hemisphere, I
realized that Nicaragua had reverted to its pre-revolution days, if it had
ever really managed to leave them. Unemployment, inequality, corporate exploitation, and unequal distribution of land wracked the nation.
In León, I saw murals depicting the bloodied hope of the 1980s, and

hopped on top of a bus to Miraflores, a farming community in the north, where the revolution's ethics and bright eyed plans are still put to use.

Within Miraflores everyone owns land, pools their labor and resources together, and makes decisions collectively. Many residents are ex-Sandinista fighters and have the missing legs or fingers to prove it. In one home, my host sat by a lantern at night and told me stories of *La Guerra* (the war). He accentuated each account with his shaking fist, from which a mine explosion had taken two fingers. Among other gory tales of death and suffering, he told of the how the Contras put heads on posts to scare the Sandinistas away. Though Nicaraguans had land, access to education and healthcare in the 1980s, many were often too busy fighting to enjoy it. His neighbors pointed to nearby hills, indicating with tears in their eyes where a brother or aunt was killed. Their stories were present, palpable. *La Guerra* was just yesterday. It was everywhere.

Nicaragua was not the only Central American country to feel the wrath of the Cold War. From 1976 to 1983, Washington supported a devastating military dictatorship in Argentina that ran all branches of government, outlawed elections, and encouraged school and business leaders to provide information on subversive people. The administration took control of the police, banned political and union organizations, and tried to eliminate all oppositional elements in the country through harassment, torture, and murder. Journalists, students, and union members faced a particularly large amount of bloody repression, thus ridding the nation of a whole generation of social movement leaders. As was the case in other Latin American countries, the threat of communism and armed guerrilla movements was used as an excuse for Argentina's dictatorial crackdowns. Hundreds of torture camps and prisons were created. Many of the dead were put into mass graves or thrown out of planes into the ocean. Five hundred babies of the murdered were given to torturers' families and the assets of the dead totaling in the tens of millions of dollars, were all divided up among the perpetrators of the nightmare. Thirty thousand people were killed in Argentina's repression.[52] In the wake of this horror, mothers of the disappeared regularly marched in Argentina's Plaza de Mayo, earning the name *Madres de la Plaza de Mayo*. These women organized for justice and human rights, demanding to know the location of their disappeared children.[53]

During this time, Latin America hemorrhaged blood. In December 1981, in the rural, indigenous village of El Mozote, El Salvador, the Atlacatl Battalion—Guatemalan soldiers trained by US military operatives—massacred 750 people, including hundreds of children under twelve. Soldiers shot, stabbed, decapitated, and amputated arms, legs and genitalia from their victims. Some reported that fetuses were cut out of pregnant women, and that children were smashed against rocks or thrown into rivers while their parents watched. Investigations revealed that the bullets used in this massacre were manufactured in the US. John Waghelstein was the leader of the US military's advisory team in El Salvador at the time. He served two tours in Vietnam and focused his military training on "going primitive." Such tactics were implemented in what turned into a thirty-five year civil conflict that left an estimated 200,000 people dead.[54]

In 1970, the socialist doctor Salvador Allende was democratically elected in Chile. The Nixon administration in the US feared his leftist projects would succeed, thus providing an example for the rest of the region. "I don't see why we need to stand by and watch a country go communist because of the irresponsibility of its people," National Security Advisor, Henry Kissinger said of Chile in 1970.[55] In the three years that Allende led the country, he nationalized the copper industry, the telephone companies, and the banks. He created universal education and health care and fought for the rights of women and workers. These were major advances, particularly taking into account the extent to which he was targeted by the Nixon administration from the start. Washington worked to destabilize his government through the CIA, funding and supporting anti-Allende groups and media in Chile. One of their key allies became the military general Augusto Pinochet, who led a successful coup against Allende on September 11th, 1973. Pinochet's 16-year dictatorship, which began in the bombed-out rubble of the government palace, left 3,000 dead and disappeared, and many more tortured and traumatized.[56]

Pinochet's rule in Chile offers one of the clearest examples of how the application of neoliberal policies in Latin America went hand in hand with dictatorial repression. Economists from the University of Chicago, known as the "Chicago Boys"—Milton Friedman, Friedrich von Hayek and Arnold Harberger—were essential architects of Chile's neoliberal economy. Their philosophy involved clamping down on labor unions and leftist political parties that posed a threat to their vision. When Pinochet overthrew Allende in 1973 and unleashed a fury of repression against union and leftist political organizers, the time was ripe for the Chicago Boys to get to work. The dictator invited them to Chile where they were placed in charge of the country's economy. From their posts they made sure the state didn't interfere in the economy and that foreign investment flourished.[57] The Chicago Boys cut state spending and removed restrictions on foreign investment. Tens of thousands of public employees were dismissed when the government sold over 400 state industries to private companies.[58] However, even Pinochet recognized that the policies were too harsh, and revoked some of the Chicago Boys' most drastic measures soon after they were implemented.

The scale of these economic policies and the brutal tactics used to enforce them were topics that military governments kept quiet about. It has taken years for citizens to gain access to information about how and why such violence was visited on them. Years after the dictatorship in Chile, the ghosts of Pinochet's rule still haunt the country. In 2003, on the 30th anniversary of Pinochet's US-backed military coup, half of the people on Santiago's busiest street were shopping. The other half were protesting against the government's reluctance to take sides in the 30-year-old argument about the events surrounding the coup. Weeks of reflection and discussion to mark the anniversary were well under way. Chile's television stations and newspapers were swamped with a mixture of nostalgic, historical, and new information regarding the coup and Allende's presidency. City-wide conferences, rallies, concerts, and lectures on the controversial events continued every day, all day.[59]

Much of the 'new' information being shown on TV and printed in newspapers was only new in Chile, and had been available to the rest of the world for decades. Aldo Casali, a history and economics professor at the Universidad de Diego Portales in Santiago, told me: "When someone asks what we have learned socially in these 30 years, I don't know because we have only recently begun to talk [about it] seriously."

For countless Chileans, allowing Pinochet and his collaborators to go free is like trying to move forward without a memory. Miguel Faure, a student activist at the Universidad de Chile, said, "For us, political stability without justice is a time bomb. People are looking for justice, not only for the dead, but to make sure that this doesn't happen again, because we are not convinced that [it] cannot happen again at any moment, in any country in Latin America."[60]

These years of dictatorships ravaged Bolivia as they did the rest of the region. Various dictators came and went in Bolivia from 1964 to 1982, crushing leftist movements with a mixture of harmful economic policies, intimidation, torture, and murder. Military General Hugo Banzer took power in 1971, leading the country with an iron fist until 1978. Luís García Meza ruled in the early 1980s with fascist tendencies encouraged by such advisors as former Nazi Klaus Barbie.[61]

In El Alto, Bolivia a theater company called *Teatro Trono* works
with homeless children and youth with family or economic troubles.
One of their plays touches upon Bolivia's years under dictatorship. A
gripping scene begins when a military official screams into the crowd,
"I smell subversives!" A few members of the audience are hauled onto
the stage, tied up, and dragged off as the military man says, "I want to
put a bullet in some commie's head." Festive Andean music—the kind
one hears at parties, parades and dances—blares ironically in the background while a handful of men and women are tied up and thrown to
the ground. The torturing begins, and screams fill the air. A metal cir-
cular saw presses against a metal bar, spraying sparks all over the stage.
The sound of grinding metal, screams of "Stop! Stop!" and the music
converge in a crescendo while a toilet is dragged onto the stage. An actor
sits down on it and says, "Neoliberalism will help us develop. It will help
our future."

Perhaps the most devastating of neoliberal policies advocated
by Bolivian leaders was applied in 1985, when poverty soared, wages
dropped, and the government was unable to pay its debt to the IMF.[62]
This insolvency was punished by international financial institutions
like the World Bank, which stopped lending Bolivia money. Luckily, the
US came to the "rescue": the economist and Harvard professor Jeffrey
Sachs drew up a plan to save the country. A priority of his strategy was
enabling Bolivia to continue making debt payments to the IMF. The plan,
called Decree 21060, included the removal of trade restrictions, freezing
public sector wages and firing thousands of public employees.

The Bolivian government adopted the decree, a move applauded
by the IMF, which subsequently gave Bolivia $57 million in credit.
Though the decree stabilized the economy for a while, Bolivia's poorest were hit hard with a rise in unemployment and a drop in wages. The
move also hurt poor farmers as it directed investment and credit toward
larger agricultural producers and lowered trade barriers to allow the
importation of cheap agricultural products. The decree's application
resulted in a rise in unemployment which sent thousands of workers to
the informal economic sector as street vendors. At the same time, a drop
in tin prices forced many mines to close, putting over 25,000 miners out
of work.[63] The neoliberal regime continued, however, and from 1993 to
1997 President Gonzalo Sánchez de Lozada privatized dozens of public
industries, redirecting the country's natural wealth into the hands of foreign corporations.[64] Sickness, malnutrition, and unemployment grew to

plague a majority of the population.[65] Currently, around half of Bolivia's population of nine million earns less than two dollars a day.[66]

Over the last 25 years, according to political analyst Noam Chomsky,

> the countries that have adhered to the neoliberal rules have had an economic catastrophe and the countries that didn't pay any intention to the rules grew and developed. East Asia developed rapidly pretty much by totally ignoring the rules. Chile is claimed as being a market economy but that's highly misleading: its main export is a very efficient state owned copper company nationalized under Allende. You don't get correlations like this in economics very often. Adherence to the neoliberal rules has been associated with economic failure and violation of them with economic success: it's very hard to miss that. Maybe some economists can miss it but people don't: they live it. ... [T]here is an uprising against it.[67]

This uprising gained momentum by the turn of the 21st century, when many Latin Americans emerged from the wreckage of neoliberalism to protest against state repression and corporate exploitation. The backlash of neoliberalism brought on a new wave of change. Social movements and labor organizations entered the new millennium empowered by the lessons and legacies of revolts such as those led by Tupac Katari, the workers in Bolivia's 1952 Revolution, and the victories of the Sandinistas in Nicaragua and Allende in Chile. Movements rose up against the looting and terror that cursed the region. However, nowhere else in Latin America did corporate globalization wreak as much havoc as it did on Bolivia. Nowhere else has the people's resistance been so strong.

(Endnotes)

1 Eduardo Galeano, *Open Veins of Latin America*, trans. Cedric Belfrage (New York: Monthly Review Press, 1973), 44–46.

2 Ibid., 20–22, 32, 34

3 Ibid.

4 The idea that wealth exists in the north because of poverty in the south is a key theme throughout Galeano's *Open Veins*.

5 For more on miners' lives in Potosí, see René Poppe, *Compañeros del Tio (Cuentos Mineros)*. La Paz: Plurals Editores, 1977.

6 Herbert S. Klein, *A Concise History of Bolivia* (Cambridge: Cambridge University Press, 2003), 74–75.

7 Benjamin Kohl and Linda Farthing, *Impasse in Bolivia: Neoliberal Hegemony and Popular Resistance* (New York: Zed Books, 2006), 39.

8   Sinclair Thomson, "'Cuando sólo se reinasen los indios': Recuperando la variedad de proyectos anticoloniales entre los comunitarios andinos (La Paz, 1740–1781)" in *Ya es Otro Tiempo el Presente*, Forrest Hylton, Feliz Patsi, Sergio Serulinikov and Sinclair Thomson (La Paz: Muela del Diablo Editores, 2005), 43.
9   Galeano, *Open Veins*, 44–46.
10 Klein, *A Concise History*, 75–76.
11 Galeano, *Open Veins*, 44–46.
12 Pablo Solón, *Bartolina Sisa* (La Paz: Fundación Solón, 1999),1–10.
13 Ibid.
14 August is one of the coldest months in the Andes.
15 Iván Ignacio, "Our Homage to Commandant Bartolina Sisa, Incorruptible Aymara Leader," *Andean First Nations Council*, http://www.pusinsuyu.com/english/html/bartolina_sisa_english.html
16 Solon, *Bartolina Sisa*, p. 10–20
17 For information on 19th century indigenous rebel Pablo Zarate, also see "¿Quién fue Pablo Zarate?," El Temible Willka, http://willka.net/Pablo%20Zarate.htm. For more information on indigenous rebellions in the Andes, see Fausto Reinaga, *La Revolución India*. El Alto: Imp. "Movil Graf," 2001. Also see Hylton et al., *Ya es Otro Tiempo*.
18 Kohl and Farthing, *Impasse*, 40–41.
19 See Chapter 7 on El Alto uprising in October, 2003
20 Luis Antezana E., *Masacres y Levantamientos Campesinos en Bolivia* (La Paz: Liberira Editorial "Juventud," 1994), 129. For more information on pre-revolutionary (1952) indigenous revolts, see Roberto Choque Canqui with Cristina Quisbert, *Historia de una lucha desigual*. Serie: Rebeliones indígenas. La Paz: Unidad de investigaciones historicas unih-pakaxa, 2005.
21 Silvia Rivera Cusicanqui, *Oprimidos Pero no Vencidos: luchas del campesinado aymara y quechua 1900–1980* (La Paz: HISBOL—CSUTCB, 1984), 104–109.
22 Pablo Solón, *La Otra Cara de la Historia* (La Paz: Fundación Solón, 1999), 22–25.
23 Kohl and Farthing, *Impasse*, 44–46.
24 Klein, *A Concise History*, 206–208.
25 James Dunkerley, *Rebelión en las venas: la lucha política en Bolivia, 1952–1982,* (La Paz: Plural, 2003), 67–69.
26 Klein, *A Concise History*, 206–208.
27 In 2003, the arrival of the miners in the October gas conflict was pivotal in forcing President Sánchez de Lozada to leave the country.
28 Dunkerly, *Rebelión*, 67–69, 70–71.
29 Solon, *La Otra Cara*, 27–29, 30–31.
30 Ibid., 32–36.
31 COMIBOL went on to produce more than 50 percent of Bolivia's minerals in the early 1980s. (Farthing and Kohl, *Impasse*, 64). For more information on COMIBOL, see Salomón Rivas Valenzuela, *COMIBOL, Una Historia de Amor*. La Paz: Imprenta Astral, 1998.
32 Domitila Barrios de Chungara with Moema Viezzer, *Let Me Speak!: Testimony of Domitila, A Woman of the Bolivian Mines*, trans. Victoria Ortiz (New York: Monthly Review Press, 1978), 25. For more on women in Bolivian mining communities and unions, see María L. Lagos, *Nos hemos forjado así: al rojo vivo y a puro golpre, Historias del Comité de Amas de Casa de Siglo XX*. La Paz: Plural Editores, 2006.
33 Rivera, *Oprimidos*, 122–123.
34 Dunkerly, *Rebelión*, 104–106. Also see Solon, *La Otra Cara*, 39–42.
35 Domitila Barrios de Chungara with Moema Viezzer, *Let Me Speak!*, María L.

Lagos, *Nos hemos forjado así: al rojo vivo y a puro golpre, Historias del Comité de Amas de Casa de Siglo XX.*

36 Kohl and Farthing, *Impasse*, 49.

37 Solon, *La Otra Cara*, 32–38, 39–42. Also see Dunkerly, *Rebelión*, 91–94.

38 Duncan Green, *Faces of Latin America* (London: Latin America Bureau, 1997), 6–7. Also see Galeano, *Open Veins*, 285.

39 Green, *Faces*, 11.

40 For more information on United Fruit in Guatemala, see Manu Saxena, "United Fruit and the CIA," Eat the State, 1999, http://eatthestate.org/03-26/ UnitedFruitCIA.htm. Also see Dana Frank, *Bananeras: Women Transforming the Banana Unions of Latin America.* Cambridge: South End Press, 2005.

41 Greg Grandin, *Empire's Workshop* (New York: Metropolitan Books, 2006), 42–43.

42 Expanded on in Stephen Kinzer, *Overthrow: America's Century of Regime Change from Hawaii to Iraq.* New York: Times Books, 2006.

43 Lesley Gill, *The School of the Americas* (Durham: Duke University Press, 2004), 14–15.

44 Grandin, *Empire's Workshop*, 14, footnote 7.

45 Ibid., footnotes, 5, 6 and 8.

46 Kohl and Farthing, *Impasse*, 15–18. For more information see Robin Hahnel, *The ABC's of Political Economy.* London: Pluto Press, 2002, Douglas Dowd, *Capitalism and Its Economics.* London: Pluto Press, 2004, and Noam Chomsky, *Profit Over People.* New York: Seven Stories Press, 1998, and *Radical Priorities.* Oakland: AK Press, 2003. Regionally, neoliberal policies had devastating affects, increasing poverty and economic inequality throughout Latin America. Also see Green, *Faces*, and Galeano, *Open Veins.*

47 Duncan Green, *Silent Revolution: The Rise and Crisis of Market Economics in Latin America* (New York: Monthly Review Press, 2003), 12–13.

48 Kohl and Farthing, *Impasse*, 32.

49 For more on Kissinger, see Seymour Hersh, *The Price of Power: Kissinger in the Nixon White House* (New York: Summit Books, 1983), and William Shawcross, *Sideshow, Kissinger, Nixon and the Destruction of Cambodia* (New York: Simon and Schuster, 1979), as well as Alex Gibney and Eugene Jarecki's *The Trials of Henry Kissinger* (London: BBC Documentary, 2002).

50 "Plan Condor," Source Watch, *Center for Media and Democracy* (February 10, 2006), http://www.sourcewatch.org/index.php?title=Plan_Condor.

51 For more information on Sandino, see "Biographical notes," Sandino.org, http:// www.sandino.org/bio_en.htm

52 See Toni Solo, "Coming Soon to the US? Plan Condor the Sequel," *Counterpunch* (October 1, 2003), http://www.counterpunch.org/solo10012003.html. Also see Renate Lunn, "Five Lessons Bush Learned from Argentina's Dirty War and Five Lessons for the Rest of Us," *Upside Down World* (January 3, 2006), http:// upsidedownworld.org/main/content/view/160/32/. For further information on Argentina's Dirty War, see Rodolfo Walsh "A year of dictatorship in Argentina, March 1976–March 1977: An open letter to the military junta from Rodolfo Walsh. Various films on the aftermath of the dictatorships can be seen at http:// www.agoratv.org/.

53 For more information on the Madres de la Plaza de Mayo, see the website http:// www.madres.org.

54 Grandin, *Empire's Workshop*, 89–91. Death estimates are as high as 200,000, see "Guatemala Human Rights Developments," *Human Rights Watch World Report* (2000), http://www.hrw.org/wr2k1/americas/guatemala.html.

55 Mickey Z., "Nothing But Human Rights," *MIT Western Hemisphere Project*

(August 16, 2001), http://web.mit.edu/hemisphere/events/kissinger-chile.shtml.
56 Members of the Military Junta bombed Chile's government palace during the
coup in 1973. For more information, see Kinzer, *Overthrow.*
57 Green, *Silent Revolution*, 33–34.
58 Grandin, *Empire's Workshop*, 163–164, 170–174.
59 Benjamin Dangl, "CHILE: Coup anniversary sparks national debate," *Green
Left Weekly* (September 24, 2003), http://www.greenleft.org.au/back/2003/555/
555p18.htm.
60 Michelle Bachelet was recently elected president of Chile and has since enacted
legislation to prevent human rights violations from repeating themselves.
61 See Kohl and Farthing, *Impasse*, as well as Barrios de Chungara, *Let Me Speak.*
62 The policies and histories of the International Monetary Fund and World Bank
are further discussed in the chapter on Bolivia's "Black February."
63 Sánchez de Lozada's privatization plan would come back to haunt his later
administration through public demands for state control of gas reserves. Green,
Silent Revolution, 74.
64 Forrest Hylton, "Popular Insurrection and National Revolution: Bolivia in
Historical and Regional Context," *CounterPunch* (October 30, 2003), http://www.
counterpunch.org/hylton10302003.html
65 Green, *Silent Revolution*, 75, 85 (footnote 52), 86.
66 John Crabtree, *Perfiles de la Protesta: Política y movimientos sociales en Bolivia*
(La Paz: Programa de Investigación Estratégica en Bolivia y Fundación UNIR
Bolivia, 2005), 7.
67 Noam Chomsky and Bernie Dwyer, "Latin American Integration: Radio Havana
Cuba Interview," Z Magazine(March 7, 2006), http://www.zmag.org/content/
print_article.cfm?itemID=9862&sectionID=1.

Chapter Two

More Than a Leaf: Coca and Conflict in Bolivia

Cocalera Leonilda Zurita dries coca leaves near her home in the Chapare.

Photo Credit: Benjamin Dangl

"This is not a war against narco-traffickers, it's a war against those who are working to survive."

—Leonilda Zurita[1]

I n the Chapare, the largest coca growing region in the country and the focal point of the war on drugs in Bolivia, security forces have been known to play soccer with *cocaleros* while waiting for the order from US officials to destroy coca crops. Once the order is received, the game ends and the conflicts begin. "It's as though our own Bolivian military here in the tropics doesn't command," *Cocalera* (coca grower) union leader Leonilda Zurita told me, "It's the North Americans that command."[2]

The coca leaf represents perhaps the most explosive culture clash in Bolivia. This natural resource has been used in the Andes for millennia to relieve hunger, fatigue, and sickness, to increase oxygen flow to the brain at high altitudes, and as a religious and cultural symbol. Bolivians chew the small green leaf like tobacco and drink it in tea. Even the US Embassy, which has initiated most coca eradication efforts, suggests chewing the leaf to alleviate altitude sickness. Besides its traditional uses, coca is also an ingredient in anesthetics, cough syrups, wines, chewing gums, and Coca-Cola. Dried leaves are sold in small bags all over the country, and coca tea is more prevalent in Bolivia than coffee. Much of the coca produced in Bolivia goes to this legal, controlled use.

To Washington, however, the coca leaf is first and foremost the key ingredient in cocaine. Since 1989, the US government has focused on stopping coca production in Bolivia and other Latin American countries. This project, known as the "War on Drugs," involves the militarization of semi-tropical coca-growing regions, such as the Chapare and the Yungas, as well as the eradication of coca crops, to stem the flow of cocaine to the US. Other methods include drug trafficking interdiction and a crackdown on cocaine laboratories. This War on Drugs in Bolivia has resulted in violence, death, torture, and trauma for the subsistence farmers whose livelihood depends on coca crops. Meanwhile, the millions of dollars that Washington has pumped into this conflict have not diminished the amount of cocaine on the streets in the US, leading Leonilda Zurita to believe that the War on Drugs is "not a war against narco-traffickers, it's a war against those who are working to survive."

For many Bolivians, the coca leaf is a symbol of resistance against direct intervention from Washington. The green leaf also sustains Bolivians on a variety of levels, from miners risking their lives in horrible working conditions, to farmers in the *altiplano*. Coca aids protestors in long, arduous marches, street mobilizations, and hunger strikes. Bolivia's most powerful social movements and political parties have emerged from the Chapare farmers' fight to grow coca and resist militarization. Though many of the policies outlined here have changed for the better under subsequent administrations, the history of this conflict offers important contextual information on movements and political leaders that have since gone on to radically change Bolivian society and politics.

Coca traveled the world freely as an ingredient in wine and medicines until 1952, when a United Nations (UN) study labeled the leaf an addictive substance detrimental to health, effectively placing it with cocaine on a list of highly illegal drugs. The UN stated that coca should be considered the same as cocaine.[3] Since then, legal exports have all but stopped, and the coca leaf has gained fame as an illegal export.

One of the main arguments of coca farmers against the eradication of their crop is that there is a big difference between the coca leaf and the refined product of cocaine. "Trying to compare coca to cocaine is like trying to compare coffee beans to methamphetamines, there's a universe of difference between the two," Sanho Tree from the Institute for Policy Studies explains. "[Coca] is almost impossible to abuse in its natural state."[4] In Bolivia, this distinction is clear, but Bolivians realize that this message has yet to gain force internationally. "I have chewed coca every day and I am not crazy yet!" Leonilda Zurita told me. "A grape is a grape and through a long process you make wine. It's the same with coca. Coca is coca and through a long process you can make cocaine." Similarly, the sassafras tree, which produces a key ingredient in the drug ecstasy, is totally legal.[5]

Silvia Rivera, one of Bolivia's leading anthropologists and an authority on the history and use of coca, spoke with me about this important resource.[6] We sat on llama furs spread out on her office floor in front of a colorfully woven blanket piled with coca leaves. She lit a cigarette, pinched the stem off a leaf and talked of coca's importance in Andean diets thousands of years ago. Andeans ate vegetables, salads, quinoa, corn and coca regularly, preventing illness and improving stamina. Because such meals were so nutritious, Andean people didn't have to eat a lot. According to Rivera, this impressed the colonial Spanish, who ate large meals. She said coca helps digestion, blood and heart problems, and increases lung capacity. "It also cures people that are addicted to crack and cocaine...with leaves, pills and capsules." Like many Bolivians, she uses coca as a cure for common ailments instead of aspirin and pharmaceutical medicines.

Besides offering sustenance and medicinal help, coca has acted as a safety net for a population wracked by poverty. In the mid 1980s, a large sector of the population either worked in the mines or farmed in the *altiplano*. That changed when a 1983 drought forced farmers to migrate elsewhere. In 1985, the closure of the state-run mining company put over 20,000 miners out of work. Though it was a result of a drop in tin prices, the closure was also part of a neoliberal plan to privatize state run industries and break the back of the miners, who made up the most powerful labor movement in the country. Many migrated to the Chapare, where they could produce coca to survive. In this way, coca saved people from neoliberalism like a ship in a stormy sea.[7] Isabel, a Bolivian migrant from a mining family, described this trauma of the mine closures: "The money was gone...The miners didn't know how to do anything else but go underground and work down there...[A]t this time we almost died of hunger."[8]

The militancy of miners' unions, exhibited most clearly in their participation in the Revolution of 1952, was transferred to social organizations in El Alto and the Chapare. Organizational skills were applied to unions, local governments and assemblies.[9] Migrants to the Chapare formed *sindicatos*, community organizations similar to unions, to fill the void of the government. The *sindicatos* organized work cycles, and distribution of land, and mediated disputes. Through obligatory communal work, roads, health clinics and schools were built. Participation in protests, meetings and blockades was also mandatory.[10] This organizational structure grew into the Six Federations, which is now an umbrella union that includes around 40,000 coca farmers in the Chapare. The Six Federations has become a powerful instrument through which farmers organize, protest and lobby the government regarding Drug War policies.[11]

The closure of the mines in the 1980s coincided with a boom in demand from the US and Europe for cocaine. Coca quickly replaced the tin of Bolivia's closed mines as the biggest exported product of the decade.[12] Coca was also easier than other products to grow, store and transport in the Chapare, which at the time did not have major roads or bridges. Other products such as yucca, rice, fruit and corn were subsistence crops, used primarily for consumption among families, not sale. In recent Bolivian history, coca—and cocaine—has been big business.

From 1980 to 1997, the business of coca and cocaine paste made $500 million annually. The industry provided more money and jobs than any other agricultural product. During this same time period, the number of people involved in coca farming reached the hundreds of thousands.[13]

The coca that goes toward cocaine production is sent to laboratories in the Chapare where it is combined with a mixture of chemicals and transformed into a paste bought primarily by drug dealers from Colombia. Once in Colombia, this paste is refined into pure cocaine and sent into the US and other markets.[14] According to Kathryn Ledebur, the director of the Andean Information Network, a drug policy think tank in Cochabamba, there is some drug production going on in the Chapare, but coca unions and communities distance themselves from it so as not to be implicated. Therefore, the majority of cocaine paste laboratories in the region are on abandoned lands. Drugs are still produced in the region, but, according to Ledebur, production is not done in the open, nor does it benefit community members, making the Drug War's focus on working farmers and communities even more contradictory.[15]

Instead of stemming the demand side of the drug business, the US government has focused money and resources on ending production of coca. Poor farmers have borne the brunt of the conflict. The Bolivian government, backed by Washington, has enforced strict anti-coca laws, criminalizing production and violently cracking down on anyone who resists eradication. Violence, human right violations, and arrests often accompanied eradication efforts, forcing *cocalero* unions to organize to defend their right to produce coca.

Few people understand the way the War on Drugs impacts Chapare communities better than Leonilda Zurita. A longtime coca grower and union organizer, she has been jailed and harassed by police and military forces in anti-narcotics efforts. After her father died when she was two years old, her mother raised Zurita and five siblings. When she was seventeen years old, her mother participated in a government program to develop alternative products in place of coca. The project failed and those involved lost money, time, and crops. As a result, Zurita had to leave school to help with her family's coca farm. In 1991, she began cooking and cleaning at coca union meetings and in 1994 was named the secretary of minutes of the male federation of coca growers. She helped form the first women's federation of the Chapare in 1995 and later the Coordinating Committee of the Six Women Peasant Federations of the

Tropics. She continues to grow coca on her small family farm after repeated eradications.[16]

I met up with Zurita and her *cocalera* colleague Apolonia Sánchez in the Chapare town of Eterazama in February, 2006. Both of them wore the wide, pleated skirts and white, mesh, wide-brimmed hats common to indigenous women in the Chapare. Zurita is a motherly but fierce social movement leader, and answered my questions with enthusiasm. Her charisma and strength of spirit helped make her one of the most distinguished organizers in the country, as well as an alternate senator in the national congress. Sánchez is a member of the union led by Zurita and, in addition to producing coca, sells clothes for a living. They brought me to the town coca market, which is organized and monitored by the local union.

The market in Eterazama, situated on a large concrete expanse, underneath a corrugated metal roof, has been operating for the past 25 years. Inside, the air was thick with the rich, pungent odor of the coca leaf. Green piles of coca up to four feet high were spread across the floor. Farmers' children played in it, rolling around and throwing leaves at each other while families unloaded tightly stuffed sacks of coca off of cars and bicycles to empty out onto the market floor.

Like elsewhere in the Chapare, Eterazama is surrounded by small coca farms. The tropical climate allows farmers to produce coca year round, harvesting their crop every three to four months. Most of the region's coca is produced by small farmers who travel for miles by bike, car, and on foot to sell their leaves at union-controlled, legal markets in towns like this. Coca purchased at town markets is usually resold in larger city markets. The union controls sales as tightly as possible, and those caught selling coca outside the legal, union-controlled market are not allowed back.

For many farmers in the Chapare, the alternative to growing coca is unemployment and hunger. "We need to take care of our coca as if it were a child so that the whole family can survive," Zurita said. "The coca gives us food. It takes care of our education and healthcare because here education and healthcare are not free. When we sell coca, we are able to buy school supplies for our children so they can study."[17]

After my trip to the Eterazama coca market, I took a bus to visit Zurita's home in the Chapare. The vehicle was teeming with sacks of rice, cooking oil, and children in white school uniforms. I squashed myself into the pile of people and bags as we barreled down the dirt road, past a military encampment where hundreds of security forces were stationed in tents for eradication efforts. We passed countless coca fields and homes with the green leaf drying in front yards.

Her house was one of the last before the road turned into jungle foot paths. Like other homes in the area, it didn't have electricity or running water. The two story structure was about ten by twenty feet wide and had no walls or floor. A loft constructed of logs lashed together and secured with wooden pegs was topped by a roof made of intertwined leaves. Though Zurita's family lives in conditions like thousands of other poor coca farmers, she still remains connected to the outside world. When we arrived, her cell phone was charging in her husband's car and rang constantly. As she spread out rice to dry in the sun, and her husband chopped wood, she answered interview questions on the phone. Afterward, I asked her who the call was from. "Someone from BBC, London," she replied nonchalantly.

The next day we bushwhacked through a thick forest behind the house to the family coca field. The main pathway was flooded, so we hacked through swampy areas, pushing through vines and clouds of insects. After a couple of miles, the shaded forest opened up to a wide, sunlit coca field. After packing golf ball-sized wads of coca in their cheeks, Zurita and her husband began to spray pesticides on the coca from plastic packs on their backs. Chewing coca, they explained, was something they did everyday to give them strength while they worked.

When Zurita had finished spraying a section of the crop, she sat down in the shade. Between gulps of water, she told me of the mobilizations she participated in as a union leader. She saw her life shaped by her struggle against militarization and coca eradication. In a women's march from Cochabamba to La Paz from December, 1995 to January, 1996, she told me, coca farmers demanded an end to the violence in the Chapare. They also demanded a meeting with President Sánchez de Lozada's wife, who refused. "They didn't understand our situation and so we began a hunger strike, which lasted twelve days," she said.

Through coca unions, numerous blockades and protests have been organized to defend the farmers' right to grow coca. A highway that goes through the Chapare links the economically booming city of Santa Cruz to Cochabamba and La Paz. Blocking this important route puts pressure on the government to meet *cocalero* demands. Blockades constructed out of dirt, rocks, logs, and tires are sometimes sustained for weeks, or are spontaneous and mobile, harder for security forces to break up. Blockade committees are developed by coca unions with a structure and leadership in place that allows blockaders to coordinate their work and activities.[18]

Yet coca unions have done much more than protest. Zurita said that a goal of her work is "to bring the women ahead, by organizing, empowering and orienting them and setting up seminars. [Many] women in the Chapare don't know how to read or write. So the best school for the women is the union. There we have empowered people. We learn about which laws are in favor of us and which are not. This has all shown us that the union organization is important to defend mother earth, defend the coca, and defend our natural resources..."

The sun grew hotter. Her husband disappeared to another part of the coca field and Zurita reached for more coca. She knows the reality of the Chapare well, but she has a second life, which also occupies her time. This other life is one of constant travel, union meetings, protests, speeches, and interviews with the media. "Sometimes I go for weeks when the only housing I have is in the buses," she said. "I have to be in one meeting one day and have to travel by night to get to the next one the following day." In the coca field, this part of her life seemed distant. Somehow she lives with a foot in both realities: "I produce coca for my children, because if I die tomorrow they will be able to continue to eat thanks to this bit of coca."

The militarization of the Chapare is a fact of life. The first time I entered the Chapare on a night bus, I woke up to one part of the War on Drugs. The bus wheels ground to a halt at a drug trafficking checkpoint. Sleeping passengers bobbed forward with the momentum of the bus, rubbed their eyes, stretched, and squinted into the foggy night.

A misty rain fell on passengers filing off the bus. Piles of crackers, candy, coca, and soda shone in street vendors' feeble lights. As people talked and wandered to bathrooms, the bus was searched by drug enforcement officials. I was calmed by the fact that they seemed more interested in the soccer game playing on a television in their office than this routine check. As cheers and narration of the match made up the night's soundtrack, the men tapped on the hubcaps of the bus, searched through the occasional bag or purse and eyed passengers lazily. A white billboard facing the checkpoint urged travelers to alert officials if they knew someone was carrying drugs: "We pay better than narco-traffickers," read the rusted words. Beyond the checkpoint's miniature city of light sat the night jungle. The bus driver whistled sharply and pressed the horn twice to inform lounging passengers it was time to leave. Our bus was approved. We lumbered off into the night just as a voice from the TV blasted: "Gooooaaaalll!"

Washington's creation of the War on Drugs in Latin America co-incided with the fall of the Soviet Union and the end of the subsequent "threat" of communism in Latin America. The War on Drugs conveniently replaced the US-backed war on communism as a reason for US military intervention in Latin American countries. In return for working with the US government against coca production, the Bolivian government has received significant amounts of funding for security forces and financial aid.

In this stranglehold scenario, the Bolivian government has buried itself in debt and put its sovereignty at risk by strengthening ties with Washington. One of the ways the US government blackmails Bolivia into stepping up its efforts in this conflict is to threaten aid cuts if eradication goals are not met.[19] Furthermore, eradication efforts are under specific management by US officials. "There is a very strict control over the eradication forces and the interdiction by officials of the narcotics affairs section of the US embassy, or the Southern Command," Ledebur said. "For each helicopter flight, Bolivian eradication officials need the specific authorization from the US embassy."[20]

The disparity between US policy and how it plays out on the ground is exhibited in the fact that many security forces chew coca during long days of eradication. A commanding officer at an eradication camp told Ledebur, "You can't really expect these guys to have the stamina to continue eradicating without the coca leaf." Police and military forces also chew coca during street confrontations with protestors.[21]

From the time of their initiation, eradication efforts have created a cycle of violence with a trail of money that leads straight back to Washington. In 1983, the US provided $4 million to start UMOPAR, a Rural Mobile Patrol Unit that deals with drug control in rural areas. The US embassy manages the bulk of UMOPAR's budget, and the Drug Enforcement Agency (DEA) coordinates drug interdiction efforts. Most human rights violations until 1997 have been attributed to UMOPAR. The Special Drug Police Force (FELCN) was created in 1987 by President Victor Paz Estenssoro. Salary bonuses, training and weapons for the group were provided by the US government. Since then the FELCN has functioned as an umbrella organization for other Washington-funded anti-drug groups, such as the Expeditionary Task Force (ETF), which operated from 2001–2002. Interdiction efforts against the trafficking of drugs and chemicals needed to make cocaine on Bolivian soil increased throughout this time through the navy's Blue Devils Task Force.[22]

Cocaleros and security forces continued to clash under an eradication program called Option Zero, which was applied by the first Sánchez de Lozada administration from 1993 to 1997. Though anti-drug police, instead of military, carried out these efforts, this changed under the Dignity Plan, implemented by President Hugo Banzer in 1998 after he was pressured by US President Bill Clinton to create a program focused on eradicating all coca.[23] The Dignity Plan combined forced eradication efforts with increased military presence, a situation that led to human rights abuses and the torture and killing of coca farmers.[24] The US had high hopes for the Plan, which prioritized coca destruction over human rights and due process. Over several years, any concept of compensation for eradicated coca crops was totally phased out.[25]

Though this militarization has resulted in nearly 60 *cocalero* deaths since the 1980s, few of the perpetrators of these crimes have faced justice.[26] Such an environment of impunity has increased the freedom with which security forces commit violent acts. At the same time, anti-drug efforts have helped the US military establish strong relationships with the Bolivian military, a strategic goal of the Pentagon.

Campaign posters of a smiling Evo Morales peeled off the walls in a union office near the Eterazama coca market where I sat down with Berto Bautizado, a coca union leader. As a coca farmer and organizer for the past 14 years, Bautizado is one many of the many coca farmers caught in the crossfire of US policies. He has been arrested and harassed by anti-narcotics security forces in the region on numerous occasions.

"There has been so much violence," he said, punctuating his statements with hand gestures. "We have suffered a lot of torture, death and jailing. Thousands of people of all ages have been affected. We have suffered this to defend our land and coca...The US government is not conscious of our reality. They have always seen us as narco-terrorists." He looked out the door, the profile of his wrinkled face mirroring that of Morales in the posters behind him. "Ending coca here isn't possible. Coca will never end. Coca has been here forever."

Isaura, another life-long coca farmer, had walked half a day to bring her bags of coca to the market near the union office. For Isaura, military violence had become part of life. She spoke of security forces arriving to pull up her coca plants and burn them. "If you sit in the middle

of the coca field while they come to eradicate it, they will kill you. You
have to just sit and watch silently," she told me. Though these policies
have since changed, the scars remain.[27]

Studies show that, in spite of the money and firepower used in the
US War on Drugs in Bolivia, the conflict has yet to produce anything
but bloodshed. A report from the US Government Accountability Office
explains that, "While the US has poured 6 billion dollars into the drug
war in the Andes over the past five years...the number of drug users in
the US has remained roughly constant." The US Congressional Research
Service stated that the US War on Drugs has had no effect on the price,
purity, and availability of cocaine in the US.[28] George Anne Potter, an
advisor to Bolivian coca union leaders, explained that even the US government admits that "Bolivian cocaine, what there is of it, does not go to
the US, but rather to Europe."[29]

Another clue that the US War on Drugs is a convenient way to
continue post-Cold War intervention in Latin American countries is the
participation of external US institutions like the School of the Americas
(SOA) in Fort Benning, Georgia. Many of those who have unleashed the
nightmare on the ground in the Chapare were educated at the infamous
SOA. Leslie Gill's book *The School of the Americas: Military Training
and Political Violence in the Americas* explains that, since its creation
in Panama in 1946, the SOA has taught combat and counterinsurgency
techniques to over 60,000 soldiers.[30] Some of its alumni have gone on
to hold key military posts in Latin American dictatorships, from which
they orchestrated massive human rights violations. Between 1970 and
1979, in the heart of the Cold War, thousands of soldiers were sent to
the SOA from dictatorial governments. The SOA officials were so happy
with SOA graduate and Bolivian dictator Hugo Banzer, that in 1988 he
was inducted into the school's Hall of Fame. Between 1967 and 1979,
the Bolivian government sent an average of 155 soldiers annually to the
SOA, where soldiers were instructed in jungle warfare techniques, anti-
communist theory, marksmanship, surveillance, and intelligence.[31]

Former Bolivian army major Juan Ricardo Pantoja described his
education at the SOA. He told Gill that he was taught "how to tie up
prisoners of war and how to torture them—techniques that you have
to utilize to get them to make declarations. [For example] you don't let
them sleep and then you get results." According to Pantoja, another lesson SOA students learned was that a "dead subversive was better than a
prisoner." Having a prisoner interfered with the subsequent operations.
The point was to take prisoners, "get information from them quickly,

put them four meters underground and continue the operation." Training with US soldiers at the SOA was enticing to a Bolivian with limited
opportunities who wanted to rise in the ranks. Ricardo said he was impressed with the technical knowledge and wealth in the US. For many
poor Bolivians, the military offers one of the few ways out of poverty.[32]

Militarization is one side of the bloody coin of the War on Drugs.
Another side is criminalization, mostly enforced through Law 1008,
which was passed in 1988 after intense pressure from US officials.[33] The
law blurs the line between the coca and cocaine business and criminal-
izes small producers and smugglers who work to survive, while big drug
bosses are left untouched. The law took away people's right to a legal
defense, leaving many in jail for long periods of time without charges.[34]
Many are sentenced with very shaky evidence; in some cases, a simple
police report is enough to send a suspect to jail.[35]

Law 1008 has filled up Bolivian jails with poor, wrongly accused
people from all walks of life. Many are in prison with their children,
others are penniless youth. In order to appear victorious in the War
on Drugs, Bolivian officials have consistently produced high statistics
regarding the number of detained narco-traffickers. As far as US officials are concerned, the higher the numbers of people in jail, the more
successful the war. When writer Christina Haglund visited a women's
jail where many had been incarcerated under Law 1008, Walter Vino, a
National Police guard, told her "I think there are more innocents here
than guilty."[36] Though the law has been topically reformed, many of its
policies have remained in effect even into the 2006 Morales presidency.

In addition to legislature such as Law 1008, alternative development projects were established to cut down on the drug trade. The goal
of alternative development is to replace coca with other crops, such as
pineapple, plantains, oranges, and rice. Hundreds of millions of dollars have been put into such programs, and many coca farmers have
lost time and money trying to produce alternative crops.[37] Besides the
lack of a market for many of the fruit and vegetable products pushed
by alternative development programs, those products are harder than
coca to produce, transport, and store. Other forms of employment and
agricultural production could perhaps be successful, but in the Chapare,
no business has shown itself to be more lucrative or viable than coca
farming.[38]

Coca farmers at the market in Eterazama emphasized their opinion about alternative development programs. A young woman named
Maria sat next to a handful of coca sacks and regularly pulled leaves

from her pocket to chew. Her eyes darted around the room while she spoke and in between sentences she smiled and laughed with an older woman standing next to her. Like many farmers, she produces rice, bananas, and yucca in addition to coca, but only for use within her family. "There is a market for coca, and nothing else," she said.

Another cause of alternative development's failure is that organizations implementing the projects—such as the US Embassy and the US Agency for International Development (USAID)—refuse to work with existing *cocalero* unions such as the Six Federations of the Tropics of Cochabamba, in spite of their powerful infrastructure, constituency, and knowledge of the area and industry. Farmers who want to receive technical help and credit have to distance themselves from coca unions. Though this relationship is changing now, it led to many of the lasting pitfalls of alternative development.[39]

"Alternative development programs were less about alleviating poverty than coercing peasants to forsake their only viable cash crop," Gill wrote. What is needed to make these alternative projects work are "stable roads, credit, technical assistance, and high prices for substitute products."[40] The money that has funded such projects could have gone to better use. "For us, the alternative development has been gas, bullets, death, injuries, and arrests," said *cocalera* Apolonia Sánchez.[41]

Like *cocalero* unions, the Movement Toward Socialism (MAS) political party was born in the Chapare out of necessity. Coca growers realized that they needed a political instrument through which they could change the policies that were destroying their livelihoods. They organized the MAS out of a general sense of indignation and in order to resist repression, eradication, Law 1008, and the failure of alternative development.[42]

The influx of migrants to Chapare in the mid-1980s invigorated coca unions and brought diverse groups together to grapple with the hopes and challenges of a growing population and increased demand for coca. Unions held regular meetings about forming a political party. In 1989, the *cocaleros* entered the electoral realm by allying themselves with the *Izquierda Unida* (IU) political party in municipal elections. They were successful in the Chapare, gaining 42 percent of the votes. Through this new political configuration, charismatic coca farmer and organizer Evo Morales won a parliamentary bench along with Román Loayza, the executive secretary of the *Confederación Sindical Única de*

Trabajadores Campesinos de Bolivia (CSUTCB). Morales recalled that "without any parliamentarian experience" he, along with three other congressmen "shared the same small apartment in La Paz." In 1992, the Six Federations of the Tropics were brought under one umbrella. Four years later, Morales was elected president of this federation by a small margin.[43]

In March of 1995, *cocaleros*—as well as other indigenous people and *campesinos*—founded the Assembly for the Sovereignty of the Common People (ASP) and the Political Tool for the Sovereignty of the Common People (IPSP) with the aim of winning political power locally and nationally. In 1999, the IPSP took on the name Movement Toward Socialism (MAS).[44] The *cocaleros* gained ground as a powerful entity, both in the streets and in electoral politics. Their decision to start the MAS party marked a major change in the Bolivian left. For decades, other leftist parties had operated under the direction of the COB, rarely pushing their own electoral topics. The MAS would change this, gradually moving to the forefront of the left's involvement in electoral politics.[45] Morales helped develop the MAS into an "anti-imperialist" and "anti-neoliberal" party that, among other platforms, advocated the decriminalization of coca production and putting natural resources, such as gas and oil, under state control.[46]

The MAS discourse is linked to the reality and struggle of its base, using the coca leaf as a symbol of struggle and Andean traditions. As sociologist Pablo Mamani explains in his book *Geopoliticas Indigenas*, MAS has utilized the coca leaf as a political tool that not only recalls ancient Andean uses among workers, but also represents the direct struggle against US imperialism via resistance to the War on Drugs. The coca leaf acted as a bridge linking many MAS campaign issues, as did the *Wiphala*, a multicolored flag of the diverse indigenous cultures in the Andes. Both symbols were present at demonstrations, political rallies, protests and road blockades organized by the MAS. *Cocalero* supporters also identified with the humble origins of MAS leaders such as Evo Morales. While other leaders of leftist unions or parties at the time focused their energy solely on *campesino*, or indigenous, issues, Morales—an indigenous coca farmer originally from the *altiplano*—spoke to *campesino*, indigenous, and *cocalero* voters.[47]

Morales was born in 1959 into a poor llama herding family in Isallavi, near Oruro, at an altitude of around 12,000 feet above sea level. This isolated area lacked access to electricity, drinking water, and health care, leading to the young deaths of three of Morales' seven siblings due to a lack of medical attention. "These are the terms of life for families or children in rural communities," Morales explained. Their home was approximately ten by thirteen feet large, with a straw roof. "We used it as our bedroom, kitchen, dining room, and just about everything."[48]

At age six he traveled with his family to northern Argentina to harvest sugar. Six years later a drought destroyed their farm, along with those of thousands of other families in the *altiplano*. "One afternoon," he recalled, "we had just finished clearing the potato field with helpers. Then at night came wind and cold. The next day, the potato field was burnt black, with a bad smell. My mother cried all day. My father was with my uncles and they all decided, 'Here we're never going to progress, we're never going to be prosperous farmers. We have to go and find land in the east of Bolivia.'" Morales walked for a month with his father and their herd of llamas from Oruro to Cochabamba. His most vivid memories of this trip were "the large buses that traveled on the highway, full of people who threw out the peels of oranges and plantains. I picked up these peels to eat. Since then, one of my biggest dreams was to travel in one of those buses."

The family migrated to Puerto San Francisco, in the Chapare region of Cochabamba. "In the Chapare life was hard," Morales recalled, illustrating his point with the comment that people worked so hard with machetes that their hands "cried blood." On the new farm, the Morales family grew oranges, papaya, plantains, and coca, more food than the young Evo had ever imagined was possible. The new coca farming life quickly became mired in violence. One event in particular had a strong effect on Morales and moved him to take action.

In Chipiriri, a *cocalero* was killed by the military for refusing to plead guilty to trafficking drugs. "Without any contemplation, [the military] covered his body in gasoline and, in front of many people, burned him alive," Morales said. The gory scene pushed him to become involved in coca unions to fight against the repression under the War on Drugs. Morales was later jailed and tortured on various occasions for this work. In 1989, he was beaten so badly by security forces during a mobilization commemorating a massacre of coca farmers that he was dumped into the bushes. The military thought he was dead. When Drug War-related violence galvanized the *cocalero* movement for change, the MAS became their tool of resistance and Evo Morales quickly grew into their spokesman.

Cocaleros protested eradication policies and government violence with road blockades and protests in the Chapare throughout 2000–2001.

In response, President Jorge Quiroga met the resistance with violent police and military repression, pushing the *cocalero* movement to a higher
level of action. Violence escalated when, in November 2001, the government passed Decree 26415, which outlawed the sale of coca leaves in
Chapare markets. On December 6th of that same year, when *cocaleros*
dumped rotten bananas and pineapples in protest of failed alternative
development, security forces killed Casimiro Huanca, a union leader
involved in the act. When *cocaleros* protested the closure of the central
coca market in Sacaba in January 2002, conflicts resulted in the death of
security officials and *cocaleros*.[49]

Throughout this period, Quiroga waged a campaign against the
cocaleros, both through repression and rhetoric, which, combined with
the death of security forces in Sacaba, pitted public opinion against the
coca movement and the MAS. In late January, 2002, 104 congressmen
accused Morales of organizing the killing of security forces in the Chapare and voted to expel him from congress. This move backfired: Morales became an icon in the fight against US imperialism and aggression
against poor coca farmers. In the 2002 elections, he rode this popularity
through a presidential campaign. Morales' opponent, Gonzalo Sánchez
de Lozada, focused much of his campaign on taking down another can-
dididate, Manfred Reyes, subsequently leaving Morales unscathed. Sánchez de Lozada's neglect, along with some comments made by Manuel
Rocha, the US ambassador to Bolivia, gave Morales a considerable boost
in the polls.

A few days before Election Day, Rocha hoped to put a dent in
Morales' increasing popularity. "Evo Morales claimed the US Embassy
threatened to kill him." Rocha said. "This vile accusation is totally false,
an absolute lie. The US has threatened to kill one man: Osama Bin
Laden. Perhaps Evo Morales, with his tremendous lie, wanted to show
his solidarity with that assassin and terrorist. Evo Morales also said in a
speech that if he is elected he'll stop the US anti-coca program. I want to
remind Bolivians, California will only buy your natural gas if Bolivia is
not involved in cocaine. Citizens of Bolivia, open your eyes. The future
of your children and families is in your hands."[50] Unfortunately for Rocha, his idea of the best future for Bolivians was not attractive to a large
percent of the voting public.

His comment had the opposite of the intended effect. It rallied
support among voters against US intervention and emphasized Morales
as a symbol of this fight. Sánchez de Lozada joked that perhaps the US
ambassador worked on Evo's campaign team. Evo said he hoped the

ambassador kept talking. The election took place on June 30th and results were very close. At the end of the day, Sánchez de Lozada received
22.5 percent, Morales trailed close behind with 20.9 percent and Reyes
came in third with 20.8 percent. MAS won eight of 27 Senate seats and
27 of 130 places in Congress.[51] The results marked a historical victory
for the MAS, and reorganized electoral politics in Bolivia. Nonetheless,
violence continued in the Chapare. On January 14th, 2003, six *cocaleros*
were killed in confrontations in protests and blockades against security
forces. Outraged *cocaleros* allied themselves with other mining, landless,
and *campesino* groups around the country.[52]

Over time, many of the coca policies outlined here have changed,
particularly under the Carlos Mesa government and the administration
of Evo Morales. There is considerably less violence and criminalization
of coca production, though the Law 1008 has so far survived. A discussion of these changes affecting Bolivian *cocaleros* will be discussed in the
final chapter of this book.

Washington dumped millions of dollars into a raging battle over
coca, one of Bolivia's most cherished natural resources. Rising from the
ashes and blood came a coalition of farmers that would fight against US
imperialism, militarization, and neoliberalism, for their right to grow
coca and live in peace. The *cocalero* movement and the MAS, both in
the streets and in the government palace, would go on to change the
political landscape of the country. Meanwhile, the leaf continues to be
a potent symbol and nexus of Andean culture, history and a direct confrontation with US imperialism.

(Endnotes)

1   Information from author interview with Leonilda Zurita Vargas in February,
    2006. Quotes and information from Zurita are from author interview, unless
    otherwise noted.
2   Information from author interview with Kathryn Ledebur, and Leonilda Zurita
    Vargas in February, 2006. Quotes and information from Ledebur are from author
    interview, unless otherwise noted.
3   *Coca Si, Cocaína no?, Opciones legales para la hoja de coca*, Drogas y Conflicto,
    Documento de Debate N.r 13, *Transnational Institute*, (May 2006), 17.
4   Michele Keleman, "Bolivian Leader's Stance on Coca Raises US Concerns,"
    Morning Edition, National Public Radio (December 29, 2005).
5   "Coca Si, Cocaína no?," *Transnational Institute*, 17.
6   All quotes and information from Silvia Rivera are from author interview in
    July, 2006.
7   Pablo Stefanoni, *Evo Morales: de la coca al palacio* (Buenos Aires: Capital
    Intelectual, 2006), 46.

8 Colectivo Situaciones, *Mal de Altura*, (Buenos Aires: Tinta Limon Ediciones, 2005), 9.

9 Sebastian Hacher, "Bolivia: Eradicate Coca-Cola," *ZNet* (February 5, 2003), http://www.zmag.org/content/print_article.cfm?itemID=2971&sectionID=20.

10 Stefanoni, *Evo Morales*, 37. Also see Alison Spedding, "Kawsachun coca. Economía campesina cocalera en los Yungas y el Chapare," (Programa de Investigación Estratégica en Bolivia, 2005). Also Álvaro Garcia Linera et al., *Sociología de los movimientos sociales* (La Paz: Diakonia-Oxfam, 2004). Also Farthing and Kohl, *Impasse*, 157.

11 Gill, *The School of the Americas*, 174.

12 Ibid., 167–168, 174, footnote 5.

13 Kohl and Farthing, *Impasse*, 73, 74. Kohl and Farthing, "The Price of Success: The Destruction of Coca and the Bolivian Economy," *NACLA*, 34(7), (2001), 35–41. Also see Madeline Barbara Léons, Harry Sanabria, *Coca, Cocaine and the Bolivian Reality* (New York: SUNY Press, 1997), 18–20.

14 Gill, *The School of the Americas*, 164–165, 168. Also see Latin American Bureau-IEPALA, *Narcotráfico y Política: Militarismo y Mafia en Bolivia* (Madrid: LAB-IEPALA Editorial, 1982.

15 Author interview with Kathryn Ledebur.

16 "Leonilda Zurita Biography," *University of Vermont* (February 21, 2006).

17 As of October, 2006, there were Cuban doctors working in the Chapare, providing free health care.

18 Pablo Mamani Ramírez, *Geopolíticas Indígenas* (El Alto: CADES, 2005), 64-65.

19 Crabtree, *Perfiles de la Protesta*, 20.

20 Author interview with Ledebur.

21 Author interview with Ledebur.

22 Kathryn Ledebur, "Bolivia: Clear Consequences," in *Drugs and Democracy in Latin America: The Impact of US Policy*, eds. Coletta A. Youngers and Eileen Rosin (Boulder:Lynne Riener Publishers, 2005),149–152. Also see James Painter, *Bolivia and coca: A study in dependency Studies on the impact of the illegal drug trade)* (Boulder: L. Reinner Publishers, 1994), 81. Interdiction information from "Bolivia: Military and Police Aid," *Just the Facts: A Civilian's Guide to US Defense and Security Assistance to Latin America and the Carribean* (September 25, 2006), http://www.ciponline.org/facts/bo.htm.

23 Stefanoni, *Evo Morales*, 39, 41.

24 Gretchen Gordon, "Bullying Democracy," *Multinational Monitor* Vol 27, N. 1 (Jan./Feb. 2006), http://multinationalmonitor.org/mm2006/012006/gordon.html.

25 Phillip Coffin, "Coca Eradication," *Foreign Policy in Focus* Vol. 3, N. 29 (October 1998), http://www.fpif.org/briefs/vol3/v3n29coca_body.html. Also see Stefanoni, *Evo Morales*, 39, 41. Information on compensation from Ledebur.

26 Jessie Gaskell, "A Coca Grower to Lead Bolivia? How US Intervention May Have Triggered a Populist Revolution," *Council on Hemispheric Affairs* (July 13, 2005), http://www.coha.org/2005/07/13/a-coca-grower-to-lead-bolivia-how-us-intervention-may-have-triggered-a-populist-revolution/.

27 Coca eradication policies changed significantly in 2004 under the Mesa administration and later with the Morales administration in 2006. See Chapter Ten for more details.

28 Keleman, "Bolivian Leader's Stance."

29 From author interview via email with George Anne Potter, 2005

30 Gill, *School of the Americas*, 6–9, 78, 79. For more information on the School of the Americas see www.soaw.org.

31 Gill, *School of the Americas*. Some the SOA's alumni include General Roberto

Viola of Argentina, who was convicted of kidnapping, torture and murder during
the Dirty War in Argentina (1976–1983); Colonel Domingo Monterrosa, who
orchestrated the El Mozote massacre in El Salvador; Honduran death squad
leader General Luis Alonso; and Colonel Julio Alpirez in Guatemala who, while
on the CIA's payroll, killed and tortured guerrillas and a US citizen.

32   Ibid, 99, 105–107, 108, 109.

33   Mamani, *Geopolíticas*, 57–59.

34   Gill, *School of the Americas*, 170.

35   Information from Ledebur. Law 1008 says that alternative development must
follow eradication—something else that was never sufficiently applied. There
are now improvements in this law, but these changes are not being implemented
well.

36   Christina Haglund, "Sliding into the Soap Dish of the US War on Drugs,"
Democracy Center, (November 2005), http://www.democracyctr.org/
blog/2005/11/sliding-into-soap-dish-of-us-war-on.html.

37   Between 1988 and 2002, USAID spent $750 million dollars in the Chapare on
alternative development projects and the construction of roads. Crabtree, *Perfiles
de la Protesta*, 26.

38   Alison Spedding Pallet, *En Defensa de la Hoja de Coca* (La Paz: Programa de
Investigación Estratégica en Bolivia, 2003), 31.

39   Gill, *School of the Americas*, 174.

40   Ibid., 173–174.

41   Quote from author interview. Also see *Kohl and Farthing, Impasse, 157.*

42   Mamani, *Geopolíticas*, 57–59.

43   Stefanoni, *Evo Morales*, 46–47.

44   "Perfil," Evo Morales, (2006), http://www.evomorales.org/.

45   Luis Tapia, 2004. *Por el Sí, Por el No: Análisis de Resultados del Referéndum 2004.*
(La Paz: Corte Nacional Electoral, 2004), 152–153. Also see Kohl and Farthing,
*Impasse,*170.

46   Stefanoni, *Evo Morales*, 60–62, 63, 69.

47   Mamani, *Geopolíticas*, 59–60.

48   All biographical material for Morales is from the following sources: Alex
Contreras Baspineiro, *Biografía de Evo Morales* (La Paz: 2005), "Perfil," *Evo
Morales*, (2006), http://www.evomorales.org/, "Evo Morales Ayma," *Centro de
Investigación de Relaciones Internacionales y Desarrollo* (February14, 2006),
http://www.cidob.org/es/documentacion/biografias_lideres_politicos/america_
del_sur/bolivia/evo_morales_ayma., "Profile: Evo Morales," *BBC News* (December
14, 2005), http://news.bbc.co.uk/go/pr/fr/-/1/hi/world/americas/3203752.stm.

49   "Conflict Flares in the Bolivian Tropics," *Transnational Institute Drug Policy
Briefing* (January 2, 2002), http://www.tni.org/drugs/index.htm. Also see
Benjamin Kunkel and Lisa Kunkel, "Who's Counting? US plan to eradicate coca
crops in Bolivia fails miserably," *In These Times Magazine* (May 13, 2002).

50   This quote from the documentary film by Rachel Boynton, *Our Brand is Crisis*
(Koch Lorber Films, 2006)

51   Kohl and Farthing, *Impasse*, 170–171.

52   Mamani, *Geopolíticas*, 56.

Chapter Three

Water War in Cochabamba: A Victory Against Fear

Security forces and protestors confront each other in
Cochabamba during the Water War in 2000.
Photo Credit: Thomas Kruse

"We're more about making money than making things."

—**Stephen Bechtel**[1]

Champagne glasses were raised to the success that the Bechtel Corporation would bring to Cochabamba. Politicians from the highest levels of the Bolivian government patted the company representative Geoffrey Thorpe on the back. It was September 3rd, 1999, a time for celebration. The contract to privatize the city's water system had been signed and Thorpe had good reason to be giddy. His company was set to make millions off of local citizens who would now have to pay for all sources of water, from raindrops to the water in community-built wells.[2]

Protest chants from the street broke the spell of the festive contract-signing. Demonstrators were not optimistic about Bechtel's plans for Cochabamba. Inside, the party continued. "I'm used to that sort of background music," Bolivian president and former dictator Hugo Banzer told his guests. That "background music," however, would grow into a roar that would crash Bechtel's party in Cochabamba for good.[3]

By the time the contract was signed, the privatization of public water systems in developing countries had become a trademark of neoliberalism. Proponents of transferring water into corporate hands promised lower costs, more efficient management and improved distribution. Privatization via Bechtel had the opposite affects in Cochabamba: costs skyrocketed, distribution faltered and the poorest citizens were hit the hardest. In response, farmers, labor groups and city residents organized a protest movement that reversed the water privatization plan, kicked Bechtel out of Bolivia and initiated a new era in the country's social movements.

The conflict that broke out in Cochabamba was part of a global water crisis. The earth's population is expanding by 80 million a year and, by 2020, is expected to reach nearly eight billion inhabitants.[4] In contrast, the amount of available fresh water is diminishing each year. In order to sustain this population, more water will be needed for drinking and crop irrigation.[5] If the population continues to grow at the current rate, total human usage of water will reach 100 percent by the middle of the 21st century.[6]

Most of the water on the planet is made up of seawater or is frozen in polar ice caps. Less than one half percent of the world's water is available freshwater. The only way freshwater is renewable is through rainfall, and global warming is limiting this.[7] Pollution, poor irrigation methods, deforestation, droughts, and urbanization are also blocking access to this vital resource, making freshwater available only to those who can afford it. More than one billion people, 20 percent of the global population, currently lack access to safe drinking water.[8] At the same time, around 70 percent of all fresh water utilized by humans from lakes, aquifers, and rivers is used for agriculture.[9] As the price of survival rises, those with less money will not be able to afford potable water, food, or shelter. This increases the likelihood of revolt among poor sectors of society against corporations and governments viewed as blocking access to such resources.[10] Corporations in the water privatization business profit handsomely off of this global crisis.

According to UNESCO Director-General Klaus Toepfer, "As [water] becomes increasingly rare, it becomes coveted, [and] capable of unleashing conflicts." More than oil and land, he said "it is over water that the most bitter conflicts of the near future may be fought."[11] This is particularly true in arid regions such as Cochabamba.

The city of Cochabamba is nestled in a valley between the tropical area of the Chapare and the *altiplano*. A giant, white statue of Jesus Christ looks down from a hilltop over the city, his arms pointing beyond the building where Bechtel's associates' office was sacked in 2000. Christ gazes past *La Cancha*, the city's massive open air market, and toward the countryside, where *campesinos* formed blockades during the water revolt. Many of the water-related conflicts took place in the city's main plaza.

Problems with access to water were not anything new for the residents of Cochabamba. For decades, politicians on the campaign trail have promised to solve the city's water problems. As corruption, scandals, and lack of funding left water issues unresolved, the population kept growing. In 1976, around 200,000 called Cochabamba home. That number grew to 500,000 by the time the Water War began in November, 1999. A year before the conflict broke out the public water network only reached about 60 percent of the population of the city. The rest received their water from self-organized wells and hookups, or bought it from independent distributors who sold the resource at high prices. Some of the most militant participants in the Water War came from poor neighborhoods without direct water connections, whose residents were forced to pay higher rates for water delivery trucks. When *Aguas del Tunari*, a subsidiary of the Bechtel Corporation, announced the rate increase, the biggest price hikes were visited on the poorest sectors.[12]

To facilitate the privatization, the Water Law 2029 was passed and implemented at roughly the same time as the contract with Bechtel. It favored the use of water by international companies for mining, agriculture, and electrical purposes over human consumption. The law did not guarantee equal access to potable water for all citizens, particularly the poorest and most isolated sectors of society. It also prohibited the function of alternative systems of water distribution, which were used throughout rural and poor urban areas. People were billed for everything from the water piped into their houses, to water collected in rain gutters, to the water in community wells. The fact that the law and contract was designed without the input or participation of social and labor groups also sent diverse sectors of the population into the streets to protest.[13]

"Each morning when I woke up, multitudes of *campesinos*, children, women, and neighbors were passing by with banners and clubs," Luis Gonzalez told me. He was an economics student in the University of San Simon during the Water War. "All of Cochabamba was up in arms....People from all different political and social groups came together in the street barricades to confront the police," he said. "They defended themselves with stones and threw back the cops' tear gas canisters." His eyes lit up while relating the story of activists who emptied out Coca-Cola bottles to use them for Molotov cocktails.[14]

The seeds of this revolt were sown in 1996, when the World Bank pressured the Bolivian government into accepting a deal to privatize the water in Cochabamba.[15] The bank threatened to withhold $600 million in debt relief if Bolivia refused to follow the proposed plan. An extensive report on the topic from the Democracy Center in Cochabamba explains that, in 1999, the Bolivian government gave the water privatization contract to *Aguas del Tunari* during a closed-door meeting. This deal promised ownership of water in Cochabamba for the next 40 years and guaranteed annual profits of 16 percent. *Aguas del Tunari* gained control of irrigation systems in rural areas and community wells, many of which had been built and financed solely by local residents. Immediately after taking over, the company drastically raised water rates, in some cases by 200 percent. In a city where the monthly minimum wage is $60, many *Cochabambinos* found meeting water costs of $15–20 per month impossible.[16]

Cochabamba-based professor and Water War expert Carlos Crespo believes the role of the World Bank in the Cochabamba conflict should not be underestimated. "The [World Bank] thinks the water

should be administrated by private companies... and subjected to the
discipline of the market," he explained. "They tell you that the state can't
administer, that it's corrupt, that it isn't transparent... They think that
the market is the best director and is the best way to manage water. But
[the market] leaves out the poor. It makes things more expensive and the
quality [of service] worse."[17]

As the conflict in Cochabamba illustrates, there is often a big
difference in what proponents of neoliberal policies promise and how
things play out on the ground. When Bechtel arrived in Bolivia, politicians in the Banzer administration were eager to work with the company, seeing privatization as a solution to Cochabamba's water problems.

"It was very strange," said Rosseline Ugarte, a young woman who
organized road blockades with the *Confederación Sindical Única de
Trabajadores Campesinos de Bolivia* (CSUTCB) in rural areas during
the Water War. "Even people who didn't have water pipes in their houses
got billed." After the water privatization contract was signed, she worked
with the CSUTCB to spread information about *Aguas del Tunari* to
rural citizens, helping to organize them for action. Due to the lack of
public infrastructure, many *campesinos* and Cochabamba residents had
organized amongst themselves to build water wells and systems with
their own labor and money. "The water laws did not allow you to have
your own well in rural communities," she explained. "You had to pay a
certain amount even for your own well. But a *campesino* doesn't even
have enough money to buy bread, let alone pay a water bill. Where were
they going to get the money?" People were outraged. "How could they
charge us for our water? Next it would be air!"[18]

One of the community-funded, cooperative wells that came under Bechtel's control was in Villa San Miguel, a small town outside of
Cochabamba. It took from 1994 to 1997 for local residents—without
the help of the government—to plan and dig the well. Fredy Villagomez,
a proud organizer of the cooperative, said that the well provided clean
water to 210 families at a low price. Households paid two to five dollars a
month to cover the costs of the pump and well maintenance. Under the
water contract, Villagomez's cooperative was placed in the hands of a
foreign company. *Aguas del Tunari* could charge for the use of this water
through meters, and even charge for the installation of the meters.[19]

The water in Mallco Rancho, a small agricultural community west
of Cochabamba, is produced by wells run by the community. When
Bechtel took over the public water system, the irrigators or *regantes* in
the area were suddenly forced to pay exorbitant rates for water available

only through a system they themselves constructed. As the population expanded, the strain became greater on these systems. Don Juan Saavedra, a resident for more than 90 years, worked for decades managing the water distribution to the various communities in the valley. "In every community someone is in charge of regulating the use of water," he said. Over time, the population expanded, as did the need for water. "It's impossible to live without water. Because of this we entered in the blockades [in the Water War]."[20]

The business that descended on these poor farmers is among the wealthiest 100 corporations in the world. Bechtel is over a century old and works in everything from railroads, mines, and oil to airports, defense, and aerospace facilities.[21] It is the largest construction company on the planet with 19,000 projects in 140 countries, including every continent except Antarctica. Over 200 wastewater and water treatment plants around the world bear the company's name.[22] For Bechtel, the sky is the limit.

Warren Bechtel founded his corporation in 1898, initially to build railroads across Oklahoma and California with Chinese and prison laborers. In 1930, the company was involved in the biggest construction project since the Great Pyramid in Giza: the building of the Hoover Dam. Warren's son, Stephen made billions constructing military bases and ships for World War II. Bechtel later entered the oil business, and eventually built US military bases in Vietnam. The company is now reaping billions for its "reconstruction efforts" in Iraq, a country whose infrastructure is in ruins due to decades of US bombing. Electric, sewage, water, and phone systems continue to be totally unreliable. Trains, schools, and roadways are barely operable. Unsanitary water is a part of reality.[23]

In most cases when governments have privatized water systems, corporations have failed to implement promised changes in infrastructure, and raised connection and monthly fees beyond most citizens' budgets.[24] So it should come as no surprise that the motto of this family empire, attributed to longtime CEO Stephen Bechtel, is "We're more about making money than making things."[25]

Bechtel's philosophy collided head-on with the people of Cochabamba. The movement against the water law and privatization plan culminated in a series of blockades and protests on November 4th, 1999. Participants in the actions demanded changes in the law and contract that would protect their traditional methods to use and distribute the water. *Regante* leader Omar Fernandez wrote that in the town of Vinto, at five am on November 4th, police intervened in one road blockade, shooting rubber bullets and tear gas at protestors. The blockaders ran, threw rocks and dodged bullets, forcing the police to shoot the tear gas upwind, so it blew back onto them. The confused security forces retreated, and blockades were organized at other points. The government ignored the action and anger among *regantes* fermented.[26]

At the end of 1999, when residents started receiving their water bills, the protests grew to include broader sectors of society, including urban residents and students. However, the general outrage was not just over the *Aguas de Tunari* price increases, it had to do with the fact the increased fees were going to a giant, multinational corporation and that many were forced to pay for a resource that had previously come from *Pachamama* (Mother Earth) for free. The powerful collaboration between rural and urban residents grew out of this shared frustration.[27]

The mobilizations in Cochabamba were organized horizontally and included diverse social sectors. Some, such as the coca farmers and irrigation workers in rural areas, organized blockades that cut off the city from the rest of the country, thus pressuring government officials to respond. Others spread information and helped organize actions among workers and neighbors. One protestor named Marcelino had seen the results of the water rate increase firsthand during his work as an employee for both *Aguas del Tunari* and *Servicio municipal de agua potable, alcantarillado y desagües pluviales* (SEMAPA), the public water company previous to privatization. This pushed him to participate daily in the protests along with his friends, family, and co-workers. He rallied 200 others from his neighborhood to join the mobilizations. They walked to the plaza together in single file almost every day.[28]

Much of the energy of these converged social forces was channeled through the *Coordinadora del Agua y Vida* (Coordinator of Water and Life), an incredibly broad coalition of groups that formed the organization on November 12th, 1999. The *Coordinadora* worked as a tool for action, bridged gaps between rural and urban citizens, and brought together diverse economic and political sectors. It played a major role in coordinating and organizing the protests, blockades, and negotiations that led to the rejection of the water law and contract. After the conflict, Oscar Olivera, a local labor organizer and a leader in the *Coordinadora*, would go on to become an internationally known spokesperson for the growing "anti-globalization" movement.

The *Coordinadora* emerged out of a need to "consolidate something among diverse groups," said Claudia Lopez, who joined the *Coordinadora* as a university student during the Water War. "So the question was—how are we going to bring them all together? The answer was to bring them all under the *Coordinadora*...which came about when the people said, 'Let's take the water issue into our own hands.'" During the Water War, Lopez was finishing her university degree in biology. Initially her work involved spreading information, setting up workshops on the water law and contract, and organizing demonstrations.[29]

According to Lopez, the *Coordinadora* learned organizing strategies from already-formed rural sectors. "The *campesinos* had a more complete picture of what was happening," she told me. "They had an organization that met through assemblies, where they made decisions among themselves." Such methods of organizing were not as deeply ingrained into the urban society. However, the two worlds united in the Water War, complementing each other. Lopez said the privatization acted as a "detonator" of social action.

In January, 2000, the *Coordinadora* began organizing protests against the water rate hike and called assemblies to discuss what kind of action to take. Members called for blockades and protests if officials didn't arrive to discuss the demanded changes to the contract and law. Officials did not respond, and blockades began on January 10th. Other groups organized city-wide strikes. The city, airport, and major highways were shut down by blockades. Protesters used rock piles and trees to build road blockades to stop all city traffic, and thousands of protestors gathered in the city's main plaza. Jim Shultz of the Democracy Center reported that "the *Coordinadora* set up its headquarters in the ragged offices of the local factory workers' union and hung a wide banner from the third floor balcony. Bright red with white letters, the banner carried the city's new rallying cry, *El Agua es Nuestra Carajo!*, The Water is Ours, Damn It!"[30]

Tension was high on January 13th when the Ministers of Economy and Commerce from the Banzer administration arrived in Cochabamba to discuss changes in the water law and contract. Representatives from the *Coordinadora* and other groups involved in the protests met with these officials. During the first round of dialogue, police gassed protestors outside, leading representatives from the *Coordinadora* to leave the meeting, refusing to negotiate while police repressed citizens. In a meeting later that same day, government officials said they would revise the privatization deal and water law, but without changing the rate hikes. By the end of the meeting, it was agreed that the government would review and respond to the changes demanded by the *Coordinadora* within three months.[31]

Many Cochabambans didn't have the patience or the money to wait three months. Citizens were defiant: instead of paying their increased water bills, they burned them in the plaza. The company responded by threatening to shut off water connections. In early February, the *Coordinadora* announced plans for a regional march to peacefully occupy Cochabamba's main plaza.[32] In spite of the pacific nature of the planned action, government officials prohibited the march. Special police forces called "Dalmations," for their spotted camouflage uniforms, were flown to Cochabamba from La Paz to deal with the expected protests.[33]

On the morning of February 4th, thousands of people marched into Cochabamba. When the demonstration arrived just one block into the city, the Dalmations appeared on motorcycles and shot tear gas into the crowd. The Quillacollo Bridge into town was blocked by security forces. Marchers sprinted across, trying to break through the line of police, but were slowed by the gas. When they eventually crossed over, the police used stronger tear gas. In response, coca farmers from the Chapare and local residents split up to charge into the plaza from different streets.[34] Fredy Villagomez, a member of the *Coordinadora*, described events: "The young men were in the city center, trying to hold the plaza. Others were...maintaining a barricade across the highway. The women were cooking for those on the barricade. There were many *campesinos* passing by, walking to Cochabamba to join the rebellion."[35] More than 1,000 police and soldiers in riot gear were in the streets, transforming the city into a war zone.[36]

One of the many leaders in this broad, grassroots movement was Oscar Olivera. I had met and listened to Olivera on numerous occasions, the first being a protest in Washington, DC against the IMF and World Bank in April of 2000, just after the Cochabamba revolt. He was a short man, who barely reached the microphone on stage, and his speech showed him to be an articulate, gifted, and passionate public speaker. These traits contributed to his role as a spokesperson for the *Coordinadora* in the Water War. During the conflict, photos showed him with intensely focused eyes shadowed by a lack of sleep and his signature short-rimmed black hat.

In *Cochabamba*, a book Olivera wrote, he describes the solidarity among citizens during the protests. During one demonstration, the

strength of the tear gas forced him and others to knock on the door of
a house for water. The family let the group in and Olivera spoke with
them about the motive of the protest. "They've raised your rates too," he
told them. "We have to go out and fight them—it's the only way." Later
on, he writes, the same family distributed water to protestors, and participated in some of the worst street fighting. Incidents such as this took
place across Cochabamba. "The greatest achievement of the February
days," writes Olivera, "was that we lost our sense of fear...[W]e started
to talk among ourselves, to know one another, and to regain our trust
in ourselves and each other."[37] As a result of the pressure in the streets,
the government signed a deal on February 6th that froze the water rate
increase. In March, the *Coordinadora* organized a referendum on the
water conflict. 96 percent of 50,000 voters supported the cancellation of
the *Aguas del Tunari* contract. Still, the government didn't budge.[38]

Street mobilizations re-emerged on April 4th. Yet, unlike those in
February, the government did not deploy police or soldiers to repress
protestors. It was a tactic to diffuse the pressure. "We became quite wor-
ried, because it seemed that the only way to maintain our resistance was
to provoke the government and get it to react," writes Olivera. Popular
assemblies were called to discuss what actions to take. At these meetings, "everybody had a chance, not just to air their complaints, but also
discuss ideas and advance proposals."[39]

"Anyone could speak, but for you to be heard required action," Olivera wrote. "This became the first requirement to speak. It was a time for
talk, but not without action...The decisions made as a result of this process were presented for validation at the next level, the *cabildos* (town
meetings)." The *cabildos* were held in public plazas and were attended by
50–70,000 people. Final decisions were made depending on the crowd's
reception to plans and ideas. "The crowd responded to different proposals by expressing a collective sentiment, by either applauding or making
disapproving noises, such as boos or whistles. Sometimes the leaders
had to follow the people." It was proposed that protesters give the government 24 hours to cancel the water contract. However, people didn't
want to wait that long and instead headed to the *Aguas del Tunari* office,
where they pulled down the company sign and peacefully occupied the
office. The next day, tens of thousands of people gathered in the plaza to
protest the water law and contract with Bechtel. They refused to leave
until their demands were met.[40]

Meanwhile, the blockades and confrontations between protestors
and security forces in rural areas were intensifying. Rosseline Ugarte

explained that while the tear gas filled the air in Cochabamba, out in the countryside the road blockades were maintained by *campesino* groups, cutting off major routes to the city. "We put stones in the road, everything we could. Every day we went out to blockade." She visited different communities to help organize and coordinate the blockades. "We'd discuss our plans until dawn. It couldn't be something we just threw together. It had to be strategic, so that the pressure got results."

The blockades were coordinated through a complex system of communication and decision making. Representatives from different communities gathered to plan actions then returned to their homes to discuss tactics with neighbors. "They were prepared," Ugarte said. "*Campesinos* aren't idiots who you can tell 'hey *compañero*, let's go blockade for this and that.' No, they've got their eyes open." After many meetings, people would come to an agreement. "The *campesinos* organized their own committees to decide on strategic blockading places." How stones, dynamite, and food would be provided was also discussed. She spoke of blockade strategies such as unattended blankets of spikes and nails on roads, which prevented traffic from passing, and others where blockaders would jump to from one road to another "like fleas" when police arrived.[41]

Besides anger at the water privatization, rage against the repression carried out by security forces also pushed citizens to action. "A huge mistake of the government was to militarize the city, and to bring in other police. It just augmented the anger," Carlos Crespo recalled.

The most tragic act of violence was the death of teenager Victor Daza, who was shot dead by a sniper on April 8th. The shooter, Captain Robinson Iriarte de La Fuente, had been trained at the School of the Americas.[42] The tragedy was amplified by the fact that Daza was not participating in a protest, but simply walking in the street. Ugarte remembered the event vividly: "I was going around in the street and just a meter away our friend [Daza] was shot. We couldn't do anything. He died instantaneously. People picked him up in a blanket and found a little car to try to take him to the plaza and protest." This violence galvanized popular anger against the government and security forces.

On April 6th, martial law was declared and the leaders of the *Coordinadora* were hunted down by police. By hiding in various houses, and changing clothes as a disguise, leaders were able to remain free and send messages to those protesting and blockading in the streets via radio and cell phones. By Saturday, April 8th, the mobilizations were enormous. Groups of young people took over the main plaza and set up barricades. Other groups took over the San Antonio jail and burned police vehicles.[43]

"Nobody wanted to be left out," Lopez told me. "All of the neighborhoods in the city were organized. They were overcome with the feeling of resistance...They collected donations [for food], delegated leaders, and organized soup kitchens in different neighborhoods. Others brought food to those in the city center who were resisting, because the protests raged day and night...It was a huge gesture of solidarity." She recalled those days with excitement in her eyes. "We were united by something that was very clear to all of us: we wanted *Aguas del Tunari* to be thrown out of Cochabamba."

Protestors who remained in the streets, maintaining blockades and defending occupied plazas, were dubbed "Water Warriors." Many of them were young and from all walks of life. Homeless kids fought next to youth from rich neighborhoods. Soccer teams took their solidarity off the field and translated it into a side-by-side fight at the street barricades.[44] "The poorest young people were always on the frontlines, throwing stones at the police," Luis Gonzalez said. "They are people who have a tradition of fighting because they have been ignored, marginalized, pushed around. They're always struggling just to survive. They inspired us to move forward."

In response to civil unrest, government officials held a meeting with the *Coordinadora* on Monday, April 10th. Officials from the Mayor's office, the Defender of the People (Ombudsman) and the President of the Municipality were in attendance.[45] Some politicians at the meeting arrived willing to listen to demands from protestors. Others proclaimed that it didn't matter how many people were killed in the streets, the contract and law would stay the same.[46] Leaders from the *Coordinadora* went to the plaza, which was packed with protestors and Water War riors. They told the people to hold the plaza and remain ready to carry out the necessary actions if they didn't get what they wanted in the negotiation meeting. Later in the afternoon, a deal was made between government officials and the *Coordinadora* to reject the contract and put the water back in public hands. The Law 2029 was changed, but had to be approved by the Parliament. Until then, pressure in the streets continued.[47]

Regante leader Omar Fernandez went to La Paz to participate in the Parliamentary session where the law, with alterations, was passed. The law placed the now-public water company, SEMAPA, in the hands of a board, that was managed in a participatory fashion, which included leaders from the mayor's office, unionized SEMAPA workers, and the *Coordinadora*.[48]

Though the water fees went back to the structure that was in place before Bechtel arrived, creating a successfully public-run water system proved to be harder than many citizens imagined. According to Cochabamba water specialist Susan Spronk, though SEMAPA has attempted to expand the water network to poorer neighborhoods in Cochabamba over the years, lack of funds has prevented them from doing so. The services of those who were previously connected to SEMAPA have not improved. Inefficient services and work on the part of SEMAPA have been denounced by clients and there have been cases of corruption in the water system's management. There have also been reports of illegal water connections being made with the consent of higher-ups in the company, creating financial losses for SEMAPA.[49]

"At least the fact that there are three elected officials sitting on the board provides a means by which the social movements can gain access to information about budgets and expansion plans," Spronk explained. However, these three people don't exert sufficient power over the management of the company because the mayor and his allies still maintain control. According to Spronk, though the water utility is autonomous in the sense that it has its own budget, the mayor is the president of the board. She believes, "the process to establish social control is long and arduous because powerful local hegemons do not just give up power, it must be wrestled from them. The slow process of democratization of the public water company is still in its beginning stages."[50]

Another challenge faced Bolivians in the wake of the Cochabamba victory. To recover what Bechtel said were losses and missed profits from the cancellation of the water contract in 2000, the company demanded $50 million from the Bolivian government. It took its case to the secretive World Bank's International Center for the Settlement of Investment Disputes, without press access or testimonies from Bolivians.[51]

In January, 2006, Bechtel dropped their claim against Bolivia after an international campaign of protests, emails and petitions demanding that the case be opened to the public. Demonstrations flared up at Bechtel offices around the world and in 2002, protestors chained themselves to the company's lobby in San Fransisco. Police and fire officials used saws to cut chains and remove the activists. After this action and others, the company board of supervisors passed a resolution to ask Bechtel to drop the case against South America's poorest country. Instead of the millions they initially asked for, Bechtel left with a symbolic 30 cents in their pocket.[52]

Cochabamba's Water War weakened the legitimacy of political parties and traditional unions, and strengthened the power and confidence of horizontally organized coalitions of workers and citizens such as the *Coordinadora*. "There is now a greater distrust of the government and the formal political system," Carlos Crespo said. "The people's self direction has repeated itself in later situations... After 2000 I am convinced that life and politics [in Bolivia] have been transformed."

The 2000 Water War took place at a high point for the growing "anti-globalization movement." The Battle of Seattle—street protests against the World Trade Organization—occurred just months before the Water War and a similar mobilization took place against the IMF and World Bank in Washington, DC in April 2000, just after the victory in Cochabamba. Oscar Olivera's presence at the protest in DC along with reports from the Water War distributed via the internet helped establish the conflict as a symbol for this movement.

Other groups against water privatization emerged in the wake of the Cochabamba victory. A contract with the French company Vivendi was terminated in Argentina because of the business's weak performance.[53] Shortly after the Cochabamba revolt, the Confederation of Indigenous Nationalities of Ecuador (CONAIE) created its own water reform proposal, which focuses on the social, community-based, and ecological aspects of water. In Ecuador's Chimborazo Province, locals organized themselves into cooperatives of water users, which defend the area against corporations, landowners, and the government.[54] In 2005, residents and social organizations in El Alto, Bolivia united to kick out the French water company, Suez.[55]

Other organizations from diverse countries linked themselves with activists from the 2000 Water War to exchange ideas and strategies. One such group came from Uruguay, where a referendum against water privatization was organized in 2004. Olivera traveled to Uruguay on many occasions previous to the referendum to meet with water rights groups. Water activists in Uruguay were inspired by the Cochabamban experience and used it as a reference point, starting their own *Coordinadora*.

The push for the Uruguayan referendum was spearheaded by the National Commission in Defense of Water and Life (CNDAV), a coalition of social groups and civic networks including unions from the state sewage and water company, State Sanitary Works (OSE). The coalition started the action in 2002 when the Uruguayan government and IMF planned to privatize water in the country. The main companies that were to profit from this deal included Suez and the Spanish *Aguas del Bilbao*. Under the deal, the cost of the connection to the water system was exorbitant and the price of the water was ten times higher than that of the OSE. Additionally, the service provided by these companies was of a much lower quality and less dependable than the state company. *Aguas de la Costa*—a Suez company—also polluted Lake Blanca, which it used in part of its sanitation procedures. The public company had serviced isolated areas to ensure that residents had access to water. To increase revenue, the private companies cut these lines off until clients paid for a new connection. Citizens who couldn't afford the reconnection had to go without access. These shady dealings contributed to the outrage and move for the referendum.[56]

In October, 2003, CNDAV presented 283,000 signatures to the parliament, which guaranteed that a referendum be held the following year, during the national elections. At the polls, Uruguayan voters rejected privatization of water and made access to the resource a human right protected by the constitution. In October, 2004, 1,440,000 Uruguayans (almost 65 percent of all voters) voted to support this constitutional amendment.[57]

The new amendment required that civil society, consumers, and citizen groups participate in all aspects of public water management.[58] A letter signed by 127 social organizations from 36 countries highlighted the fact that the constitutional amendment passed in the Uruguayan referendum "secures the protection and sovereignty of this natural resource against attacks from transnational corporations transcending the national limits of Uruguay and setting a strong political precedent for the whole region."[59]

Besides invigorating social movements in Bolivia by providing an example of what was possible through popular protest, the Cochabamba Water War inspired activists around the world fighting against corporate exploitation. The conflict provided a clear-cut example of the failure of neoliberal policies that pit large corporations against working people. Instead of an improved water system, privatization of the city's water produced a rebellion that would change the political environment in Bolivia for years to come. As Uruguayan Eduardo Galeano writes of his country's movement for water rights, "More than five centuries have passed since Columbus. How long can we go on trading gold for glass beads?"[60]

(Endnotes)

1 Jeffrey St. Clair, "Straight to Bechtel," *CounterPunch* (May 9, 2005), http://www.counterpunch.org/stclair05092005.html.

2 Thomas Kruse, "Bechtel versus Bolivia: the next battle in the "Water War,"" *Public Citizen*, https://www.citizen.org/print_article.cfm?ID=8114

3 Kruse, "Bechtel versus Bolivia: the next battle in the "Water War,""

4 *World Resources 1998–99: Environmental change and human health* (Washington, D.C.: World Resources Institute, 1998),141–45, 244–45.

5 Peter H. Gleick, *The World's Water, 2000–2001: The Biennial Report on Freshwater Resources* (Washington, DC: Island Press, 2000), 63–92.

6 Michael T. Klare, *Resource Wars: The New Landscape of Global Conflict,* (New York: Owl Books, 2002), 19.

7 M. Barlow and T. Clarke, "The Struggle for Latin America's water," *NACLA Report of the Americas* 38, no. 1 (July, 2004).

8 Mark Kinver, "Water policy 'fails world's poor,'" British Broadcasting Corporation News (March 9, 2006), http://news.bbc.co.uk/2/hi/science/nature/4787758.stm. Also see, Barlow and Clarke, *Blue Gold: The fight to stop the corporate theft of the world's water* (New York: The New Press, 2002).

9 Sandra Postel, *Last Oasis: Facing Water Scarcity*, The Worldwatch Environmental Alert Series (New York: W. W. Norton & Company,1997), 19–20, 48–59. From Klare, *Resource Wars*

10 Klare, *Resource Wars*, 24.

11 Interview with Klaus Toepfer, "Water Wars Forecast If Solutions Not Found," *Environmental Science and Technology* (January 1, 1999.) From Klare, *Resource Wars*

12 Crabtree, *Perfiles de la Protesta*, 10. Also see Thomas Kruse, "La "Guerra del Agua" en Cochabamba, Bolivia: Terrenos Complejos, Convergencias Nuevas." In *Sindicatos y nuevos movimientos sociales en América Latina,* (Buenos Aires: CLACSO, 2005), 121–161.

13 Carmen Peredo, Carlos Crespo, and Omar Fernández, *Los Regantes de Cochabamba en la guerra del agua, Presión social y negociación* (Cochabamba: CESU-UMSS, 2004), 114–115.

14 All quotes and information from Luis Gonzalez are from interview with author in February, 2006.

15 Often the World Bank not only makes privatization of water a condition for lending money, but it tells the government of a country which water company to work with. In order to provide water to the population and receive loans, many governments are left with no other choice but to follow orders. For more, see Jeff Fleischer, "An Interview with Maude Barlow," *Mother Jones* (January 14, 2005), http://www.motherjones.com/news/qa/2005/01/maude_barlow.html. Corporations that deal with water management such as Bechtel and the French company Suez often use their clout to influence policy in their favor among lending institutions such as the World Bank and the International Development Bank (IDB). They do this to acquire financing or profitable contracts. For example, some of the IDB's largest loans have gone to companies for the privatization of water in Latin America. The World Bank has recently tripled its

budget for financing privatization projects. Behind such policies lies the belief in neoliberalism. See Barlow and Clarke, "The Struggle for Latin America's Water."

16 Jim Shultz, "Bolivia's War Over Water," *The Democracy Center* (2004), http://democracyctr.org/bechtel/the_water_war.htm.

17 All quotes and information from Carlos Crespo are from an interview with the author in February, 2006.

18 All quotes and information from Rosseline Ugarte are from an interview with the author in February, 2006.

19 William Finnegan, "Leasing the Rain," *The New Yorker* (April 8, 2002), http://www.newyorker.com/printables/fact/020408fa_FACT1.

20 Crabtree, *Perfiles de la Protesta*, 9. Also see Thomas Kruse, "La 'Guerra del Agua' en Cochabamba, Bolivia: Terrenos Complejos, Convergencias Nuevas." In *Sindicatos y nuevos movimientos sociales en América Latina*, (Buenos Aires: CLACSO, 2005), 121-161.

21 Bechtel website, www.Bechtel.com.

22 Barlow and Clarke, "The Struggle for Latin America's water," and *Blue Gold: The fight to stop the corporate theft of the world's wate.* Also see Vandana Shiva, "Bechtel and Blood for Water: War As An Excuse For Enlarging Corporate Rule," *ZNet* (May 12, 2003).

23 St. Clair, "Straight to Bechtel."

24 Arnie Alpert, "Is Another World Possible? A Water Activist Reports from Porto Alegre," *Common Dreams* (February 23, 2005), http://www.commondreams.org/cgi-bin/print.cgi?file=/views05/0223-29.htm.

25 St. Clair, "Straight to Bechtel." Ibid.

26 Fernandez, *Los Regantes de Cochabamba*, 128–130.

27 This information on reasons for shared outrage between urban and rural areas is from an email interview with Susan Spronk, November, 2005.

28 Ana Esther Ceceña, *La Guerra por el agua y por la vida* (Buenos Aires: Madres de Plaza de Mayo, 2005),105.

29 All quotes and information from Claudia Lopez are from interview with author in February, 2006.

30 Shultz, "Bolivia's War Over Water."

31 Fernandez, *Los Regantes de Cochabamba*,132 and Oscar Olivera, *Cochabamba: Water War in Bolivia*, trans. Tom Lewis (Cambridge: South End Press, 2004), 31–32.

32 Shultz, "Bolivia's War Over Water."

33 Fernandez, *Los Regantes de Cochabamba*, 135.

34 Ibid.

35 Finnegan, "Leasing the Rain."

36 Shultz, "Bolivia's War Over Water."

37 Oscar Olivera, *Cochabamba*, 34–36.

38 Finnegan, "Leasing the Rain."

39 Olivera, *Cochabamba*, 37.

40 Ibid., 38.

41 In the 2000 Water War, *regantes* also used skills learned in previous mobilizations regarding water issues.

42 For more information on this school's work, see School of the Americas Watch website: www.soaw.org, also Gill, *The School of the Americas*.

43 Fernandez, *Los Regantes de Cochabamba*, 146.

44 Cecena, *La Guerra por el agua*, 103–104.

45 Fernandez, *Los Regantes de Cochabamba*, 149.

46 Olivera, *Cochabamba*, 44–45.

47 Fernandez, *Los Regantes de Cochabamba*, 149.

48 Ibid, 150–151.

49 From Susan Spronk, "Roots of Resistance to Urban Water Privatization in Bolivia: The 'New Working Class', the Crisis of Neoliberalism, and Public Services," Fifth draft submitted to *International Labor and Working Class History*, Special issue on Privatization of Public Services (August 25, 2006). Union problems have also arisen. According to author email interview with Spronk, "Various activists in Cochabamba are particularly frustrated with the union, which struck a deal with management to increase the number of employees sometime after the new manager (Gonzalo Ugalde) was hired in 2001. The union also seems to have power over hiring practices (not of managers, which are selected by the board of directors)." Also see Belén Balanyá, Brid Brennan, Olivier Hoedeman, Satoko Kishimoto and Philipp Terhorst eds., *Reclaiming Public Water Achievements, Struggles and Visions from Around the World* (Netherlands: Transnational Institute and Corporate Europe Observatory, 2005), http://www.tni.org/books/publicwater.htm., Also see Food and Water Watch: http://www.foodandwaterwatch.org/water.

50 From author interview with Spronk.

51 Paul Harris, "Bechtel, Bolivia resolve dispute: Company drops demand over water contract canceling," *Chronicle Foreign Service* (January 19, 2006), http://www.sfgate.com/cgi-bin/article.cgi?file=/c/a/2006/01/19/MNGM8GPJAK1.DTL&type=printable. Also see Jim Shultz, "Bechtel vs. Bolivia: The People Win!" *PeaceWork* (February, 2006), http://www.peaceworkmagazine.org/pwork/0602/060208.htm.

52 Harris, "Bechtel, Bolivia resolve dispute." And Shultz, "Bechtel vs. Bolivia."

53 Finnegan, "Leasing the Rain."

54 Rutgerd Boelens and Hugo de Vos, "Water War and Indigenous Rights in the Andes," *Cultural Survival Quarterly* (January 6, 2006), http://209.200.101.189/publications/csq/csq-article.cfm?id=1867.

55 The story of El Alto's revolt against Suez is told in Chapter Nine.

56 Belén Balanyá, Brid Brennan, Olivier Hoedeman, Satoko Kishimoto and Philipp Terhorst eds., *Por un modelo público de agua: Triunfos, luchas y sueños*, trans. Beatriz Martinez Ruiz (Netherlands: Transnational Institute / Corporate Europe Observatory / El viejo topo, November 2005), 179.

57 Balanyá et. al., "Por un Modelo Publico de Agua," 178.

58 Ibid., 180–181.

59 Raúl Pierri, "Uruguary, Referendum Gives Resounding 'No' to the Privatization of Water," *Inter Press News Service* (November 1, 2004), http://www.ipsnews.net/interna.asp?idnews=26097.

60 Eduardo Galeano, "Where the People Voted Against Fear," *Common Dreams.org* (November 13, 2004), http://www.commondreams.org/views04/1113-20.htm.

Chapter Four

IMF Backlash:
Que Se Vayan Todos!

Protestors demand that former Bolivian President
Gonzalo Sánchez de Lozada be tried for the deaths
caused by police and military repression under his
administration. The signs read: "What have you
done to ensure that the crimes of this man don't go
unpunished?"

Photo Credit: Julio Mamani

"It didn't occur to the President of Bolivia to do anything else than to follow the rules of the IMF."

—Eduardo Duhalde[1]

A single rock crashed through a window of the Presidential palace in La Paz around noon on February 12th, 2003. The tension between the striking police and the military had reached a climax. The rock, tossed by a high school student, set in motion a bloody conflict that would leave over 30 people dead and hundreds wounded.

The conflict was the result of the International Monetary Fund (IMF)'s pressure on the Bolivian government to apply an income tax increase. Instead of reducing the government's deficit, the move plunged Bolivia into chaos. The country's police force, already demanding higher wages, went on strike when the tax hike was announced. Student, labor and social organizations followed their lead, and a two-day civil war broke out between demonstrators allied with police and the military, which was protecting the interests of the government. In the bloody mayhem that ensued, young, inexperienced military recruits were pitted against policemen fighting for decent wages. The IMF, along with the neoliberal Sánchez de Lozada adminstration, dug its own grave in a country that echoed with the street cries of Argentina's uprising against similar IMF-backed policies just two years earlier— *Que se Vayan Todos!* (Kick them all out!)

Like thousands of other Bolivians, Abraham Bojórquez, a young rapper from El Alto, was swept up into the two-day turmoil. I met him in *Wayna Tambo*, a youth cultural center with a radio station, music studio, café, and library. Bojórquez dresses like a hip-hop artist from the US, with baggy pants, a baseball cap tilted to the side, and a hefty coat. Before being sent off with a rifle to guard the presidential palace on February 12th, he had already had been through several adventures that took him from El Alto to Brazil and back, and into the IMF conflict in an unexpected way.[2] We talked on the second floor of *Wayna Tambo* as a rock band practiced downstairs. The sun was setting on one of the highest cities in the world, and cold wind from snowcapped mountains in the distance blew in through the cracks in the window pane.

He was 12 years old when he hopped on a bus to Brazil from Bolivia. Economic and family problems forced him to leave his home in El Alto and try his luck in Sao Paolo. He found his first job working in front of a sewing machine at a Korean tailor's shop from six in the morning to midnight each day. Financial troubles weren't his only challenges. "I had a gun pulled on me five times in Brazil," he said. The first time was because he unknowingly danced with a Brazilian's girlfriend. The second was during a fight in defense of a Bolivian friend who was being harassed by a Brazilian. "Everybody carried guns there, even kids who were just 10–13 years old."

When he arrived back in Bolivia, tired of the lifestyle in Brazil, he signed up for his obligatory military service, partly out of curiosity. Completing military service also makes it easier to get a job or enter college in Bolivia. As he was training in the military, Bolivian President Gonzalo Sánchez de Lozada worked with the IMF to lower the country's deficit in order to gain a long-term loan from the institution. Early in his military training, Abraham was sent to secure the Presidential palace from police and students protesting the tax hike. Like many neoliberal plans before it, this one was applied to the country through the barrels of guns, one of which ended up being held by Bojórquez.

The man behind the orders that sent Bojórquez into the crossfire was Sánchez de Lozada. It was his second term as president after spending the first 22 years of his life living in the US, where he not only developed a US-accented Spanish, but studied the gospel of the free market, a religion he followed so fervently that his friends in Washington called him "the most intelligent neoliberal in Latin America." Because of this, and his accent, many Bolivians referred to him as *El Gringo*. He amassed enormous wealth in two of the country's most infamous areas of exploitation—land ownership and mining—emerging later as a political leader in the Senate, Ministry of Planning, and the government's economic advisory groups.[3] Before his first stint as president from 1994–1997, he left his position as director of his mining company, *Minera del Sur*, which had become one of the ten largest businesses in the country.[4]

The documentary *Our Brand is Crisis* follows Sánchez de Lozada's 2002 presidential campaign, offering a revealing look at this peculiar character.[5] To give a much-needed boost to his campaign, the 73-year-old candidate hired a group of consultants from Greenberg, Carville and Shrum (GCS) Political Consulting, based in Washington, DC. The company has worked in polling, campaign management, strategy and advertising in elections all over the world. Their idea of democracy is wrapped up in the belief that free market economics bring benefits to their candidates' constituencies. The movie documents the chasm between the wealthy Bolivian elite, represented by Sánchez de Lozada's campaign team, and the impoverished majority, which the consultants manipulated, lied to, and promised solutions that they never intended to deliver.

GCS was hired to sell a candidate whom polls indicated the citizens did not want to buy. Jeremy Rosner, the chief architect of the campaign, told Sánchez de Lozada plainly, "You've still got over half the electorate who can't stand you... I mean, [for] probably 55 percent the only question is 'how high should the gallows be?'" In spite of these odds, Sánchez de Lozada won the presidency with Evo Morales coming in just 2.5 percent of the votes behind him.

As a re-elected president, Sánchez de Lozada had a heavy hand in transforming Bolivia into a lab rat for neoliberal economics. In 2002, Sánchez de Lozada was entering a crisis he helped develop. From 2000 to 2003, the income of the poorest 10 percent of the population declined by 15 percent, while that of the richest 10 percent increased by 16 per cent. In the highlands, over 90 percent lived in poverty.[6] From 1997 to 2002, Bolivia's budget deficit rose from 3.3 percent of the national income to 8.7 percent.[7] In July, 2003, a governmental report indicated that the quality of life for Bolivians was worse than it had been five years ago. Unemployment had risen and people were earning less. In 1998, there were 2.3 million Bolivians without electricity. By the 2002 election year, that number had risen to 3.1 million.[8]

The IMF had a plan to reverse the crisis. Representatives from the institution told the Sánchez de Lozada administration that, in order receive a vital loan, the country's deficit had to be lowered from 8.5 percent to 5.5 percent.[9] The government was between a rock and a hard place; they were starving for money and not in a position to turn down the loan. On the other hand, the policies they were to apply to lower the deficit would prove to be disastrous for the country. George Gray Molina, one of Sánchez de Lozada's key economists, said that his administration was "up against the wall every month" with the IMF. Without the loan, they would not be able to pay the salaries of public employees.[10]

When the IMF told Sánchez de Lozada he had to lower the deficit, his economic team devised an income tax plan, which would generate the funds the government needed to overcome the deficit crisis. To accomplish this, they planned to apply a 12.5 percent income tax on citizens with the lowest salaries in the country.[11] According to Jim Shultz of the Democracy Center, Sánchez de Lozada's tax plan was calibrated to make people with the lowest incomes pay an extra two dollars per month, which in many cases pays for two days' worth of food.[12] Once again in Bolivia, the poor were to bear the burden of the neoliberal economic system.

The IMF officials, on the other hand, said that they were not pressuring the Bolivian government into applying the tax. "On paper that is no doubt true; in reality it is widely known that the IMF takes an active role in proposing solutions to the problems it identifies," a press statement from the activist group *50 Years is Enough* explained. "The introduction of new taxes on the working population was widely known to be the IMF's favored remedy for the deficit."[13]

The tax forced a discontented population into the streets. Interestingly enough, the revolt was led by the very people who in other cases would have been called on to suppress it: the Bolivian police force. On a cold July morning, I hopped into a taxi for a meeting with police Colonel José Villarroel, a participant on the front lines of the February revolt.

Villarroel worked in a special police force for a number of years and later as the director of intelligence for the city of La Paz.[14] His uniform was clean and ironed and his haircut was short. The way he carried himself and communicated with his co-workers exhibited a sense of honor and respect. Each person in the building saluted him as I followed him to his office. I looked around to the policemen whose salaries this tax plan would have affected. They would have been shoved into poverty along with their friends and family whose wages would be slashed so that the neoliberal model could continue to flourish in Bolivia.

The rest of the building bustled with morning activity, but Villarroel's office was quiet and orderly. His smile suggested a sense of humor, kindness, and boredom with his work, perhaps explaining his eagerness to talk with me as a break from his normal routine. Like many who participated in the revolt of February, 2003, the experience had changed his life and outlook. He now had a different job in migration and viewed protests in a new light.

"The police salary is very low," Villarroel explained to me. "In January, 2003 there was a rise in salaries for government officials, but there was no increase for us." This created discontent, forcing a group of policeman led by Major David Vargas to decide to go on strike in a demand for higher wages. "Various classes and levels of policemen went on strike, and the unity and participation in the strike grew. The police just didn't go to work. It was a strike all the way from El Alto to the South of La Paz," Villarroel said.

The same methods the police utilized to repress protests were used to start this one. Except this time, their organizational capacity as a police force was put into effect to resist state policies, not to enforce them. "There is a national leadership within the police, each department has a leader and they communicate with each other. Through this system it is decided what action to take…In this case, Major Vargas was the leader. The command was to go on strike, so the unity was very strong," Villarroel said. "There was a movement within the police force to begin the strike and stop working. These orders were coming from our superiors, from above." The officers were in lock step with one another.

On February 9th, Sánchez de Lozada announced the 12.5 percent income tax increase. Many workers and social organizations in the country immediately rejected the move. For the police force, the tax increase was the last straw. They hadn't even received their salaries for January when the president rejected their demand for a 40 percent salary increase. With David Vargas as their leader, the police met with the Minister of Government, Alberto Gasser. Their central demand was a modification of the tax hike to apply to those with salaries of $660 a month and higher, thus taking the burden off poorer citizens. According to Vargas, the minister replied, "[The tax hike] can't be withdrawn. The President can't do that. We have a commitment with the International Monetary Fund. We can't go back on this because it would say that the government isn't serious."[15] What the government did not realize was that the police were equally serious.

The way in which these policies were applied to Bolivia was business as usual for the IMF, a notoriously undemocratic institution where voting power is based on financial clout, putting 17 percent of economic decision making into the hands of US representatives. Though IMF policies deeply affect the world's most impoverished nations, such as Bolivia, the institution has always had a European president. Such a system leaves those people most affected by the policies totally out of the decision making process.[16] While IMF officials may think that they are working in a country's best interest, they are often not open to alternatives. The policies they advocate are structured to help a country participate in global trade, increasing its buying or export potential. Many times, local elites like Sánchez de Lozada are happy to go along with these recipes.[17]

As the Nobel Prize-winning, former chief economist and senior vice president at the World Bank, Joseph Stiglitz, points out in his book, *Globalization and its Discontents*, part of the problem with the IMF is that "it does not acknowledge that development requires a transformation of society." He argues that, instead of rapidly enforced free trade policies, the IMF should focus on programs in education, land reform and health care to generate social and economic improvements.[18] In vintage IMF style, Sánchez de Lozada did exactly the opposite. Yet he was far from the first president to follow the dictates of the IMF to tragic ends. Two years before he tried to apply the income tax on the poorest sectors of society, a similar IMF-inspired crisis hit the booming Argentine economy.

In a matter of days, Argentina went from being one of the richest nations in the region to one of the poorest. The roots of this crash can be traced to previous dictators allied with the IMF. The Argentine dictatorship of Jorge Videla in 1976 developed strong ties with the institution, adopting policies of privatization and debt accumulation that improved the dictatorship's standing with rich countries, particularly the US. The US Federal Reserve was supportive of the Videla regime because most of the borrowed money was put into US bank accounts.[19]

When the Videla dictatorship ended in 1984, Raul Alfonsin was elected president. His economic policies were roughly the same as Videla's, and many of the dictatorship's economic and financial officials remained in their governmental posts. Under the Videla regime, Argentine subsidiaries of companies such as IBM Argentina, CitiBank, Bank of America, Renault Argentina and others had been encouraged to go into debt. The Alfonsin government paid off these companies' debts with taxpayers' money. Carlos Menem, Alfonsin's successor, proceeded to privatize everything in sight, selling most of the country's state-run companies and resources at low prices to foreign buyers. For example, the Boeing 707s of the airline company *Aerolineas Argentinas*, which are still in use today, were sold to a French company for $1.40 each. Meanwhile, the government's debt grew at a rapid rate, from $8 billion in 1976 to nearly $160 billion in 2001. This forced the government to spend an enormous percent of tax revenues on loans and interest, instead of on maintaining social programs, education, and health care.[20]

In order to combat inflation, the Argentine government set up an economic plan in 1991 that pegged each peso to the US dollar. This allowed the government to distribute only pesos that were backed in the reserves by dollars. In order to keep this system stable throughout the 1990s, Argentina had to borrow yet more money.[21] Menem's privatization of public works, combined with deregulation and free capital flow, essentially made the government lose control over the economy. Most of Argentina's domestic banks ended up in the hands of foreign companies, which favored lending to their traditional multinational corporate clients rather than small and medium sized Argentine businesses. This stunted national growth considerably. At the same time, the IMF pushed for cutbacks in social spending and raised taxes, spinning the country out of control.[22]

The IMF had formerly referred to Argentina as a success story. In its own words, the IMF "programs are intended to help a country adopt policies that will help it regain market confidence and thereby have access to private capital, which are essential for growth and jobs."[23] Furthermore, as Stiglitz points out, "[I]nside the IMF it was simply assumed that whatever suffering occurred was a necessary part of the pain countries had to experience on the way to becoming a successful market economy..."[24] While the economy "improved" under the neoliberal leadership of Videla, Alfonsin, and Menem, lower class Argentines endured the ravages of that "success."

Abraham Leonardo Gak, Rector of the School of Business at the University of Buenos Aires, explained that, during the 1990s, the Argentine government's control over the economy gradually shifted into the hands of the market. "There's an idea that the market is the best way to manage resources," Gak said. "It's been preached continuously for more than 27 years. It was installed, not just in the economy, but in the minds of the people. Imports replaced local manufacturing and investment capital could go in and out of the country at any moment. It seemed like the economy was growing..." But wealth was actually becoming concentrated in the hands of a few while unemployment rose and business became less regulated. This was supposed to allow the private sector to boost the economy.[25]

The neoliberal party ended on December 19th, 2001. Argentina defaulted on $100 billion of debt and the banking system crashed. Many Argentine citizens woke up on December 19th unable to access their savings accounts. In an attempt to stop the flow of dollars out of the country, the government had frozen citizens' bank accounts. Middle class people became poor, the poor went hungry and unemployment skyrocketed. Thousands hit the streets in protests, and twenty-one people were killed in confrontations with police. The country went through five presidents in two weeks.[26]

Out of the wreckage, people attempted to construct a new world. Citizens countered poverty, homelessness and unemployment with barter systems and alternative currency. Neighbors organized assemblies and provided food to the neediest in their communities. Unemployed workers took over their factories and businesses, running them as co-operatives. The economic depression pushed neighbors in Argentina together, unified social movements and created a space for further mobilizations and progressive electoral victories. A similar transformative experience took place in Bolivia two years later. IMF-backed policies in that country weakened the government, strengthened social movements' capacity to mobilize, and galvanized national outrage against the Sánchez de Lozada administration.

"It didn't occur to the president of Bolivia to do anything else than to follow the rules of the IMF," said Argentine president Eduardo Duhalde, pointing out the parallels between the two conflicts. In spite of the lessons offered by the Argentine crash, the medicine prescribed by the IMF in Bolivia only made the ailing country sicker.[27] Yet even before the tax increase hit the paychecks of the poorest workers, blood filled the streets of La Paz in protest against it.

MAS party and *cocalero* leader Evo Morales, emboldened by his near victory in the 2002 presidential elections, called for protests, strikes, and blockades against the tax increase. Labor and social organizations across the country joined his call to action. The Special Security Group (GES), the police force led by Major Vargas and the one José Villarroel belonged to, led the movement with a national strike and protest. Approximately 100 members of the GES gathered in the Plaza Murillo in front of the Presidential Palace at 10 am on February 12th. Students from the Ayacucho high school arrived at 11 am to join the march.[28]

Bojórquez, the hip-hop artist, was in the Presidential Palace when the situation exploded. Though his superiors regularly woke him up early in the morning to do spontaneous training for combat and social conflicts, he was surprised when they told him to go to the Presidential Palace to put those skills to use. Normally military students are sent into shooters' positions in the field after three to four months of practice. They sent Abraham to do this job after barely two weeks of training. "I wasn't prepared," he told me.

He felt solidarity with protestors outside in the plaza, yet as a member of the military, he was trapped. He said military superiors sent the younger, less-trained students to carry out the thankless task of shooting at their fellow citizens. "The saddest thing was that the soldiers were utilized, controlled to defend a president that lamentably wasn't doing things correctly...a lot of the military inside the palace wanted to leave during the conflict," he said. "They didn't believe in what they were told to do." Other soldiers in the February conflict were similarly ill-prepared. In the confusion, some of them shot their guns by mistake. One soldier accidentally shot himself.[29] Villarroel, who was based in the Plaza Murillo with other police throughout the conflict, also criticized the palace security, blaming the soldiers' lack of experience for many of the deaths.[30]

Around noon, students from the Ayacucho and Felipe Segundo Guzman High Schools started throwing rocks at the Presidential Palace.[31] The act was met with applause from the police.[32] In response, the military shot tear gas toward the police barricades. Provoked by the gas shot by the military, the police returned fire with their own gas canisters.[33] Armed reinforcements from both the police and military arrived at the plaza and the shootout began.[34] Ceasefires were attempted, but the violence continued, peaking around two in the afternoon with exchanges of lethal fire between police and soldiers while military snipers shot from rooftops.[35]

One of the victims caught in the crossfire was 16-year-old Julián Huáscar, a student at the Colegio Italo Boliviano Cristobal Colon. On February 12th, Julián skipped breakfast and rushed out the door. His mother, artisan Maria Calcina, wondered why he was in such a hurry. Later that day, after his mother had heard about the shooting in the Plaza Murillo, she, like many other parents, went out searching for her son. She found him at the morgue. "Get up," she told him, but he had been killed by a bullet to the heart.[36]

Villarroel said the lack of police working in the streets created chaos, which was taken advantage of by many people. People broke into ATM machines, businesses, and government offices. This mayhem spread to Cochabamba, Santa Cruz, and other areas of the country. At 3:30 in the afternoon on February 12th, protestors attacked the Vice Presidential Palace and burned documents and furniture. Later in the evening, looters broke into banks, political party offices and one state run TV station.[37] The level of violence forced government officials to negotiate with Major Vargas.

"In the afternoon a ceasefire was called," Villarroel said. "Ambulances arrived for the dead and wounded. The police marched peacefully around the Plaza Murrillo, and snipers on the roofs stopped shooting." However, tempers were high and the ceasefire did not last long. Villarroel said that soon "the army began to shoot more civilians, thinking they were disguised as members of the police department. The army used high caliber weapons... transporting guns, tear gas, and ammunition in ambulances. They were decidedly out to kill people." Police uniforms turned into military targets that night as army tanks rolled in and police fortified their street barricades.

Whereas under dictatorships and during protests it is often the bearded and scruffy people who are singled out by the police or military, in this conflict it was the people with trim haircuts like those of police-men who were targeted. Such was the case with 22-year-old civilian Jorge Mauro Franco Miranda, who, on February 12th, went to the center of the city to pick up his ID card, which was being refurbished at a store. He never retrieved it. According to his wife, Rosa Mamani, Miranda had a short haircut similar to that of a uniformed policeman. Rosa called his cell phone at 3 o'clock but he didn't answer. He had already been shot down in the street.[38]

Throughout the day of February 12th, El Alto was flooded with tear gas from the military and smoke from road blockades. Protestors constructed street barricades and bonfires out of furniture and garbage to block the passage of the military and other vehicles.[39] For two days, marches organized by students, workers, and civic organizations came and went from El Alto to La Paz. Though a great deal of destruction did take place in El Alto, union organizations and neighborhood groups or-ganized watches and lines of defense to protect their communities and businesses from the military, looters, and others taking advantage of the chaos.[40]

Angry *Alteño* protesters attacked symbols of corporate and politi-cal power during the days of chaos. Protestors burned down the office of the mayor, an ally of the president, while others destroyed and robbed banks, water, and electrical company offices.[41] When a group of protes-tors tried to take over the Coca-Cola plant in El Alto, security forces arrived and fired into the crowd, killing six.[42] The next day, the La Paz streets were transformed into battle zones. Snipers shot from rooftops and protestors tossed dynamite, their thunderous explosions rattling buildings.[43]

Though her parents had asked her not to go out on the streets because of the violence, 24-year-old student nurse, Ana Colque, the single mother of a 22-month-old child, had been helping the wounded all day on February 13th. She left her child in the care of her parents.[44] Carpenter Ronald Collanqui, who was working on the roof of a building near Plaza San Fransisco that day, was shot by military snipers across the street. Colque, dressed in a white nurse outfit, climbed the stairs to the roof to attend Collanqui and was shot in the chest by the snipers. An ambulance arrived ten minutes later to bring her to the hospital where she died shortly afterward. The snipers said they believed the two victims posed a threat and so had fired in self defense.[45]

That same day, demonstrations by farmers, workers, students, and miners gained momentum in Cochabamba, Potosí, Santa Cruz, and the Chapare. They mobilized against the tax increase and demanded the president's resignation. Villarroel spoke of the solidarity between the police and Bolivian citizens. "Many people supported us and joined the protest. They sang songs when we passed. Wherever we went, the people applauded."

When peace finally settled into the streets on Friday the 14th, thirty-one people had been declared dead, the majority of them younger than 25 years old. [46] The IMF officials, however, were not around to see the results of their suggestions. As soon as the conflict began, they checked out of the five star Plaza Hotel and flew out of the country.[47] The IMF later denied there were any connections between the institution's policies and the violence in Bolivia.[48] In response to protests and violence, Sánchez de Lozada cancelled the tax increase and announced, "Our budget will not be a budget of the International Monetary Fund."[49] Neither Villarroel nor Bojórquez was harmed during the conflict. Villaroel went on to a less stressful job with the migration police, in part to spend more time with his family. Bojórquez left military service just in time to switch sides and join the street mobilizations in October, 2003 against President Sánchez de Lozada and his gas exportation plan.[50]

Instead of molding the country into an easily exploitable cog in the machine of corporate globalization, the IMF agenda created a violent social backlash in Bolivia. The IMF-prompted conflicts in Argentina and Bolivia spurred on new eras of social movements in both countries. Emerging from the economic crash, social movements in Argentina grew, solidarity was built between neighbors and factories were occupied and run by unemployed workers. In Bolivia, social movements strengthened their collaborative efforts against the Sánchez de Lozada administration.

Reports from a poll conducted by the television company Unitel in August, 2003 indicated that Sánchez de Lozada was supported by only nine percent of the population. The primary causes for discontent included the deaths that took place on the 12th and 13th of February, his handling of the economic crisis and corruption. "It's been a horrible year," admitted the president in early August.[51] It was just about to get worse.

(Endnotes)

1   "Chronologia de febrero de 2003," in *Para Que No Se Olvide: 12–13 de febrero 2003*, APDH, ASIFAMD, DIAKONIA (La Paz: Plural Editores, 2004). This book includes reports from the OEA, and Bolivian newspapers, *Pulso*, *La Razon* and *La Prensa*.

2   All quotes from Abraham Bojórquez are from and interview with author in February and July, 2006.

3   Biographical information about Gonzalo Sánchez de Lozada is from the following sources: "Gonzalo Sánchez de Lozada," Interview with *Public Broadcasting System* (March 20, 2001), http://www.pbs.org/wgbh/commandingheights/ shared/minitextlo/int_gonzalodelozada.html#top, "Gonzalo Sánchez de Lozada," *Fundacion CIDOB* (September 7, 2006), http://www.cidob.org/es/ documentacion/biografias_lideres_politicos/america_del_sur/bolivia/gonzalo_ Sánchez_de_lozada., Also "Sánchez de Lozada," *Latin Trade* (November, 2004).

4   Klein, *A Concise History*. 258–262.

5   Rachel Boyton, "Our Brand Is Crisis" *Koch Lorber Films* (2005).

6   Tom Kruse, "The IMF's Impact on Bolivia," *Americas.org*, http://www.americas. org/item_64.

7   Jim Shultz & Lily Whitesell, "Deadly Consequences: How the IMF Provoked Bolivia into Bloody Crisis," *Multinational Monitor* (May/June 2005), http://www. thirdworldtraveler.com/IMF_WB/IMF_Bolivia_Crisis.html.

8   "Empeora la calidad de vida de los bolivianos," *Econoticiasbolivia.com* (June 24, 2003).

9   Kohl and Farthing, *Impasse*, 172–173.

10 Jim Shultz, "Deadly Consequences: The International Monetary Fund and Bolivia's "Black February"," *Democracy Center* (April 2005), http://www. democracyctr.org/publications/imfindex.htm.

11 Kohl and Farthing, *Impasse*, 172–173.

12 Shultz & Whitesell, "Deadly Consequences."

13 Emad Mekay, "IMF Policies at Root of Riots, Say Activists" *Inter Press News Service* (February 13, 2003), http://www.globalpolicy.org/socecon/bwi-wto/imf/ 2003/0213riot.htm.

14 This quote and all others from Colonel José Villarroel are from an interview with author in July, 2006.

15 Shultz, "Deadly Consequences."

16 This system is explained at length in by Joseph E. Stiglitz, *Globalization and its Discontents* (New York: W. W. Norton & Company, 2003).

17 For more history on the IMF, see Eric Toussaint, *Your Money or Your Life* (Chicago: Haymarket Books, 2005).

18 Stiglitz, *Globalization*, XIV.

19 Toussaint, *Your Money*, p. 313–323

20 *Ibid.*

21 Part of the IMF packet that hurt the debt problem was the privatization of pensions. In the previous pension plan, working citizens paid for the pensions of others. Under the privatized plan, each person paid for his or her own pension. During the transition to the new plan, the government did not receive funding

for the pensions, and had to pay for the pensions itself, contributing to greater deficit. Green, *Silent Revolution*, 14–15.

22 Stiglitz, *Globalization*, 69.

23 *International Monetary Fund*, http://imf.org/external/np/exr/ccrit/eng/crans. htm#q08

24 Stiglitz, *Globalization*.

25 Mark Dworkin and Melissa Young, *Argentina: Hope in Hard times* (Reading: Bull Frog Films, 2004).

26 Green, *Silent Revolution*, 13, 14–15.

27 "Chronologia de febrero de 2003," in *Para Que No Se Olvide*, 21–28.

28 Chronologia de febrero de 2003, p21–28, Chapter in book, *Para Que No Se Olvide*, includes reports from the OEA, and the Bolivian newspapers, *Pulso*, *La Razon* and *La Prensa*

29 Victor Orduna said the obligatory military service was "shamefully" used in February. According to Orduna, superior officers put the young students in the thankless position of shooting at their own fellow citizens, Victor Orduna, "Los Jovenes desde el 12 y 13 de febrero," in *Para Que No Se Olvide*, 163–164.

30 Information from interviews with Bojórquez, Villaroel.

31 Without much pre-planning, the students had become key protagonists in the conflict. The throwing of rocks at the government palace, which Orduna describes as a "catharsis," did not last long, but did operate as the breaking point in a tense situation, Orduna, "Los Jovenes," in *Para Que No Se Olvide*, 12–13.

32 Chronologia de febrero," *Para Que No Se Olvide*.

33 It is unclear who fired the first bullet. The military contends it was the police, and the police say the army fired first. See Shultz, "Deadly Consequences."

34 "Chronologia de febrero de 2003," in *Para Que No Se Olvide*, 21–28.

35 Ibid. Also, José Antonio Quiroga T., "Antecedentes y Contexto de la Crisis de Febrero" in *Para Que No Se Olvide*, 43–44.

36 "Testimony of Maria Calcina, Representative of the Association of Families of Victims of the 12 and 13 of February," *Fundación Solon*, Tunapa publication, #9, 2003, 5–6. Calcina later began organizing marches in the Plaza Murrillo for Justice for her son's death, in the style of the marches of the Madres de la Plaza de Mayo in Argentina.

37 "Chronologia de febrero de 2003," *Para Que No Se Olvide*.

38 Testimony of his wife, Rosa Mamani in Quintana, "Policias y Militares," in *Para Que No Se Olvide*, 136.

39 Prensa Altena, Año 2, #8 (February, 2003), p 3–11.

40 Ibid.

41 "Chronologia de febrero de 2003," in *Para Que No Se Olvide*.

42 Orduna, "Los Jovenes desde el 12 y 13 de febrero," in *Para Que No Se Olvide*, 178.

43 Sebastian Hacher, "Gringo Go Home," *ZNet* (February 14, 2003), http://www. zmag.org/content/print_article.cfm?itemID=3044&sectionID=20.

44 Shultz & Whitesell, "Deadly Consequences."

45 "Chronologia de febrero de 2003," in *Para Que No Se Olvide*. Sniper responses from Shultz, "Deadly Consequences."

46 Of the 31 people that died in those two days, 22 were under 25 years old, seven were 20 years old, and five were younger than 19. The dead included 16 civilians, 10 policemen and five soldiers, all from bullet wounds. One hundred and eighty-nine people were wounded, including 106 civilians, 53 military personnel, and 30 policemen. Information from Orduna, "Los Jovenes desde el 12 y 13 de febrero."

47 Shultz, "Deadly Consequences."

48 Mekay, "IMF Policies at Root of Riots."

49   Shultz & Whitesell, "Deadly Consequences."

50   Regarding the protests in October, Bojórquez said, "If I'd been in the military during that revolt I would have been ready to join the people of El Alto with my gun. The people were just fighting with sticks and rocks."

51   "Solo el 9 % de los bolivianos apoya a Goni," *Econoticiasbolivia.com* (August 5, 2003).

Chapter Five

Occupy, Resist, Produce

Members of *campesino* and indigenous organizations
occupy the Plaza Murillo in front of the Presidential
Palace in La Paz to demand the distribution of unused
land to landless farmers.

Photo Credit: Benjamin Dangl

"If you want to take power and you can't take over the state, you have to at least take over the means of production."

—Candido Gonzalez[1]

On April 20th, 2000, hundreds of Bolivian landless families peacefully took over land in Pananti, an area in Tarija, and began a precarious new life. They pooled their labor to cultivate the land, which had been abandoned for eight years, and built their homes close together for protection from the thugs hired by local cattle ranchers who claimed the land was theirs. The residents devised shifts to keep watch on the community while others slept, worked in the fields, or gathered water from faraway sources. In early November, 2001, 60 armed men hired by local cattle ranchers attacked landless farmers in the Pananti settlement, burned down their homes, and unleashed a barrage of gunfire that killed five men and one 13-year old boy, and wounded 22 others. In response, landless farmers killed a leader of the attack.[2] Police arrested five landowners linked to the violence and nine landless farmers. Juana Ortega, who had given birth just three days beforehand, was one of those arrested. Ortega occupied the land for her children, "I decided to do it for them, for the land they will need to survive."[3]

This violence reflects an ancient system of exploitation in which land is concentrated in the hands of a few rich landowners while poor farmers are left to tenant farming slavery or starvation. In Brazil, Bolivia, and Paraguay, the occupation of land by landless farmer movements has been met with repression from governments and large landowners. In Paraguay, the presence of the US military has been linked to this violence. When colonial and neoliberal oppression takes away people's rights to land and work, they are often left with no other choice than to occupy and reclaim those spaces that promise them a chance to survive.

In recent years, Latin America has seen a flourishing of occupation and recuperation movements as farmers, factory workers, and community members reach out to take back what is theirs. In Venezuela, dissidents in a poor neighborhood occupied a jail where they were formerly imprisoned and transformed it into a community radio station. In Argentina, the economic crisis in 2001–2002 forced unemployed workers to take over the means of production and employment at hotels, businesses, and factories. In most cases, workers and families were reclaiming spaces and resources that had been taken over by corporations, dictatorships, or governments enacting neoliberal policies. The cases outlined here offer powerful examples of people confronting corporate exploitation and empire in concrete, physical ways that can be applied anywhere else in the world.

A look at these examples of occupation and recuperation of political, agricultural, and work space in Latin America illuminates the convergence between neoliberalism and popular social movements in Bolivia and elsewhere in Latin America. From land and prisons to factories and hotels, citizens have fought against this displacement under the motto: Occupy, Resist, Produce.

The wealth of Latin America's large landowners has been built on the backs of the region's poor, landless farmers. Since the Spanish colonists arrived on the continent plantations were largely powered by slaves, though land was sometimes lent to workers in exchange for money, crops, or labor. It was common for owners to rule every aspect of life on their plantations—from communication with the outside world, to internal commerce and justice. These colonial chains still grip the continent. With the application of neoliberal policies, old plantations were turned into modern industrial farms owned by US and European corporations. *Campesinos* fed up with working conditions or unable to compete with large farms increasingly migrated to the city. Currently, Latin America has some of the most unequal land distribution in the world.[4]

In Bolivia, a country largely dependent on agriculture, conflicts over land have arisen on numerous occasions. Leading up to the Revolution of 1952, one of the only ways *campesinos* survived was through their work in horrible conditions on large farms. In return for the use of their own small plot of land, *campesinos* served the owner's family day and night, cleaning, cooking, and tending to livestock and crops. The Revolution of 1952 offered a glimpse of hope to these small farmers. Large land holdings, mostly in the western provinces—which are called departments in Bolivia—were broken up and distributed to landless farmers, and various forms of exploitation on large farms were outlawed. Some indigenous communities were given land titles.[5]

Since then it has been uphill battle for most of Bolivia's landless. General Hugo Banzer gave his allies and friends thousands of hectares of land, much of which is in the fertile department of Santa Cruz.[6] In the 1990s, when neoliberal policies were applied in full force to Latin America, privatization and foreign investment was encouraged, and small farmers were ignored by governments. Their credits were slashed and land was sold off to foreign owners. "Modernization" of the agricultural industry favored exports and cheap labor, goals that were threatened by empowered *campesinos*.[7]

Seventy percent of the productive land in Bolivia is owned by a wealthy five percent of the population.[8] Cattle ranching, the expansion of the soy industry, and mineral exploration have put a strain on land use and distribution. Brazilian soy companies have taken over significant portions of land in northeastern Santa Cruz, displacing the Guarayo indigenous populations. In southern Santa Cruz, ranchers compete with the Guarani indigenous communities for land. Conflicts between small farmers and industrial producers are common elsewhere in this department.[9]

Various areas of indigenous land were not officially recognized until lowland indigenous people from Santa Cruz and Beni began a march in 1990 to demand legal recognition. Their cause was motivated by the fact that the land they traditionally used was being threatened by increased logging, cattle ranching, and soy production. Their demands were eventually met by President Paz Zamora who created decrees legally recognizing indigenous land.[10] However, indigenous populations have often had trouble making the government enforce and enact the decrees that are made to soothe social conflict. Furthermore, the titles given to indigenous communities were only allowed to have one owner, instigating internal disputes as well as facilitating the sale of indigenous land by the individual owners.[11]

Protests and violent confrontations continued across the country over this valuable resource, forcing the government to take action in 1996 with the passage of the National Agrarian Reform Service Law (INRA). The law included a plan to grant collective titles to indigenous communities, resolve conflicts, and distribute state owned, unused, or illegally obtained land to landless farmers. However, as an investigation by the Andean Information Network reports, successive governments failed to enact this legislature due to vague definitions of unproductive land and standards for determining the legality of land holdings. During the nine years following the passage of the law, land titles were certified on only 18 percent of the targeted areas. Corruption and lack of initiative to fully implement the law resulted in few victories for Bolivia's landless.[12]

Another aspect of the INRA Law that angered small farmers was a change in the article of the land law, established in the Agrarian Reform of 1953, which said that "The land belongs to those who work it"—meaning that the land had to be used productively or else the state could take the rights to it. Under INRA, landowners were allowed to keep their unused land as long as they paid a one percent property tax on the entire value of the land. Yet it was up to the landowners themselves to establish that value, leaving loopholes for corruption.[13]

In the face of such inequality, landless farmers have organized to take unused land regardless of official sanction. On June 14th, 2000, a march of farmers demanding land arrived in the town of Entre Rios, in the department of Tarija where a representative of the Prefect asked to meet with leaders of the march. It was then that farmers decided to form the Bolivian Landless Movement (MST). From this beginning, the MST has coordinated actions, marches, and land occupations, inspiring others across the country to do the same. The first land occupations usually involved 34–40 families who took unused land and set up tents or homes with log walls and plastic tarps for roofs. Communities then began cultivating subsistence crops on land that had often been unused for decades.[14]

The land in Timboy Tiguazu, a humid area 65 kilometers outside of Yacuiba, in the department of Tarija, was totally abandoned and unused when 13 landless families occupied it in 2000. After the takeover, men prepared the land for cultivation and women looked for the best places for homes. Though the poor quality of roads made the zone nearly inaccessible, it had plenty of water sources and good land for farming. In the beginning, family members took turns working for large landowners outside their area and in cities and towns to buy supplies for the new community. They divided work duties and organized shifts to protect themselves from thugs hired by local landowners. By 2001, a total of 40 families lived there, many of them producing surplus vegetables to sell in local markets.[15]

In the wake of such success, landless farmers occupied land elsewhere, primarily in Santa Cruz and the Chaco where there are vast expanses of unused land. Wilfor Coque of the MST participated in a land occupation in 2000 in Ichilo, northeast of Santa Cruz. According to Coque, land there had been sold illegally, leaving little for indigenous people and small farmers in the region. Coque said that the community will continue occupying unused land until the "state gives us back what is ours."[16] Many farmers take part in the occupations to work the land for survival, as in the past, labor for large landowners barely has paid enough to survive. "There are still haciendas where 30 peons work from sunrise to sunset for a completely inadequate salary," said Ermelinda Fernández, an MST member in the Chaco. Some laborers are paid only $1.41 per day, but, according to Fernández, "...they have no alternative because they have no land of their own."[17]

Silvestre Saisari, a leader of the Santa Cruz MST, was brutally attacked in 2005 while giving a press conference in the city's main plaza—which he calls "the most fascist plaza in Bolivia"—about landowners' use of armed thugs to suppress landless farmers. To prevent him from denouncing these violent acts to the media, people reportedly tied to landowners pulled his hair, strangled, punched, and beat him.[18] I met him at the MST office in Santa Cruz, a building with tall, barbed wire topped walls. It looked like a military bunker from the outside. This made sense, given the treatment Saisairi and other like-minded social and labor leaders received from the city's right-wing elite. Saisari, a bearded, soft spoken young man, said, "Land is a center of power. He who has land, has power....we are proposing than this land be redistributed, so their [elites'] power will be affected."[19]

The plight of the landless *campesinos* is region-wide, and knows no borders. Though Brazil has an enormous amount of unused land, many farmers there remain landless. Isolated struggles for land among Brazilian farmers gained momentum in the late 1970s, when neoliberal policies concentrated land ownership, and farmers were faced with the option of taking over land or migrating to cities.

Brazil's MST was officially created in 1984, and organized subsequent meetings and land occupations. Since its inception, the MST has occupied unused land and built houses, cooperative farms, schools, and health clinics. Their communities are based on sustainable environmental and agricultural plans that help a majority of the community.

When Brazil's military dictatorship ended in 1985, a constitution was passed that allowed the expropriation of large tracts of land that either were unused or did not provide a social function. Though landless farmers hoped that this would lead to redistribution, land remained in the hands of a few who were willing to use violence to defend their property. Since 1985, over a thousand MST activists have been killed in confrontations during land occupations.[20] However, at that point the movement had grown too large to suppress. Brazil's MST now includes around 1.5 million members who have not only occupied land, but also acted as a conduit to pressure the government for change; they organized marches and blockades against genetically modified crops, occupied buildings and other spaces in protest of economic policies, and demanded access to credit, health care, and education. Hundreds of thousands of Brazilian families have now received land as a result of the MST's work.[21]

Many in Brazil's MST hoped that presidential candidate Luiz Ina-
cio Lula da Silva would assist the change they were working toward, so
the organization put their efforts into Lula's 2002 presidential campaign.
During the campaign, Lula's Workers Party demanded that the MST
stop all direct action land occupations, as they would be used by the
right against Lula and cost his party important votes from the middle
class. The MST complied. After his electoral victory, Lula turned his
back on the movement and took a hostile position on land occupations.
Instead of working with the MST, he criminalized the movement and its
tactics and increased the division between large agricultural producers
and small producers, favoring the former with subsidies, tax breaks, and
credit. The smaller producers could not compete in this atmosphere.
Lula's aggression toward landless farmers forced many to take matters
into their own hands. In Lula's first year in office, the number of families
occupying land jumped from 26,958 to 54,368. The number of rural conflicts over land also increased during this time.[22]

Like water, land is something that many can't live without. However, in terms of international press, private property is the golden
fleece of neoliberalism, and governments that have redistributed land
or nationalized formerly private businesses have often been short-lived.
It is the very mention of land redistribution in Venezuela and Bolivia
that has sent elites babbling with fear about socialists and wire editors
scurrying to title articles with the word "dictator." For this reason, many
leftist presidential hopefuls who have led their campaigns with a swell of
support from landless and indigenous groups are too timid to approve of
land redistribution once in office.

Governments often interpret land and factory occupation as a direct
threat to their authority. This has motivated many leaders to use military
force, instead of dialogue, in order to resolve conflicts. In some cases,
the US military has offered its services against occupations. In Paraguay, human rights organizations have linked US military exercises to
an increased violence against landless farmers. While traveling across
this country in 2002, I met welcoming farmers who let me camp in their
backyards. I eventually arrived in Ciudad del Este, known for its black
markets and loose borders. Now the city and farmers I met are caught in
the crossfire of the US military's "war on terror."

On May 26th, 2005, the Paraguayan Senate was bullied into letting
US troops train their Paraguayan counterparts in total immunity.[23] The

US threatened to cut off millions in aid to the country if Paraguay did not grant the US troops entry. In July, 2005 hundreds of US soldiers arrived with planes, weapons, and ammunition. Washington's funding for counterterrorism efforts in Paraguay soon doubled, and protests against the military presence hit the streets. Argentine Nobel Peace Prize laureate Adolfo Perez Esquivel commented on the situation in Paraguay, "Once the United States arrives, it takes it a long time to leave. And that really frightens me."[24]

The US government has often used the excuse of security support for their military presence in Latin America—typically, this translates to *economic* security for corporations in their quest for cheap raw material and new markets. Paraguay offers many natural resources, such as the Guarani Aquifer, one of the largest sources of fresh water in the hemisphere, gas reserves in neighboring Bolivia and Argentina, and extensive land for the expanding soy industry.[25] After US troops arrived, conflicts quickly emerged over one resource: land. As in most Latin American countries, disputes over land ownership are nothing new in Paraguay, where one percent of the population owns 90 percent of usable land.[26] Recently, as agribusinesses have boomed and Paraguay has become the last pro-American stronghold in South America, small farmers have once more become the losers in these clashes. The security of these interests is protected at the cost of civil rights.

Paraguay is the fourth-largest producer of soy in the world. As this industry has expanded, an estimated 90,000 poor families have been forced off their land. The use of toxic insecticides, genetically modified seeds, and the expulsion of *campesinos* go hand in hand in areas where businesses want to operate. This desperate situation forced many *campesinos* to occupy land, which has led to violent confrontations since 2003. After initial military deployments to areas of unrest, the Paraguayan military established outposts to monitor and control the landless movement.[27]

Campesinos have organized protests, road blockades, and land occupations against displacement. These efforts have earned them considerable repression from military and paramilitary forces. According to the Rural Reflection Group (GRR), an Argentine organization that documents violence against farmers, on June 24th, 2005, in Tekojoja, Paraguay, hired policemen and soy producers kicked 270 people off peacefully occupied land, burned down 54 homes, arrested 130 people, and killed two.[28]

Another example of this violence is the death of Serapio Villasboa Cabrera, a member of the Paraguayan *Campesino* Movement. His body was found, riddled with knife wounds, on May 8th, 2006. Cabrera was the brother of Petrona Villasboa, who was spearheading an investigation into the death of her son, who died from exposure to toxic chemicals used by producers of genetically modified soy. According to Service, Peace and Justice (Serpaj), an international human rights group with a chapter in Paraguay, one method land and agribusiness owners used to force farmers off their land was to spray toxic pesticides around communities until sickness forced residents to leave.[29]

GRR said Cabrera was killed by paramilitaries connected to large landowners and soy producers, who are intent on expanding their holdings. The organization explains that owners hire paramilitaries to pursue *campesino* leaders organizing against the occupation of their land. Investigations by Serpaj demonstrate that the worst cases of repression against farmers have taken place in areas with the highest concentration of US troops.

These repeated proportions demonstrate the influence the US military currently has in the region. "The US military is advising the Paraguayan police and military about how to deal with these farmer groups.... They are teaching theory as well as technical skills to Paraguayan police and military. These new forms of combat have been used internally," says Orlando Castillo of Serpaj. Tomás Palau, a Paraguayan sociologist at BASE-IS, a Paraguayan social research institute, described to me the relationship between the repression against landless farmers and the new US military presence in his country. Like Castillo, Palau said there is an association between the US military presence and the increased violence against *campesinos*: "The US is teaching counterinsurgency classes and preparing the Paraguayan troops to fight internal enemies...These classes are led by North Americans, who answer to Southern Command, the branch of the US military for South America."[30]

Castillo described intelligence methods that the military uses to find landless leaders: "The US troops talk with the farmers and get to know their leaders and which groups and organizations are working there, then establish the plans and actions to control the movement and advise the Paraguayan military and police on how to proceed...." Castillo believes that the US and the Paraguayan governments are using the rhetoric of terrorism to suppress national movements for social justice. "US troops form part of a security plan to repress the social movements in Paraguay. A lot of repression has happened in the name of security and against 'terrorism,'" he said.

The US embassy in Asunción rejects all claims that the US military is linked to the increased repression of *campesino* and protest groups, either through exercises or instruction. In an e-mail response to the charges, Bruce Kleiner of the embassy's office of public affairs wrote that "the US military is not monitoring protest groups in Paraguay" and that "the US military personnel and Paraguayan armed forces have trained together during medical readiness training exercises (MEDRETEs) to provide humanitarian service to some of Paraguay's most disadvantaged citizens." However, Kleiner's statements are contradicted by the deputy speaker of the Paraguayan parliament, Alejandro Velazquez Ugarte, who said that of the 13 exercises going on in the country, only two are of a civilian nature.[31]

A group of representatives from human rights organizations and universities from all over the world, including the *Madres de la Plaza de Mayo* in Argentina and a group from the University of Toulouse, France, traveled to Paraguay in July, 2006 as part of the Campaign for the Demilitarization of the Americas (CADA) to observe and report on the repression going on in the country linked to the presence of US troops.[32] Interviewed *campesinos* said they were not told what medications they were given during the US medical operations. *Campesinos* reported that patients were often given the same treatments regardless of their illness. In some cases, the medicine produced hemorrhages and abortions. When the medical treatment took place, patients reported that they were asked if they belonged to any kind of labor or social organization. Military filming of communities, people, and homes was conducted in conjunction with the interrogation of residents.

Throughout the Cold War, the US government used the threat of communism as an excuse for its military adventures in Latin America. Now, the United States is using another "ism" as an alibi for its military presence: terrorism. The Pentagon currently has more resources and money directed to Latin America than the Departments of State, Agriculture, Commerce, and Treasury combined. Before September 11th, 2001, the annual US military aid to the region was around $400 million. It's now nearly $1 billion. Much of this goes to training troops.[33]

Conflicts related to the US military presence in Paraguay fit under the banner of the US "War on Terror." Washington has justified its military presence in Paraguay by stating that the Triple Border area at Ciudad del Este, where the borders of Paraguay, Argentina, and Brazil meet, is a base for Islamist terrorist funding. In a June 3rd, 2006, Associated Press report, Western intelligence officials, speaking anonymously, claimed that if Iran is cornered by the United States, it could direct the international network of the Lebanese Shiite group Hezbollah to assist in terrorist attacks. The Justice Department indicted nineteen people in 2006 for sending the profits from the sale of counterfeit rolling papers and Viagra to Hezbollah. "Extensive operations have been uncovered in South America," the AP article states, "where Hezbollah is well connected to the drug trade, particularly in the region where Argentina, Brazil, and Paraguay meet."[34]

Another claim that terrorist networks operate in the Triple Border region is based on a poster of Iguaçu Falls, a tourist destination near Ciudad del Este, discovered by US troops on the wall of an Al Qaeda operative's home in Kabul, Afghanistan, shortly after September 11th, 2001. Aside from this, however, the US Southern Command and the State Department report that no "credible information" exists confirming that "Islamic terrorist cells are planning attacks in Latin America."[35] Luiz Moniz Bandeira, who holds a chair in history at the University of Brasília and writes about US-Brazilian relations, said, "I wouldn't dismiss the hypothesis that US agents plant stories in the media about Arab terrorists in the Triple Frontier to provoke terrorism and justify their military presence."[36]

According to BASE-IS, Paraguayan officials have also stepped up the threat of terrorism to justify their aggression against *campesino* leaders. One group, the *Campesino* Organization of the North, has been accused of receiving instructions from the Revolutionary Armed Forces of Colombia (FARC), that country's largest leftist guerrilla movement. The Association of Farmers of Alto Paraná (ASAGRAPA), a *campesino* group near the Triple Border, reported that a local politician offered one of the organization's leaders a month's pay to announce that other members in the organization were building a terrorist group and receiving training from the FARC. BASE-IS reports suggest that this type of bribery and disinformation is part of an effort to guarantee the "national security of the US" and "justify, continue, and expand the North American military presence."

Wild allegations about landless Paraguayan farmers' links to terrorists are a convenient way to justify the increased spending and military presence in the region. "The US government is lying about the terrorist funding in the Triple Border, just like they did about the weapons of mass destruction in Iraq," said an exasperated Castillo of Serpaj. The streets I walked through in Ciudad del Este, and the farmers I met along the way, seemed to pose as much of a threat to US security as the pirated Tom Petty CDs and bottles of counterfeit whiskey sold in the country's black markets.

While landless farmers have resisted pressure against their right to survive and work their own land in Paraguay, a different kind of occupation has gone on in Argentina, where workers took over the means of production and employment. Instead of land, the resources available to these unemployed workers were hotels, textile factories and businesses that could offer a source of survival in an urban setting.

When Argentina's economy crashed in 2001, citizens protested, despaired, and began to take matters in their own hands. They organized community assemblies and barter fairs, built urban gardens, and used alternative currency. Perhaps the most well known of these initiatives was the recuperation of bankrupt factories and businesses which were occupied by workers and run cooperatively. There are currently around two hundred worker-run factories and businesses in Argentina, most of which started in the midst of the 2001–2002 crisis. Fifteen thousand people work in these cooperatives and the businesses range from car part producers to rubber balloon factories. Three recuperated businesses with stories that are representative of this movement are the Chilavert book publishing company, Hotel Bauen, and the Brukman textile factory.

Chilavert is located outside the center of Buenos Aires in a quiet neighborhood. On the front of the building is a colorful mural with the slogan of the recuperated business movement: "Occupy, Resist, Produce." The factory itself is divided into offices, a kitchen, and a cultural space for film screenings, dances, poetry readings, and art exhibits. The largest area is full of printing and bookbinding machines from the 1950s–1970s. When I visited the factory, one woman was editing a Chilavert journal while a musician used a nearby computer to print out fliers for an upcoming concert. Teenagers who worked in the factory as interns listened to a worker explain the intricacies of book layout and design. Toward the end of the day, dozens of people showed up for salsa classes. The factory had a festive, communal feel to it, but work was still going on and the machines were printing away. While I was there, a book of poetry and a science textbook were being printed.

When the factory was started in 1923 it was called Gaglianone, after the family who ran the business for decades. Following the worker takeover nearly 80 years later, the factory was renamed Chilavert, for its street address. Gaglianone was well known in Buenos Aires as a producer of high quality art books and material for major theaters. However, in the 1990s, business went into a slump and much of the equipment was sold off, salaries were lowered, and workers were fired. In April of 2002, the factory closed its doors. Out of necessity and a desire to keep their place of work in operation, the workers decided to occupy the factory. At first, they clandestinely produced books—as illegal occupants of the building. After printing the books, workers snuck them through a hole in the factory's wall and into the neighbor's house, from where they were shipped for distribution. Though the hole has since been repaired, Chilavert workers have proudly placed a frame around this exposed brick section of the wall.

A climactic moment came on May 24th, 2002 when eight police patrol cars, dozens of policemen, eight assault vehicles, two ambulances, and one fire truck showed up at Chilavert to kick the workers out. Though only eight workers occupied the building, they were accompanied by nearly 300 other people, including neighbors, students, and workers from other cooperatives who were there to help defend the factory. The massive group intimidated the police and, when it became clear that blood was about to flow from both sides, the police retreated. The workers had won.[37]

Candido Gonzalez worked at Chilavert for 42 years before participating in the worker takeover. After a recent heart attack he attributed to stress and overwork, he said he planned to take it easy. Still, that didn't stop him from attending the fifth annual World Social Forum in Brazil just before my visit. While we talked, he joked with many workers in the building and was in high spirits. Our interview lasted a couple of hours and he touched upon topics from earthquakes to whiskey. "Occupy, resist, and produce. This is the synthesis of what we are doing," Candido said, as he passed me a glass of iced tea. "And it is the community as a whole that makes this possible." He spoke of the policemen's attempt to evict them. "But we, along with other members of the community, stayed here and defended the factory." He recalled this fight with tears in his eyes. "It is normal for you to fight for yourself, but when others fight for your cause it is very emotional."

Local community members had a good reason to stand up for the Chilavert workers: part of the local economy depends on Chilavert for business. "We get our transportation, ink, food, coffee, and paper—there is a paper factory fifteen blocks from here—all in this neighborhood.

Chilavert helps the economy and if this factory closes, the neighborhood suffers."

"Every decision, every assembly, every book published, has something to do with politics," Chilavert worker Julieta Galera explained. "The idea is to make books and works of art that have something to do with our political vision. There is a lot of prejudice against recuperated factories in Buenos Aires. People think we don't work hard enough. But Chilavert does some of the best work in the business." Twelve people work at the factory and, unlike other cooperatives in the city, everyone has the same salary. Major decisions are made in assemblies and community-based activities play an important role in the weekly agenda. Since the worker takeover, Chilavert produced numerous books on social and political themes, with titles such as "The Unemployed Workers Movement," "What are Popular Assemblies?" and "Piquetera Dignity."

Though Chilavert is one of the most famous of the recuperated businesses, its story is still unknown to most Argentines. "We almost don't exist in the newspapers or the TV programs because we aren't with the government," Candido explained. "There are some two hundred recuperated, cooperative businesses in Argentina. That's not a lot compared to all the others that are not run this way."

Candido didn't think much of Argentine president Nestor Kirchner, and didn't attribute Chilavert's success to any politician.[38] "We didn't put a political party banner in the factory because we are the ones that took the factory. All kinds of politicians have come here asking for our support. Yet when the unions failed, when the state failed, the workers began a different kind of fight...If you want to take power and you can't take over the state, you have to at least take over the means of production." Candido pointed across the room to a giant safe in the corner. Across the top of the safe was the name, Gaglianone. He laughed and shook his head. Perhaps that's where the old boss hoarded all of his money. "Now," Candido explained, pulling out a bottle, "this is where we keep the whiskey."

Another example of this worker cooperative movement is Argentina's Hotel Bauen. The hotel first opened during the military dictatorship in 1978, when Buenos Aires hosted the World Cup. From that time on, the hotel was a meeting place for big business owners, people connected to the dictatorship, and right-wing politicians such as former Argentine President Carlos Menem. Ironically, whereas it used to be a hangout for the right-wing elite, since the worker takeover in 2003, Hotel Bauen has been a center for left-leaning activist groups and union members. When the city's subway workers went on strike in 2005, much of their decision-making and organizing was coordinated from the hotel.

Marcelo Iurcovich ran the hotel until 1997 when he sold it to Solari, a Chilean company. In 2001 the hotel went bankrupt and on December 21st of that year, Solaris fired all of its workers. The majority of the ninety employees went without work for twelve to fourteen months. "Our decision to take over the hotel wasn't capricious," Horacio Lalli, a member of the hotel's cooperative, told me. "A lot of the people here were fathers and mothers of families. There was no work. We had to do something, so after a lot of meetings we decided to take the hotel back."

On the night of March 21st, 2003 after a meeting in Chilavert, Hotel Bauen's workers gathered at the intersection of the streets Corrientes and Calloa in downtown Buenos Aires. They walked the short distance to the hotel and entered the building. Cheers filled the air. The lights were switched on. Workers hugged each other and wept. They had succeeded in the first step of the recuperation process: occupation. Yet the hotel was far from being in working condition. A lot of the material and equipment had been sold by the previous owners or stolen. The workers still faced months of cleaning and repair work in order to get the hotel back on its feet. "Businesses and students in Buenos Aires helped us out by gathering money for us so we could eat," Lalli explained. "Yet we were afraid the hotel bosses would come back and kick us out. This period of time was full of fear."

Once under worker control, the hotel became a bustling center for political and cultural events. The workers ran their business as a cooperative. Not everyone received the same salary, but all major decisions were made in assemblies attended by all the hotel's workers. Fabio Resino has been working at the hotel since it was taken over by the workers in 2003. "If the hotel had been run as a cooperative for all these years it would not have closed," he explained. "There was a lot of corruption and bad management with the previous owner. You could ask all ninety people that work here today and they'd all respond that they prefer this system to working for one boss."

Resino noted that there is a difference in worker morale now that running the hotel is a collaborative effort. "Before, we worked for a boss," he continued. "Now we work for ourselves. And when it is a cooperative you want to work better because it is your business, your own process. Before workers were numbers. Now we are people." Even in the face of harder work, Resino had no qualms about the change. "It takes more time this way, you have to work for more hours with fewer resources," he said, "but it's worth it."

Two days before Hotel Bauen's workers were fired, another Argentine business came under worker control. On December 19th, 2001, 52 employees at the Brukman clothing factory, the majority of them women, refused to continue working until their bosses handed over their back-wages. Plagued by debt and gradual bankruptcy, the owners hadn't paid the workers their weekly paychecks for 15 days. The bosses demanded that the workers return to their stations, but the sewing machines remained silent.[39]

Jacobo Brukman, the owner of factory, fled the building. The workers, many of whom didn't even have the two pesos needed for the bus ride home, remained in the factory, placing banners out the windows that said, "We Want Our Salaries!" Protesters in support of the workers showed up the following day. In a telephone conversation, the Brukman owners offered the workers two suits apiece instead of their salaries. The employees refused and constructed a road blockade in front of the building in protest. Afterwards, a Brukman client contracted a large order of Bermuda shorts. The workers produced them, using the money from the deal to pay the gas and electric bill of the factory. They soon began running the business themselves, organizing contracts, salaries and general management. What started out as a simple demand for back-wages turned into a fierce struggle for worker-control. Driven by a need to survive and support their families, the workers tried to gain ownership through legal means, fighting against politicians, judges and police in riot gear.

Celia Martinez, a worker at Brukman, was part of this struggle from the beginning. A former right-winger, her experience in the worker controlled Brukman quickly radicalized her. Sitting down in a room outside the factory's lobby, she told me of the current horizontal organization of the factory: "We all charge the same for our work and each person has one vote. The assemblies are held once every week or every fifteen days, depending on the need."

Celia's co-worker Matilda Adorno described early assemblies, just after the factory was taken over: "For many of us it was difficult to understand how to live with each other, and treat each other equally. Now we know what it is like in the other person's shoes and we have made peace. In the assemblies we would be able to pull each other's eyes out in order to defend our respective points of view. But afterwards we'd drink maté [tea] together."[40]

Miles outside Buenos Aires is one of the most prominent of the recuperated, worker-run factories in Argentina. The Zanon ceramics factory was taken over in 2001 and has since been economically successful. However, as a major symbol of Argentina's recuperated factory movement, it has been a target for right-wing hostility. In March, 2005, a woman who worked at Zanon was kidnapped and tortured by a group workers believe is linked to the local government.[41]

In the afternoon on March 4th in Neuquen, a city outside Buenos Aires, the woman—whose name was not released—was leaving the factory when a group of people forced her into a green Falcon car, the same type of vehicle used during Argentina's dictatorship in the seventies to kidnap and torture "leftists." The group in the car began to insult her, saying that they knew where she lived, where her family worked and where her daughter plays after school. Then they began to cut her with a knife, taunting with comments like "cut her more so that the blood will flow in Zanon..." After cutting her arms and face they threw her out of the car and said they were going to go after her daughter next.

The woman called the workers at Zanon and the police. Police surrounded her house to protect her family throughout the night. By morning, however, there was only one policeman on guard. At 9 am one of her kidnappers returned through the back door and repeated the same actions as in the car, insulting her and cutting her with a knife. When the man left, the one policeman who was on guard said he did not hear or see anything.

"This is one of many things that have happened to Zanon workers. Last year Pepe, a Zanon worker, was seriously injured in the eyes with pellets from police during a protest," said Esteban Magnani, author of *El Cambio Silencioso* (*The Silent Change*), a book about worker cooperatives in Argentina. "In Neuquen you have Jorge Sobisch, a right-wing governor who wants to be the new Carlos Menem.[42] Sobisch wants to show how tough he is, so he is trying to get rid of Zanon." The governor had recently declared he would run for president in the next elections.

At a press conference held by Zanon workers regarding the kidnapping, Alejandro Lopez, the general secretary of Neuquen ceramic workers, said, "The police have not helped Zanon...nothing goes on in Neuquen without the consent of the local government." Hundreds of people were in attendance at the press conference, which was held in Hotel Bauen. The mood at the conference was somber. The memory of the dictatorship's killings and torture still weighed heavy in the hearts and minds of Argentines. This kidnapping was a harsh reminder that after years of fighting against such horrendous acts, they still do occur. Evoking the fear many thought was long gone in Argentina, Lopez said, "Neuquen is not an island."

While workers battled the economic woes of neoliberalism in Argentina, Venezuelans in a neighborhood in Caracas fought another kind of enemy through occupation. In both cases, symbols of repression and exploitation were reclaimed and used for the community. In Venezuela, local residents took over and transformed a local jail into a community radio station.

The neighborhood of El 23 de Enero is like many of the improvised neighborhoods in Caracas clinging to the hillsides of the city. Multi-colored apartments made of brick and cement stack on top of each other forming labyrinthine alleyways and streets. One of many barrios in Caracas, the community was self-assembled by immigrants from the countryside, most of whom began by squatting land on hills outside the city's center, and assembling houses next to and on top of each other. As in most barrios in Caracas, the approximately 15,000 residents of El 23 are accustomed to corporate media stereotypes of their barrio as a dangerous, drug-ridden slum. They have also become adept at building their own community infrastructure, at times by hand, and at times over radio waves.

In January of 2006, community media activist Gustavo Borges, a big, mustachioed man with a smile that doesn't always come easily, led me from the subway toward the barrio's new radio station, *La Emisora Libre al Son del 23 de Enero*. Borges, a lifelong resident of the neighborhood, pointed to the roof of an enormous apartment building with laundry flapping in the windows. "We attacked the police station with guns from the roof of that building," he explained, referring back to his days as a guerrilla fighting against right-wing governments. "This is the police station we were shooting at," he smiled, pointing to a white building with murals of Che Guevara and Simón Bolívar. Outside, people set up chairs for a community event, and from the second floor, festive music blasted over speakers. There was nothing to suggest that the building's former incarnation was that of a police station and jail where, for 40 years before the presidency of Hugo Chávez, political activists and dissidents like Borges were detained.

Inside the building, construction was underway. The sound of pounding hammers and saws filled the air. On the second level, the

broadcasting had already started. Borges led us up the stairs to a recording studio where we met with one of the radio producers, Juan
Contreras. Like Borges, Contreras had also been jailed in this building.
Contreras, with short hair and a green T-shirt, looked tired but excited.
Standing in the soundproof recording studio, he said this was "a concrete political act" that had to do with transforming the nightmare the
neighborhood had lived through under previous right-wing governments. "This building was constructed in 1975 under the first government of Carlos Andres Perez and was put in the heart of El 23 de Enero
in order to detain popular protests, to repress, persecute, punish, and
assassinate the people."

He explained that the residents of El 23 de Enero led the charge to
transform this symbol of repression into something for the community.
After having various meetings and gaining the legal support from the
mayor, locals occupied the building, but police resisted. "They played
with us, stalled and stalled, and refused to move out," Contreras recalled.
Residents told the police chief they would not leave until all the police
agreed to clear out completely. The tactic worked. The police gave in,
and the community members began working on the building, stripping
down the floor, redoing the rooms and bathrooms and turning it from a
jail to a radio station and community center. Plumbers, carpenters, and
locals arrived with supplies and skills to contribute to the transformation. They started broadcasting on August 22nd, 2005. "In six months
look what we've done!" Contreras said.

To start a program on the station all people have to do is write a
clear proposal of what they would like to produce. The radio now has
shows on hip-hop, folk music, social and political issues, as well as on
regional, Latin American integration and history. One program provides
a space for community members who have complaints about the government, another teaches health for senior citizens. The radio is coordinated by a committee of El 23 residents of all ages. "Everyone has their
responsibility...We all mess up sometimes, we're human, but we try to
function in a horizontal way," explained Contreras.

Contreras said that their radio fights against misinformation from
Venezuela's corporate media. "All the mass media does is censure and
stigmatize what's being done [in our neighborhood]. For the big media
monopolies, we are some terrorists who have a radio, who kicked out
the police..." Opposition media in Venezuela issues a constant stream
of criticisms and slander campaigns against poor neighborhoods such
as El 23 de Enero. This media monopoly played an important role in

the short-lived, Washington-backed April, 2002 coup against President Hugo Chávez. During this conflict, corporate radio and TV stations refused to report on the massive pro-Chávez uprising during the coup and framed Chávez supporters for violent acts they did not commit. In Venezuela, as in many other countries, media are used by the elite as political weapons. Community radio stations in Venezuela are localized responses to this threat.[43]

"This place was a symbol of repression, of the 40 dark years of our country," Contreras said. "So we took that symbol and made it into a new one, a tangible part of the revolution. It is evidence of the revolution made by us, the citizens," he said. "The institutions need to play a role and the government needs to play a role, but we can't hang around waiting for the revolution to be made for us; we have to make the changes."

Throughout the region, workers, families, and farmers organized to take back what was rightfully theirs. Citizens united to recuperate natural resources and entire governments. In Bolivia, a movement to take gas reserves out of corporate hands and put them under state control turned the entire nation upside down. In cases of land, jail, and factory occupations many people were left with no other choice but to utilize the resources available to them to survive and overcome the lasting affects of police repression. At the heart of each of these occupations was the question of property and ownership, and whether or not a privileged elite or poor majority should use these resources. The striking examples of recuperation outlined here are being put to use all over the world, where people are acting on this simple slogan: Occupy, Resist, Produce.

(Endnotes)

1 From author interview with Candido Gonzalez in February, 2005.

2 Omar Mendoza C., Zedin Manzur M., David Cortez F. and Aldo Salazar C., *La Lucha por la tierra en el Gran Chaco tarijeño* (La Paz: Fundación PIEB, 2003), 81–87, 119–132.

3 Peter Lowe, "Bolivian Landless Give Birth to a Movement," *Resource Center of the Americas*, May, 2005, http://www.nadir.org/nadir/initiativ/agp/free/imf/bolivia/txt/2002/0501bolivian_landless.htm.

4 "In a recent study of land distribution in developing countries, four countries in the region topped the list. They had the highest land distribution Gini Coefficients in the world. Eleven of the top 16 countries in the same list came from Latin America. No Latin country was in the group of low or even medium inequality. . . The FAO estimated that around 1970 the biggest 7% of land holdings in the region (those above 100 hectares) owned 77% of the land." Samuel A. Morley, "Distribution and Growth in Latin America in an Era of Structural

Reform," *International Food Policy Research Institute: Trade and Macroeconomics Division* (January 2001), http://www.ifpri.org/divs/tmd/dp/papers/tmdp66.pdf. Also see Pauline Bartolone, "Land For Those Who Work It: Can committing a crime be the only way to uphold the constitution?," *Clamor Magazine* (September 5, 2005) and Green, *Faces of Latin America*, 24–27.

5 Rafael Reyeros, El pongueaje: La servidumbre personal de los indios bolivianos (La Paz: Universo, 1949)., Also Green, *Faces of Latin America*, 25, 33.

6 "Bolivia's Agrarian Reform Initiative: An Effort to Keep Historical Promises," *Andean Information Network* (June 28, 2006), http://ain-bolivia.org/index. php?option=com_content&task=view&id=22&Itemid=27.

7 Green, *Faces of Latin America*, 32–33.

8 This land distribution statistic for Bolivia is provided by the *Comisión Especial de Asuntos Indígenas y Pueblos Originarios*, cited in "Los peces gordos de la tierra: Familias Latifundistas," *El Juguete Rabioso* (November 27th, 2006), 8. "Struggle for land in Bolivia," *British Broadcasting Corporation* (September 14, 2006), http://news.bbc.co.uk/2/hi/americas/5303280.stm.

9 Crabtree, *Perfiles de la Protesta*, 32–36, 36–38.

10 "Bolivia's Agrarian Reform Initiative ," *Andean Information Network*.

11 For more information, see Kohl and Farthing, *Impasse*.

12 "Bolivia's Agrarian Reform Initiative" *Andean Information Network*. .

13 Information from author interview with journalist and Bolivian Landless Movement researcher Wes Enzinna.

14 Mendoza C., et. al., *La Lucha por la* tierra, 73–76.

15 Ibid., 89–95.

16 Crabtree, *Perfiles de la Protesta*, 38–39.

17 "Landless Step up Occupations," *Americas.org* (March 18, 2006), http://www.americas.org/News/Features/200205_Bolivian_Landless/20020501_index.htm.

18 Raquel Balcázar, *Repressión Fascista en Santa Cruz*, (Santa Cruz: Video Urgente, 2006)

19 From author interview with Silvestre Saisari in September, 2006.

20 Jeffrey Frank, "Two Models of Land Reform and Development," *Z Magazine* (November, 2002), http://www.landaction.org/display.php?article=22.

21 "About Brazil's Landless Workers Movement," *MST*, http://www.mstbrazil.org/

22 James Petras, Henry Veltmeyer, *Social Movements and State Power: Argentina, Brazil, Bolivia, Ecuador* (London: Pluto Press, 2005), 92–93, 111–113, 130–131. For an excellent resource on current issues within Brazil's MST, see Raúl Zibechi, "Landless Workers Movement: The Difficult Construction of a New World," *IRC Americas* (October 4, 2006), http://americas.irc-online.org/am/3547.

23 In October of 2006, the Paraguayan Senate it would not allow the troops immunity past their December deadline.

24 COHA Memorandum to the Press, "Washington Secures Long-Sought Hemispheric Outpost, Perhaps at the Expense of Regional Sovereignty," Council on Hemispheric Affairs (July 20, 2005), http://www.coha.org/NEW_PRESS_RELEASES/New_Press_Releases_2005/05.78_Washington_Secure_Long_Sought_Military_Outpost_Perhaps_At_the_Expense_of_Regional_Soverignty.htm., Also "Inquietud por una base de EEUU en zona fronteriza de Paraguay," *El Deber* (July 7, 2005), http://www.eldeber.com.bo/20050707/nacional_2.html, and Pablo Bachelet, "4 nations that won't sign deal with U.S. risk aid loss," *Miami Herald* (December 18, 2004), http://www.latinamericanstudies.org/us-relations/loss.htm. Since 2002, US troops have had 46 exercises in key areas such as borders with Brazil Argentina and Bolivia. Stella Callón, "Enviada Asesinato de indígenas paraguayos tendría nexos con operaciones de soldados de EU,"

La Jornada (November 27, 2005), http://www.jornada.unam.mx/2005/11/27/ 031n1mun.php. Also see Benjamin Dangl, "US Military Descends on Paraguay," *The Nation*, (July 17, 2006), http://www.thenation.com/doc/20060717/dangl

25 Ana Esther Cecena and Carlos Ernesto Motto, "Paraguay: eje de la dominacion del Cono Sur," in *Conflictos sociales y recursos naturales* (Buenos Aires: Consejo Latinoamericano de Ciencias Sociales, 2005), 275–277, p278–279, 280–281. Also see Chapter 3 for more information.

26 Esther Cecena and Ernesto Motto, "Paraguay," in *Conflictos sociales*, 275–276.

27 Tomas Palau Viladesau, " El Movimiento *campesino* en el Paraguay: conflictos, planteamientos y desafios," in *Reforma agraria y lucha por la tierra en America Latina: Territorio y movimientos sociales* (Buenos Aires: Consejo Latinoamericano de Ciencias Sociales, 2005), 41–42.

28 See Javiera Rulli, "GMO Soy Growers commit Massacre in Paraguay," *The Activist Magazine*, (June 29, 2005), http://activistmagazine.com/index. php?option=com_content&task=view&id=383&Itemid=56 and Grupo de Reflexión Rural http://www.grr.org.ar/

29 Information based on author interviews with Orlando Castillo, 2005 and reports from Grupo de Reflexión Rural http://www.grr.org.ar/

30 Information based on author interviews with Tomas Palau, 2005.

31 Author email interview with Bruce Kleiner in July, 2005. Ugarte quote from Charlotte Eimer, "Spotlight on US troops in Paraguay," *BBC News*, (September 28, 2005), http://news.bbc.co.uk/2/hi/americas/4289224.stm. ·

32 See Campaña por la Desmilitarización de las Américas, CADA, "Conclusiones generales de la Misión Internacional de Observación," *America Latina en Movimiento* (July 15–20, 2006), http://alainet.org/active/12453&lang=es.

33 Greg Grandin, "The Wide War: How Donald Rumsfeld Discovered the Wild West in Latin America," *TomDispatch*, (May 7, 2006), http://www.tomdispatch.com/ index.mhtml?pid=82089.

34 Katherine Shrader, "U.S. Studying Iran's Retaliation Options," (June, 3, 2006), *Associated Press*, http://www.cbsnews.com/stories/2006/06/03/ap/world/ mainD8I0JOC00.shtml.

35 Bureau of Political Military Affairs, "Foreign Military Training: Joint Report to Congress, Fiscal Years 2004 and 2005," *US Department of State*, (April, 2005), http://www.state.gov/t/pm/rls/rpt/fmtrpt/2005/45677.htm

36 Kelly Hearn, "Patrolling America's Backyard?," (November, 4, 2005), *AlterNet*, http://www.alternet.org/story/27775/

37 All information and interviews on the worker cooperative movement in Argentina are from interviews with the author in February and March, 2005.

38 Argentine President Nestor Kirchner was believed by many at that time to not be enacting the radical changes in the economy that many demanded in the 2001–2002 protests

39 For full interview, see: Benjamin Dangl, "An Interview with Celia Martinez of the Worker Controlled Brukman Textile Factory in Buenos Aires," *Upside Down World* (August 29, 2005), http://upsidedownworld.org/brukman-interview.htm.

40 La Vaca, *Sin Patrón: Fábricas y empresas recuperadas por sus trabajadores* (Buenos Aires: La Vaca Editora, 2004)

41 All reportage on Zanon repression from: Benjamin Dangl, "Member of Worker-Run Factory in Argentina was Kidnapped, Tortured," *Upside Down World* (March 24, 2005), http://upsidedownworld.org/main/content/view/22/32/.

42 Menem was the president of Argentina during the nineties and enacted numerous neoliberal policies which many believe greatly contributed to the country's 2001–2002 economic crisis.

43 For more information on the 2002 coup in Venezuela, see Eva Gollinger, *The Chávez Code: Cracking U.S. Intervention in Venezuela* (Caracas: Editorial Jose Marti, 2005) and Kim Bartley & Donnacha O Briain, *The Revolution Will Not Be Televised, "Chávez: Inside the Coup"* (Del Rey: Vitagraph Films, 2003).

Chapter Six

The Wealth Underground

Protestors in El Alto during the 2003 Gas War haul train cars off tracks with their bare hands, pushing them onto the highway to block military and police forces from entering the city.

Photo Credit: Julio Mamani

"Many don't see any particular point in having their culture and lifestyle destroyed so that people can sit in traffic jams in New York."

—Noam Chomsky[1]

Fireworks greeted the morning of September 19th, 2003 in Cochabamba, with the first major mobilization of what came to be called the Gas War. Tens of thousands of people filled the streets, waving signs and cheering *El Gas No Se Vende!* (The Gas is Not For Sale!). Babies wrapped in colorfully embroidered cloth peered from the backs of their mothers who marched in the already hot sun. Most protesters were *cocaleros* from the Chapare. They looked exhausted but determined, veterans of this kind of activity. Major intersections were blockaded with piles of rocks, flaming tires, and garbage. Dark smoke from bonfires hung over the central plaza, where the crowd converged. Placards bobbed above the sea of people, whose cheers rose to a fevered pitch. Shaking his fist from a balcony above the uproar, Evo Morales called for continued protests, threatening, "If the government decides to export the gas, its hours are numbered!"[2]

The conflict that manifested itself in Bolivia was part of a larger global resource crisis. Whether over water, land, or food, resource wars have grown in recent years, the bloodiest focusing on access to oil in the Middle East. As the human population increases, so does the demand for oil and gas. Yet these resources are running out, causing prices to rise and countries to invade or exploit one another.[3] Meanwhile, those who cannot afford to pay the price of fire continue to rise up in protest.[4] As the Gas War unfolded in the Andes, bodies were also falling to the ground Iraq, Afghanistan, and Venezuela in conflicts over control of oil and gas.[5]

The question of how to best use Bolivian gas unified diverse social and labor groups into a one month long, nationwide mobilization for change. After decades of corporate exploitation of raw materials, Bolivians united to say *"Basta!"* Rather than sell their gas at a low price to foreign corporations, Bolivian people demanded that the resource under their feet be used for national development.[6] An explanation of the history of state control of resources in Bolivia and Venezuela shows ways in which the paradigm of elite exploitation of oil and gas industries has been constructed, and how it can be reversed.[7]

The September 19th march in Cochabamba was the affirmation of a new movement.[8] By the time the conflict ended a month later, the president had fled the country and confrontations between protesters and security forces resulted in 67 deaths and hundreds of injuries. The day after this initial march, one event ignited the national outrage that led to those bloody results.

At the same time protestors marched in Cochabamba, the US, German, and English embassies found out that several of their citizens had been stuck in road blockades for a week in Sorata, a town north of La Paz. US ambassador David Greenlee pressured the Bolivian government to take action.[9] Bolivian security forces were dispatched immediately for a "rescue" operation.[10] On September 20th, just before dawn, the military forces on their way to Sorata approached the small town of Warisata, surprising the residents blockading the road in protest of the gas exportation plan and other local issues.[11]

Making no attempt to reach an agreement, security forces opened fire indiscriminately on *campesinos*, shooting into homes and schools. Some of the *campesinos* returned fire with their own weapons—often no more than stones. In the end, the confrontation left seven dead from bullet wounds, including two soldiers, a 60-year-old man, a student, a professor, and a mother and daughter. Nearly 25 injuries were reported from both sides.[12] Bolivia was standing at a precipice and these deaths tipped it over the edge. Once the first domino fell in Warisata, there was no turning back.

After the news of the Warisata massacre spread throughout the country, protests, road blockades, hunger strikes, and militant rallies were organized by social and labor organizations. The security forces had not been provoked into attacking, but had actually ambushed the largely unarmed residents of the town. Mauricio Antezana, the spokesman for President Sánchez de Lozada, said that "they had spoken with the *campesinos* that were blockading Sorata, and had reached an agreement that allowed the numerous buses to leave." Yet when the security forces arrived, the tension rose and the agreement was ignored.[13]

Though government officials maintained that the security forces were ambushed by *campesinos*, human rights investigators from the Defensor del Pueblo (Ombudsman), Bolivia's Permanent Assembly of Human Rights and the Congressional Human Rights Commission stated that there was no evidence of an ambush, and that the military had been securing the area around Warisata from early morning. Later in the afternoon, though talks with the *campesinos* to end the blockade were in progress, the military had aggressively moved in for the confrontation. In the midst of a national debate regarding the confrontation—during a ceremony in which the US gave the Bolivian government $63 million in development aid—US ambassador David Greenlee said that the intervention of the security forces in Warisata was justified.[14]

In response to repression in Warisata, activists marched to major intersections in Cochabamba to construct road blockades out of rocks, tires, dumpsters, and bonfires. Students blockaded an intersection just outside the central plaza. The traffic, usually congested day and night in this part of the city, was at a standstill. Angry taxi drivers pressed on horns while activists fueled blockade fires. Suddenly, a mass of policemen on motorcycles appeared toward the end of one street and sped toward the blockade. They fired tear gas into the crowd of students, leapt from their motorcycles, and brought their nightsticks crashing onto the bodies and heads of the young activists. Many students were immediately thrown into the backs of the police trucks and handcuffed. A woman ran into the street, screaming at the policemen, "Who are you defending? Who are you defending?"

The deaths in Warisata galvanized public anger against the Sánchez de Lozada administration and his gas exportation plan. As violence against the movement increased, so did participation. Repression brought resistance, the opposite of the government's objective. The more the nightsticks crashed, the more people were filled with fury, went on strike, constructed road blockades, and marched. The gas exportation issue proved to be a spark that fueled a much larger fire of national discontent. Protesters in the Gas War demanded higher wages, reforms in coca laws, the release of jailed political prisoners, and solutions to land distribution problems. In the end, many Bolivian activists combined their demands into one unified call for the resignation of President Sánchez de Lozada. Above the din of this varied, nearly chaotic social movement, one chant was present everywhere: *"El Gas No Se Vende!"*

Demands for gas nationalization emerged out of a long history of corporate exploitation and successful examples set by the state-run gas company. A look at the history of Bolivia's gas and oil illustrates how a country with so much resource wealth in its subsoil came to be one of the poorest above ground.

Grandparents of the Guarani indigenous people tell stories of oil, or "magic water," being used years before the arrival of the Spanish.[15] The black liquid cured wounds on people and animals, kept fires going and battle arrows aflame. When the Spanish arrived, law declared

the black liquid property of the King of Spain.[16] When new importance
was given to this resource for use in automobiles, Standard Oil, a New
Jersey-based company, gained control of Bolivian gas.[17] Competition
with the company's arch-rival, Royal Dutch Shell of Britain, led to the
Chaco War (1932–1935), which pitted Latin America's poorest countries
against each other.

The seeds of this war were sown by Standard Oil and Royal Dutch
Shell as both companies sought reserves in disputed border territories
between Paraguay and Bolivia.[18] In spite of subsequent tension between
the nations, Standard Oil explored and discovered enormous deposits
in these areas with Bolivia's permission. Paraguay, in turn, granted Royal
Dutch Shell access to the same land in question. Under pressure from
the feuding companies, a war broke out between the two countries.[19] As
a result of the conflict, Bolivia lost hundreds of thousands of kilometers
of land in the Chaco to Paraguay, and thousands of lives. Eduardo Galeano wrote of the Chaco War, "It was a quarrel between two corporations,
enemies and at the same time partners within the cartel, but it was not
they who shed...blood."[20]

After the Chaco War, an enraged Bolivian public demanded that
Standard Oil leave the country. The government eventually sent the
company packing for clandestinely exporting Bolivian gas to Argentina,
completing the first expropriation of property from a US multinational
corporation.[21] With the Standard Oil contract cancelled, gas went into
state hands. *Yacimientos Petroliferos Fiscales Bolivianos* (YPFB), the first
Bolivian state-owned oil company, was created to run the industry in
1936. In four years, YPFB produced 882,000 barrels of oil, more than
Standard Oil had produced in 15 years in Bolivia. In 1953, the company
produced enough to provide for the national consumption of oil.[22] For
over 60 years, YPFB generated enormous funding for the government,
contributing 55.7 percent of total exportation in 1985.[23] Though the
industry went in and out of state hands over the years, it was through
YPFB that the technology, expertise, and infrastructure was developed
to sustain the state run industry, a success that contributed to recurring
demands for nationalization.

In March of 1994, during his first term as president, Sánchez de
Lozada designed and passed the Law of Capitalization. This law was
intended to boost the Gross Domestic Product (GDP) and save the
country from an economic depression, but had the opposite results, particularly on the gas industry. The law approved the privatization of the
country's telephone company, airlines, trains, and oil and gas companies.

Before the law was passed, these businesses had produced around 60 percent of the government revenues. In 1997, YPFB went into the hands of American, Dutch, Spanish, and Argentine companies.[24] The state business was sold for $844 million to British companies, $100 million under its valued price.[25] Between 1997 and 2003, the official amount of known natural gas in Bolivia increased by ten times. Yet the more gas Bolivia produced, the poorer the country became.[26] As Roberto Maella, the Executive of the REPSOL/YPF gas company in Bolivia said, "The profit of the oil and gas industry in Bolivia is very high: for every dollar invested, an oil company gains ten dollars."[27]

The divisive gas exportation plan that led to the 2003 Gas War began with the administration of Hugo Banzer in 1997. When Banzer resigned, vice president Jorge Quiroga carried the neoliberal torch. The plan to export Bolivia's gas through Chile to the US was to be executed by Pacific LNG, a consortium organized in June, 2001 of British Gas (BG), British Petroleum (BP) and Repsol/YFP. These corporations controlled Margarita, the largest area of gas reserves in Bolivia, and planned for the project to involve the daily export of 36 million cubic meters of gas to the US for 20 years. The first phase of exportation was to consist of a gas duct from Tarija, Bolivia to Patillos, a Chilean port on the Pacific Ocean. A plant would then be constructed at this port to liquefy the gas before carrying it by boat to a Mexican port where it would be re-gasified for transportation to and distribution in the US.[28]

According to Carlos Arze, the director of The Center for Studies of Labor and Agrarian Development, (CEDLA), based in La Paz, the plan allowed for the gas to be sold at more than 20 times the price paid to the Bolivian government.[29] Because of the cost of transportation and refinement in this plan, the gas would be purchased as a raw material in Bolivia for approximately $.18 per thousand cubic feet and then sold in California for around $3.50–4.00 per thousand cubic feet. Chile would also make money for processing the gas in its port, another stage of the sale from which the Bolivian government would not profit.[30] Not the least of the reasons for outrage among citizens was the fact that Chile had stolen Bolivia's access to the sea in a territory war in 1879, an event that still angers many Bolivians.[31]

Environmental problems have also emerged in the wake of the corporate takeover of gas. In January, 2000, Transredes, a subsidiary of Enron and Shell, was responsible for an oil spill in Bolivia's Desaguadero River. The water, which many locals rely on for their livestock, turned black. According to researcher Christina Haglund, animals in the region died as a result of the spill and green plants around the river were destroyed.[32] Haglund writes that Transredes "disregarded warnings about an old, eroded, and rickety pipeline...The gush of Enron/Shell petroleum that poured into the shallow river was enough to fill more than two Olympic-sized swimming pools." 30,000 residents of the region were affected. [33]

Besides the historical, environmental, and economic reasons for protesting corporate control of gas and the 2003 exportation plan, many Bolivians hoped that the gas, one of its last major resources, could be used for national development. The gas within Bolivia's soil, which has created so many conflicts above ground, has no color or odor. Natural gas—which is the bulk of the hydrocarbons that Bolivia calls its own—contains butane, propane, and ethane and is the cleanest of all fossil fuels in terms of pollution and carbon emissions. Despite its name, natural gas is not the liquid gasoline that people put into cars. It is most often used for cooking, heating, and the generation of electricity, and it makes up around 1/3 of energy use in the US and 25 percent of global use. Natural gas is primarily distributed locally through pipelines due to the expensive process of compression and liquification needed for transport in ships or trucks. Most of Bolivian gas leaves the country through pipelines to Argentina and Brazil.[34]

Protestors in the 2003 conflict demanded cheaper access to gas-related products, such as diesel for tractors and agriculture. In Bolivia, more than half of the diesel used is imported from abroad. Diesel could be locally produced from natural gas, and offered at a low price to farmers, but development efforts up to 2003 focused on exportation, not on national use or access. Natural gas can also be used in the production and local use of fertilizers, paper, cement, textiles, explosives, plastics, glass, heat, and electricity.[35] Better local distribution and use of the resource was another protestor demand. Many Bolivians don't have direct access to gas in Bolivia for use in kitchens and heating.[36] Over 90 percent of the gas is exported and of the ten percent that goes to Bolivian use, a very small amount goes to people's homes. Most goes to thermo-electric plants, where electricity is generated that is prohibitively expensive and doesn't arrive to most of the population which, according to Arze, is, "still living as if in medieval times."

One of protesters' biggest complaints is that, to date, corporate investment in the Bolivian gas industry has not significantly benefited Bolivia. Foreign investors focus on making money by selling to external markets instead of developing the infrastructure for national use and industrialization. For example, the biggest gas duct to Brazil from Bolivia is 40 times bigger than the one that goes to the capital city of La Paz. The older ducts created by YPFB are in disrepair and cause regular environmental problems. This means that the country with one of the largest gas reserves in the region has some of the worst distribution and industrialization methods for its own citizens.[37] Such movements for the recuperation of natural resources in Bolivia led political analyst Noam Chomsky to say, "Many don't see any particular point in having their culture and lifestyle destroyed so that people can sit in traffic jams in New York."[38]

Many protestors called for the expropriation of foreign companies operating in the country, the end of Sánchez de Lozada's hydrocarbon law and re-nationalization of the gas industry through the recuperation of YPFB.[39] As the amount of known gas in the Bolivian subsoil continues to rise, so does the price and demand for this resource, creating an opportunity to gain much needed capital to rebuild YFPB.[40]

However, putting resources into government hands is far from a foolproof alternative to corporate control. Though YFPB offers hopeful examples for state control of gas, the government-run industry has the potential to be just as exploitative, corrupt, and inefficient as corporations. Much would depend on YFPB management. Ecological destruction from any gas or oil industry is nearly inevitable, whether it is in state hands or not. In the case of the Cochabamba Water War, corporate control of water horribly affected a majority of the population, and yet, after Bechtel was kicked out, the subsequent public control has also left much to be desired.[41]

In order for the state to take responsible control over the gas industry, social movements, channeling the will of the people, will have to exert their influence over the state to ensure that resources would in fact benefit the people. Both the input of experts from other nationalized industries and methods of creative, participatory public management would be in order.

These complications do not change the fact that, for many Bolivians, gas had become a magic word in 2003, a symbol of all past resources lost and all possible wealth for the future. Like coca and water, the gas was viewed as a natural resource for survival. Not only was it needed for heating and cooking, many wanted it to open doors to development, education and health care. As citizens mobilized for this change in September and October of 2003, they were met with violent repression.

Mobilizations against the gas exportation plan gained momentum as a historical pact developed between labor and social organizations. Groups normally at odds with each other unified against the gas plan and the Sánchez de Lozada administration, paralyzing the country with strikes, marches and road blockades. Workers and farmers blockaded roads in El Alto, La Paz, and the Chapare. Miners entered the fray in a march from Oruro to La Paz.[42] Routes to other cities—as well as borders with Chile and Peru—were cut off and confrontations between protesters and the army and police forces escalated. A general strike completely shut down La Paz on October 8th. In El Alto, *Econoticias Bolivia* reported that "for more than three hours, throughout this young and impoverished city, tear gas, rocks, and dynamite rained down."[43]

On October 9th, 2003, near El Alto, 40-year-old miner, Jose Atahuichi, was killed after a stick of dynamite exploded near him. Later that same day, 22–year-old Ramiro Vargas Astilla died from a gunshot wound from security forces during a protest near El Alto.[44] The government called for the military to use force to open the route between Oruro, Potosí, and Cochabamba, and to stop the marches from entering La Paz. In El Alto, residents paraded the body of Atahuichi angrily around the community. When Sánchez de Lozada was asked at a press conference to comment on these deaths, he refused to respond and left the room.[45]

Confrontations in the Gas War were cyclical. In the event of a large demonstration or blockade campaign, conflicts between protestors and security forces erupted, followed by a ceasefire and attempts at negotiation. High tempers and a lack of dialogue pushed opposing factions further from each other. The government refused to communicate with protest group representatives, choosing to fuel the growing fire with repression. The result was a shift in power from the government palace—which many citizens viewed as unrepresentative and corrupt—and into the streets. When commenting on the social unrest dividing Bolivia at that time, Sánchez de Lozada said to reporters, "These problems and difficulties are born of what I consider a very radical group in Bolivian society that believes they can govern from the streets and not from Congress or the institutions."[46]

Yet the Bolivian government left the people no other choice, as they were blocked from articulating their opinions and needs within the political system. Traditional parties in the government were more concerned with conserving their own power than representing the views of the opposition and citizens in the country. For example, in a meeting over congressional appointments, traditional party members fought over key posts in the state house while opposition parties, such as the MAS, were left waiting in congress for over twelve hours without being able to take part in the meeting.[47] Such undemocratic procedures pushed a discontented populace to direct action.

The government appeared unable and unwilling to address the social unrest. Regular violent confrontations in street protests caused protestors and government officials to become entrenched in their own positions, making dialogue between the two groups nearly impossible. The Interim Human Rights Ombudsperson, Carmen Beatriz Ruiz, warned that "if the parties in conflict do not begin dialogue, the situation will spin of control at any moment."[48]

According to press reports, Sánchez de Lozada's support resided only in "the US ambassador, the foreign petroleum companies, and the uncomfortable bayonettes of the military."[49] Just as the protests in the country reached a new high water mark, the president made the following announcement: "I will not resign from the presidency because my wife wants to keep on being the first lady of the nation."[50]

As I witnessed the conflicts from the city of Cochabamba, I saw a city paralyzed by its own people. While the conflict wore on, shops and restaurants in Cochabamba shut down either because owners were on strike or because they were afraid a protester would throw a rock through their window if they did not strike. Often, taxi and bus drivers wouldn't go on the streets out of fear of running into road blockades. Cochabamba became a ghost town; blockades kept the streets empty.

Olga was the mother of the family who ran the hostel where I lived at the time. Though her husband had voted for Evo Morales in the 2002 election, and the political beliefs of the couple leaned toward the left, they did not sympathize with the protesters in the Gas War. Their money came from tourism, and when social conflicts rocked the country, tourists avoided Bolivia. "Our hostel used to be full all week long," Olga lamented, "now it is not even half full on the weekends. We can't feed ourselves. People who depend on transportation of goods and food are also suffering because they can't work while the roads are blockaded. These protests and road blockades are hurting the economy a lot more than any gas exportation plan ever would."[51]

Pickup trucks full of security forces in riot gear looking for protesters and blockades roamed the streets. Tear gas blew through the air day and night, and flaming blockades constructed out of anything that could impede traffic, including garbage, tires, and wood, covered the streets. When the police showed up, they shot tear gas into crowds and beat up protestors. Occasionally, while these violent battles raged, the police marching band practiced on the second floor of their office. Loud, patriotic songs blasted through trumpets and tubas, mixing with the sound of protest chants.

These days of mobilizations strengthened camaraderie between protestors. After a day of marching and blockading, people gathered to relax, dance, play music and discuss the country's crisis. At one of these many parties, I met protest movement leaders Felipe Quispe and Roberto de la Cruz. On the first Friday of each month on the outskirts of Cochabamba, *Tinku*, a youth activist collective, held a raucous party powered by Andean folk music and *chicha*, an alcoholic drink made from fermented corn.[52] The party took place in a low lying building with a tin roof and a concrete floor with ditches on the side for an easy cleaning after the event. People packed into the room, chewing coca and passing around buckets of *chicha*, which they drank out of gourd bowls. Hours after the party started, Quispe and De la Cruz walked in wearing leather jackets and smiling nervously.

The indigenous leaders were ushered into a ritual for *Pachamama*. The ceremony consisted of a small fire covered with incense and auspicious objects and herbs. One person after another bowed toward the West, where the sun set, made a request from *Pachamama*, and splashed *chicha* in the four corners of the fire. Some asked for success and less violence in the Gas War. It was a smoky affair, and people gave speeches that moved others to tears. Quispe and De la Cruz grabbed handfuls of the coca leaves that were offered to them and dashed their bowls of *chicha* around the fragrant flames.

Quispe appeared restless and uncomfortable, as if holding in some kind of internal hurricane. He is often referred to as *El Mallku*, which in the Aymara language means prince, leader, or condor. He founded the political party the Pachakutik Indigenous Movement (MIP) and in 1998 was elected the General Secretary of the indigenous *Confederación Sindical Única de Trabajadores Campesinos de Bolivia* (CSUTCB).[53] A central goal of the MIP has been the formation of an indigenous state in which indigenous people control the territory and natural resources of the area.[54] An outspoken critic of neoliberalism and the Bolivian elite, Quispe participated in the Tupac Katari Guerrilla Army in 1984, which led a failed insurrection against the government.[55] In 1992, he was arrested for involvement with the group and since his release has been a militant advocate of an indigenous state.

Both Quispe and De la Cruz participated in the 2003 Gas War protests and blockades in El Alto. After they had shaken dozens of hands at the party, I settled into the seat between the two leaders. Quispe smiled as buckets of *chicha* were set in front of him. When I told him I was from the US, he smirked and yelled, "Oh, a gringo!" He took a big gulp from his bowl. "*Queremos sangre gringo!*" (We want gringo blood!). He raised his fist and gave me a solid, but good natured punch that knocked me off my chair. I climbed back into my seat and asked "What is it like to be leading some of the most intense road blockades in the country?" He looked at me. "We will fight with our tooth and nail until all the politicians are out of the government."

Gas War protestors demanded a state-run gas and oil industry that could industrialize gas within Bolivian borders to benefit the population. This meant not only better access to gas, but more revenue for social programs. "Bolivia could impose the kind of initiatives that state companies have used in Venezuela," explained Arze of CEDLA. Venezuela offers an example of the kind of changes that could be possible in Bolivia if nationalization took place and profits from the sale of oil and gas were redirected to social programs instead of foreign corporations.

The largest oil and gas reserves in Latin America are found in Venezuelan subsoil. For decades a small elite profited from the industry while the majority of citizens lived in poverty. With the rise to power of President Hugo Chávez in 1998, this vicious cycle began to change. Through a renegotiation of contracts with foreign petroleum industries, Chávez transferred much of Venezuela's oil into state hands. Once the new contracts were in place, the revenue from the business was redirected away from the country's elite and into projects to benefit the poorest communities.

Economic inequality, rampant in Venezuela throughout the 20th century, came to a breaking point in 1989, when right-wing President Carlos Andres Perez arrived in office.[56] Perez implemented harmful IMF structural adjustments, accepted a massive loan and subsequent debt which plunged the country into an economic recession. The Caracazo, a February, 1989 uprising in Caracas against the Perez government and his economic policies, was met with brutal military repression. Hugo Chávez, then a young colonel in the army, refused to participate in the Caracazo crackdown and in 1992 led an attempted coup d'état against the Perez government. When the coup failed Chávez took the blame for it and was imprisoned until 1994.[57]

Soon after his release Chávez began a presidential campaign that took him across the country, gaining support from diverse sectors of society. He started out with little financial backing, often traveling in a broken-down pickup truck and giving speeches out of the back. His humble background—he grew up in a poor family—and fiery speeches offered a radical alternative to the wealthy, right-wing politicians in power and gave hope to a disenfranchised population, 60 percent of which lived below the poverty line.

Shortly after winning the 1998 presidential election, Chávez renationalized the country's oil reserves in a process that could be applied by the Bolivian government. Under the new constitution, the state was granted full ownership of the *Petroleos de Venezuela SA* (PDVSA) gas and oil company.[58] This keeps the government, instead of corporations, in control of the industry. The law stipulates that "all state activity related to oil exploration and production is to be dedicated to the "public interest" and toward supporting "the organic, integrated, and sustainable development of the country..."[59] The constitution also establishes that revenue from the oil business should be used primarily to finance health care and education. Additionally, a change in the tax system was designed to generate more income for the government. The change created a tax raise from 16.6 percent to 30 percent per barrel of oil, with royalty payments directed to the government. The newfound funds have been largely spent on programs in health care, literacy, education, and subsidized food for poor communities.[60]

Not only is the oil revenue helping to create important social programs, the economy has received a boost from Chávez's new policies. Mark Weisbrot, a director at the Center for Economic and Policy Research, (CEPR) in Washington, wrote that under the Chávez administration, the country's economy has grown by 9–18 percent in recent years, making it the fastest growing economy in the hemisphere. This is not all due to oil wealth, either. In the 1970s, prices for the resources were high, but from 1970 to 1998, income fell by 35 percent, one of the worst declines in the region. Weisbrot attributes the current economic rise in part to more efficient tax collecting on the part of the Chávez administration, as well as benefits caused by social programs.[61]

Social programs developed out of oil wealth are empowering the nation's poor and improving educational and employment opportunities. According to government statistics, these programs have reached

54 percent of the population.[62] Chávez's government began literacy campaigns, undertook land reform, constructed free dentist offices, hospitals and schools in the poorest neighborhoods and created systems of subsidized supermarkets and business cooperatives all over the country.

In 2003, I visited a newly built community center in a Caracas neighborhood. In one room, women over the age of 70 were attending literacy classes decorated with murals of Chávez. Such profound changes in poor communities can take place in Bolivia if the gas revenue is redirected toward such programs. The literacy campaign, known as Mission Robinson, has reached millions of people of all ages, bringing the literacy rate in 2004 to an impressive 99 percent. Over a million people have enrolled in programs to receive high school diplomas. Occupational classes teach carpentry, auto repair and other skills to help people gain employment.[63] Programs in education and literacy have also lowered Venezuelan poverty rates by giving citizens new skills with which to gain employment and better their living situations.[64]

Nearby the literacy classrooms were the octagonal health clinics that are located throughout the country. In the clinics, Cuban doctors offer emergency medical care, vaccinations, check-ups, and medicine for common illnesses. Free health care improves the quality of life for many Venezuelans. The use of Cuban doctors in Venezuela's new clinics and health care systems has allowed for the quick expansion of services. In some cases, poor families are able to visit the doctor or a dentist for the first time in generations. A lack of health care causes an increase in poverty as poor citizens wait to go to the doctor until they are so ill that drastic and expensive measures have to be taken. This can lead people to be sick more often, and can affect their ability to support their families.[65]

A local resident led me to a building under construction that was soon to be a *Mercal. Mercals*, government subsidized supermarkets providing basic food for low prices, are now all over the country. Beans, bread, milk, vegetables, and other products, largely from Venezuelan producers, are available in the markets.[66] As a result, according to Weisbrot, household poverty rates are declining.

Alicia Cortez works as the Coordinator of the Local Health Committee in La Vega, another traditionally poor neighborhood in Caracas. She has run a government-funded *Comedor Libre*, or Free Cafeteria, from her home since 2002. Cortez explained the system to me while simultaneously stirring a pot of soup and slicing carrots. "Around 150 people come here each day to eat," she told me. "We go around and look for families that seem the neediest and invite children who live in the street, sick people, pregnant women and so on."

Her daughter Ayari works in the *Comedor Libre*, but also teaches at Mission Robinson. According to Alicia, "The meals are free and the food is served from 12–2 pm. Four women, including myself, work all morning to prepare the meals. In all the sectors of the barrios [a sector is an area of about five blocks] there is at least one *Comedor Libre*. With this program, people can depend on at least one good meal six days out of the week."

Though these programs affect many citizens, the entire political process in Venezuela revolves around Chávez as a central figurehead, putting at risk the participatory, democratic system that Venezuelan *Chavistas* celebrate. Nachie, a writer with the *Red & Anarchist Action Network* (RAAN), who traveled around Venezuela in 2006 to interview people and learn about the political and social environment under Chávez, illustrated this dilemma well with the following question: "What interests us most is the extent to which Chávez will allow himself to become obsolete. That is, will his projects of self-management and self-reliance in specific communities and the country as a whole transcend the need for a figurehead?"[67] Nachie contended that, while the social programs were clearly not "bad," they engender a kind of dependence on the state, bringing all civic work under the umbrella of the Chávez administration.[68]

Unfortunately, the energy industry is inherently ecologically dangerous and, equally unfortunately, various environmental disasters have taken place or are immanent under Chávez's watch. One example is the trans-Amazonic gas pipeline planned to be constructed from Venezuela to Argentina. PDVSA itself has admitted the operational risks of the plan, and Venezuelan government-funded studies predict an *"ecological catastrophe."*[69] Furthermore, Chávez announced that Venezuela would triple its coal production through open pit mining, primarily in Sierra del Perijá, where hundreds of Wayuú, Yukpa, Barí, and Japreria indigenous tribes live. This contaminating operation has already displaced many of these families, putting their survival, land, water, and biodiversity at risk. In March of 2005, indigenous activists marched in Caracas to protest the destruction from open pit mining in ancestral lands. Chávez, who was meeting with Argentine soccer legend Maradona at the time, refused to meet the protestors.[70]

In a similarly egregious move, Chávez happily welcomed ChevronTexaco to do business in Venezuela. When company representatives arrived, Chávez said, "We are good friends, good partners, and good allies of many US companies who work with us and every day we are more aligned in our work." ChevronTexaco, the 5th largest company in the world, is known for its human rights abuses, environmental destruction, and harsh tactics against indigenous communities.[71] ChevronTexaco's multi-million dollar Hamaca project, based in Venezuela's Orinoco river basin, is taking place in tandem with PDVSA. The environment and indigenous populations in the river basin are expected to be devastated by the project.[72]

Both Venezuela and Bolivia illustrate the dilemma posed by corporate versus state control of natural resources, and the dangers inherent in the highly profitable and inevitably polluting energy industry. In question during the 2003 Gas War was the road that Bolivia would take in terms of gas industrialization, how the profits would be directed and managed, and what effects those uses would have on the population. Similar issues will follow the Venezuelan model when Chávez leaves the presidency, whether in a matter of years or decades.

These and other questions would face Bolivians after the Gas War ended. During the chaotic month of October, 2003, however, the nation came close to an all out civil war in the movement against the Sánchez de Lozada administration and his gas exportation plan. In this revolt, the highland city of El Alto reclaimed its history as a powerful and targeted center of resistance to government control, as community organizations transferred their infrastructure into what would be one of the country's most powerful uprisings.

(Endnotes)

1 Chomsky and Dwyer, "Latin American Integration."
2 Further reports on this protest and stage in the Gas War are available in Benjamin Dangl, "Bolivia's Gas War: Seven Dead in Protests" *CounterPunch* (September 29, 2003), http://www.counterpunch.org/dangl09292003.html.
3 The US government, allied with corporations, has invaded Afghanistan and Iraq and has attempted to secure the oil fields in Venezuela through a coup in 2002. All of this is related to the growing gas and oil crisis. For more information, see The Association for the Study of Peak Oil and Gas: www.PeakOil.net.
4 In this context, the price of fire refers to the cost of heating and cooking gas, as well as gasoline for car engines and the production of electricity through natural gas. Fire, in this sense, means that on a stove, in a furnace, engine or light bulb.
5 A key reason for the Bush administration's invasion of Iraq was to gain control of the country's oil reserves. In Venezuela, that country's elite allied itself with the United States to retake control of the government and oil industry through a coup and strikes. A 2002 coup against the Chávez administration took place with

support and financing from the US.

6 This resource crisis and subsequent global conflict is extensively discussed in Michael Klare, *Resource Wars*.

7 On May 1st, 2006, the Morales administration partially nationalized Bolivia's gas reserves. A more extensive discussion of this nationalization will be presented in chapter ten. For more information, also see, Benjamin Dangl, "The Wealth Underground," *Upside Down World* (May 7, 2006), http://upsidedownworld.org/main/content/view/282/1/.

8 The initial march in September was organized primarily under a coalition of groups which was called the "Coordinator for the Recuperation and Defense of the Gas." The organizers of this organization were also key leaders in the 2000 Water War in Cochabamba, and in the formation of the Coordinator in Defense of Water and Life.

9 Greenlee has helped promote neoliberal policies in Bolivia. He is perhaps most infamously known for his harsh anti-coca eradication policies which have militarized the Chapare in Bolivia, resulting in human rights violations paired with a lack of alternative development for coca crops.

10 For more coverage of this massacre, see Dangl, "Seven die."

11 They were also demanding the release of local political prisoners.

12 For more coverage of this massacre, see Dangl, "Seven die."

13 For more information see *La Razon* (September 21, 2003).

14 This quote is from Greenlee illustrates his own detachment from the reality of the conflict. A similar attitude was taken by the Bolivian president, contributing to his unpopularity and leading to his eventual downfall. For information on Greenlee quote and meeting, see *El Diario* (September 23, 2003).

15 The Guarani indigenous group is primarily located throughout the Chaco, Santa Cruz and Tarjia region in the eastern part of the country.

16 Much of this history of gas in Bolivia is drawn from two excellent publications, which provide analysis and important background information which help in understanding the current issues facing Bolivian gas privatization and nationalization: *La Gestion de los Recursos Naturales no Renovables de Bolivia* (Cochabamba: CEDIB, 2005), 64., and *Los Hidrocarburos en la historia de Bolivia* (La Paz: (CEDLA), 2005), 5.

17 Though Bolivia did gain independence, much of the same class structure existed, which prevented an egalitarian society from developing. Though the Spanish royalty ceased to govern the country, descendents of the Spanish and mestizo (Spanish and indigenous) continued to rule most aspects of life and politics in the country. Systems of exploitation of labor remained, as did the lack of access among indigenous people to education, workers' rights and health care. The 1952 Revolution and other major legislation eventually helped revoke some the lasting impacts of the Spanish colonial period. Information on Standard Oil's history in Bolivia is available from CEDLA, *Los Hidrocarburos*, 8–9.

18 The history of both these companies in Bolivia is outlined in Mirko Orgaz García, *La Nacionalizacion del Gas* (La Paz, C & C Editores, 2005), 91., and CEDLA, *Los Hidrocarburos*, 10.

19 Another position is held among historians about how and why the war was initiated. Some contend that it was a move on the part of the Bolivian government to divert the public's attention from economic problems. See Farthing and Kohl, *Impasse*.

20 Galeano, *Open Veins*, 163.

21 Farthing and Kohl, *Impasse*, 45.

22 CEDLA, *Los Hidrocarburos*, 12.

23 García, *La Nacionalizacion del Gas*, 138.
24 This period of privatization under Sánchez de Lozada is explained in Kohl and
    Farthing, *Impasse*, 109-112. For example, "YPFB went from a high of 9,150
    workers in 1985 to around 600 by the end of 2002."
25 A new Hydrocarbons law introduced by Sánchez de Lozada in 1996 stipulated
    that companies had control of resources as soon as they came out of the ground.
    The law brought well head royalties from 50 percent to 18 percent. Where such
    royalties were applied was also expanded, making it more attractive for investors
    interested in Bolivian gas. See García, *La Nacionalizacion del Gas*, 132., and
    CEDIB, *La Gestion*, 68., CEDLA, *Los Hidrocarburos*, 21–24.
26 Ibid., 25.
27 *Los Tiempos* (May 5, 2002).
28 This deal is discussed at length in Iriarte, *El Gas: Exportar o Industrializar?*,
    (Cochabamba: Grupo Editorial Kipus, 2003), 30–31. This final gasification
    phase might have also happened in the US, in California, depending on how the
    contract was organized.
29 Some of the best information on the gas industry in Bolivia is available from
    Carlos Arze and *El Centro de Estudios para el Desarrollo Laboral y Agrario* at
    www.Cedla.org. All information from Arze on Bolivia's gas industry is from an
    interview with the author in February, 2006.
30 At the time, Chile was buying gas from Argentina for a higher price than what
    Bolivia would receive through the deal with Pacific LNG. Iriarte, *El Gas*, 84–87.
31 Arze said, "The topic of the [access to the sea] is a very simple issue in Bolivia.
    There is a lot of xenophobia and patriotic chauvinism. The military in the
    government always used the topic of the ocean to calm down social protests.
    People knew [the gas exportation deal] was something done by companies. But
    the fact that it was through Chile...woke up the fury of the people." Protestors
    demanded that the gas be exported through Peru instead, a more costly option
    than the government-favored plan to go through Chile.
32 Christina Haglund has done extensive research on this topic. For more
    information on the oil spill and its consequences, see Christina Haglund, "Enron/
    Shell and Hard Lives made Harder: A Front Line Account of an Environmental
    Disaster Imported from Abroad," *The Democracy Center* (August 15, 2006),
    http://www.democracyctr.org/blog/2006/08/enronshell-and-hard-lives-made-
    harder.html.
33 After the spill, Haglund reported that "Community leaders signed agreements
    with Transredes binding them to a compensation process determined by
    Transredes. The affected people along the river were compensated only for
    direct losses for which proof could be provided...Each community member who
    was evaluated as "affected" received bricks, concrete, a metal door, one window
    and aluminum roofing. The construction was left to the community members
    themselves." Residents could not opt for cash and were instead just given the
    building materials. "They broke something without fixing it," Dona Ignacia, a
    resident of the area, told Haglund. See Haglund, "Enron/Shell and Hard Lives
    made Harder."
34 Brian Yanity is a doctoral student at the University of Alaska studying alternative
    sources of energy. The information presented here on natural gas is from Brian
    Yanity, "The Alaska Gas Pipeline: A Critical Analysis," *Insurgent 49*, (February 17,
    2006), http://www.insurgent49.com/yanity_pipeline.html.
35 After nationalizing the oil industry in Venezuela, the government set up oil
    and gas connections to homes. Iriarte advocates the gas being industrialized
    for use in Bolivia, and sold for a higher price abroad to stimulate the Bolivian

economy, This is at the heart of president Morales gas nationalization plan. The
facts and figures outlined here are from Iriarte, *El Gas*, 8–10, 37, 72–73, 84–87,
89–93., Also see Luis Alberto Echazú A., "El Gas No Se Regala," (La Paz: Editorial
Liberación, 2003). The details of this demand are from an interview with Arze.

36 However, even if all of the houses and kitchens in Bolivia had access to gas, the
country would use less than 1.5 percent of the reserves.

37 From interviews with Arze.

38 Chomsky and Dwyer, "Latin American Integration."

39 Many of these joint risk contracts were set up by Sánchez de Lozada in the 1990s,
see García, *La Nacionalizacion del Gas*, 147–148.

40 Iriarte argues that as the amount of global gas reserves decreases, the demand
will increase, putting Bolivia in a good financial position if the state starts taking
advantage of its role as a major gas producer. According to Iriarte, in 2020, the
US will demand 50 percent more gas than it uses currently. Meanwhile, the
gas reserves in Argentina—which Chile depends heavily on—will dry up in 17
years. Bolivia is already exporting most of its gas to Brazil. Over time, there will
be more interest in Bolivian gas, putting Bolivia in a great position to negotiate
prices, contracts, and industrialization. Even better news for Bolivia is that the
known amount of gas in the subsoil keeps rising. Studies have shown that in 1997
the amount of gas in Bolivia was estimated to be 5.7 trillion cubic feet. In 2003,
that figure rose to 54.9 trillion. Much of the argument for industrialization of gas
in Bolivia presented here comes from Iriarte, *El Gas*, 17.

41 See chapter three for more details on SEMAPA public water management in
Cochabamba.

42 The presence of the miners in these mobilizations pushed the Gas War to a new
level. The militant history of the miners, and their use of dynamite, intimidated
a lot of the right-wing politicians who eventually fled in part because the miners
arrived in La Paz. "Los Mineros Avanzan Hacia La Paz," *Econoticiasbolivia.com*
(October 7, 2003).

43 "Se Cierra El Cerco Sobre La Paz," *Econoticiasbolivia.com* (October 8, 2003).

44 This number included the deaths during February 2003. For more
information, see Benjamin Dangl and Kathryn Ledebur, "Thirty Killed in Gas
War," *Znet* (October 13, 2003), http://www.zmag.org/content/showarticle.
cfm?ItemID=4342.

45 "Se Cierra El Cerco Sobre La Paz," *Econoticiasbolivia.com* (October 8, 2003).

46 This number included the deaths during February, 2003.

47 These deaths significantly increased participation in the streets. People from
diverse sectors of society were fed up with the repression of the Sánchez de
Lozada administration. "Ejercito Frena Avance de Mineros: Dos Muerto y Ocho
Heridos," *Econoticiasbolivia.com* (October 9, 2003).

48 See Elliott Gotkine, "Unrest rocks Bolivia," *British Broadcasting Corporation*
(October 1, 2003), http://news.bbc.co.uk/2/hi/americas/3157032.stm.

49 Dangl and Ledebur, "Thirty Killed in Gas War."

50 *La Prensa*, (October 3, 2003).

51 This media source provides regular reports which are critical of neoliberalism
and state repression. Tabera Soliz, "Goni, El Prisionero del Palacio,"
Econoticiasbolivia.com (October 2, 2003).

52 Tabera Soliz, "Goni, El Prisionero del Palacio," Econoticiasbolivia.com 10/2/03

53 The gas war had taken a serious toll on the economy. Some of the lost money
from the conflicts included $90,000 a day from the Aerosur airline company
because the problems with flights to and from La Paz and the lack of jet fuel. The
Camara Boliviana of Transportation said they had to cancel a 1.5 million dollar

contract to carry goods. There was also a high cost of reconstructing damaged roads and businesses. Andrade, *Agonia y Rebelion Sociale*, 212–214.

54 For more information on the Tinku youth group, see Benjamin Dangl, "Gringo Go Home!" *Upside Down World* (December 15, 2003), http://upsidedownworld. org/main/content/view/40/31/.

55 The CSUTCB is one of the leading *campesino*/indigenous groups in the country.

56 For more information on Felipe Quispe, see Petras, "Social Movements and the State," 187–188.

57 The Tupak Katari Guerrilla Army involved many intellectuals and activists who went on to play leading roles in the country's politics. For example, Álvaro García Linera, the current vice president of Bolivia, was a member of the group.

58 In 1992, Perez was forced from office on corruption charges.

59 This history is strikingly similar to that of Fidel Castro, who led a failed revolt against the Bautista government in Cuba. His subsequent imprisonment helped him gain support from the population for a later uprising.

60 Venezuela's oil industry was nationalized from 1943 to 1974. For more information on this history, and the current situation with the oil industry in Venezuela, see www.Venezuelanalysis.com. This brief history of Venezuela's re-nationalization, and information from the new constitution relating to the oil industry, is from Gregory Wilpert, "The Economics, Culture, and Politics of Oil in Venezuela" *Venezuelanalysis* (August 30, 2003), http://www.venezuelanalysis. com/print.php?artno=1000. After Chávez's 1998 presidential victory, he helped organize a constituent assembly to rewrite the country's constitution. Many of the progressive policies enacted by the administration were first articulated and established in this constitution. This information is from the Constitution of the Bolivarian Republic of Venezuela: Article 303

61 Cited in Wilpert, information from Article 5 of the "Ley Organica de Hidrocarburos."

62 Wilpert, "The Economics, Culture, and Politics."

63 Mark Weisbrot, "Economic Growth is a Home Run in Venezuela," *Center for Economic and Policy Research (CEPR)* (November 1, 2005), http://www.cepr.net/ columns/weisbrot/2005_11_01.htm. Weisbrot wrote that, "The official poverty rate has fallen to 38.5 percent from its most recent peak of 54 percent... But this measures only cash income; if the food subsidies and health care were taken into account, it would be well under 30 percent..."

64 Venezuelan poverty rates and other information cited in Weisbrot, "Economic Growth." Also Rodolfo Rico y Cristóbal Alva R., *Las misiones sociales venezolanas promueven la inclusión y la equidad. La revolución bolivariana corprenda al mundo*, Fundación Escuela de Gerencia Social (Caracas: Ediciones FEGS, 2005).

65 Stephen Lendman, "Venezuela's Bolivarian Movement: Its Promise and Perils, Pt. I," *Upside Down World* (January 3, 2006), http://upsidedownworld.org/main/ content/view/161/35/.

66 The main argument in this article is that poverty rates are lowering under the Chávez administration and that free health care and education improve the standard of living in Venezuela, but this improvement is not reflected in standard measures of poverty. For more information see Weisbrot, "Economic Growth," Mark Weisbrot, Luis Sandoval and David Rosnick, "Poverty Rates In Venezuela: Getting The Numbers Right," *Center for Economic and Policy Research* (May, 2006), http://www.cepr.net/publications/venezuelan_poverty_rates_2006_05.pdf.

67 Weisbrot, "Economic Growth."

68 Cited in Weisbrot, "Economic Growth., "Mercal es el lugar más visitado para comprar alimentos," *Datanalisis* (May, 2006), http://www.datanalisis.com.ve.

69 Nachie, "Bolivanarchism: The Venezuela Question in the USA Anarchist Movement," *Red & Anarchist Action Network (June 24 2005)*, http://www.anarkismo.net/newswire.php?story_id=770.

70 Nachie, "Venezuela, Socialism to the Highest Bidder," *Red & Anarchist Action Network* (July 11, 2006), http://www.anarkismo.net/newswire.php?story_id=3378.

71 Nachie, "Venezuela, Socialism."

72 Ibid.

73 Hanna Dahlstrom, "Macho Men and State Capitalism—Is Another World Possible?," *Upside Down World* (January 17, 2006), http://upsidedownworld.org/main/content/view/175/35/.

74 Ibid.

Chapter Seven

El Alto: The City That Contains a Nation

A boy stands on the scaffolding of a home he is
working on with his father in the self-constructed city
of El Alto.

Photo Credit: Dustin Leader

"The army can enter the city, they can kill many people, but they cannot take the city...During the uprising, the state was broken, it stopped existing. It died in El Alto."

—Pablo Mamani[1]

At the peak of mobilizations in the 2003 Gas War, citizens in El Alto organized a barricade on Juan Pablo II Street. The residents-turned-guerrilla fighters had pots on their heads for protection, slingshots, and both real and fake guns to intimidate security forces. Instead of confronting this militant group, security forces went into the nearby Villa Ingenio neighborhood and shot innocent people that were not prepared for a confrontation. In response, enraged citizens hauled train cars off tracks with their bare hands, shoving them onto the highway to block the passage of military and police.[2]

Residents of El Alto, or *Alteños*, emerged at the forefront of the 2003 Gas War. Their militancy and persistence is based on a history of self-reliance in a poor city where the void of the state has been filled by autonomous community organizations. Dozens of unarmed citizens were killed and hundreds wounded by security forces in this fight against a repressive administration and a neoliberal plan to export Bolivian gas. As repression worsened, rage against the government and military violence pushed the self-made city to its full capacity for mobilization, eventually toppling the Sánchez de Lozada administration and forever changing the balance of power between social movements and the state.

Central El Alto smells of exhaust, fried chicken, and cold mountain air. Muddy water flows down drain gutters while pedestrians pack against each other on sidewalks, holding hands and scolding kids. Spider webs of electric lines weave from building to building and salsa and techno music booms from apartments above and buses below. Bits of food and garbage are pounded into the dirt roads by the constant traffic. Taxis and buses compete for space and passengers, their chauffeurs chanting out destinations through open windows. An incessant chorus of horns blends with calls from vendors selling herbs, potatoes, shoes, notebooks, and coca leaves. Beyond the city, the vast *altiplano* stretches toward snow-capped mountains.

An older vendor with a gnarled face and green coveralls, selling shampoo and silverware from his stand, explained, "Everyone in El Alto is organized into some kind of union or community organization. When a problem arises we all get together and organize to fight, protest, and blockade." He repeated a phrase I had heard from nearly everyone I spoke to in the city: "Individually, we have no power. Together we can do anything." This motto has served *Alteños* for centuries, from the indigenous rebels who took siege to La Paz in 1781, to the miners of the Revolution of 1952 and the community organizations that took to the streets during the 2003 Gas War. Rebellion, self-sufficiency and social organization run in the veins of the people and the city itself.

"Welcome to the highest city in the world, where God watches us closely," reads a sign at the entrance to El Alto. At this altitude, winters are hard and cold wind from the Andes Mountains blasts through city streets. On warm days the temperature rarely goes above 68 degrees Fahrenheit. However, this hasn't stopped people from moving there. Migration to El Alto has skyrocketed in recent decades, and it now has the highest growth rate of any city in Latin America. The population in 1950 was around 11,000. By 2006 it had reached nearly 800,000. Sixty-five percent of the city's residents are younger than 25 years old and over half of the population works in the informal street vending economy.[3] One of every ten Bolivians lives there; by 2010 El Alto will be bigger than La Paz.[4]

The same forces that sent miners and farmers from the *altiplano* to the Chapare to grow coca sent thousands of Bolivians to El Alto. The closure of the state-owned mines and a massive drought in the mid-1980s made people migrate to survive. Faced with the hardships of eking out a living through the back-breaking and low-paying work of mining and rural subsistence farming, many Bolivians chose, and continue to choose, to try their luck in the city. Migrants arrived in El Alto to areas without schools, hospitals, plazas, electricity, roads, or running water. Out of necessity, families picked up their tools, combined their funds and labor and built the infrastructure of the city themselves.

Freddy Sarmiento was one of the many that moved to El Alto when the mines shut down. He worked in the mines of Potosí and, in 1985, migrated to El Alto with twenty-five other families and settled what is now called Unificada Potosí. On a warm February day, I spoke with him on a bench outside the mayor's office. The wind was cool but, because of the altitude, the sun was strong and hot. He wore a cowboy hat, leather coat, and had a rough, bohemian look about him.

"When we came to El Alto from Potosí, all the miners put their money together to buy land," he explained. The electricity, school, plazas, water system, and homes were all constructed with their own money and time. Sarmiento said that the miner's skills and habits helped them to settle in the new city. "We knew how to demand things and how to organize. We knew how to work together. That's how we got things like water quickly. We had to use our own tools, buy our own cement, everything. The state wasn't around in that time. I had the luck to have 25 *compañeros* from the mines there with me. It's our neighborhood, we made it...Even today we don't have help from the state."

His experience was like thousands of others in El Alto. Whether migrants were miners or farmers, they put their organizational skills to work in the construction of a city. They met their lack of services with camaraderie and tools, pooling their money and labor together to survive. What they couldn't build themselves, they demanded from the government in protests for roads, schools, and potable water. Out of this solidarity arose organizational strength and cohesiveness, which sprung residents into action in October, 2003.

The neighborhood organizations that emerged in El Alto during periods of massive migration were based, as in Sarmiento's case, on the experience of miner unions and community groups in rural areas.[5] One organization that has been transplanted successfully into city life is the rural *ayllu,* a group of neighbors or families that organize to discuss and act on issues that pertain to them. If there is a problem with the cost of electricity, they organize to lower the rates. If the garbage collection system is not working, they improve it among themselves. If there is a thief in the neighborhood they kick him or her out. They deal with these issues because the state does not.[6] This tight knit, responsive community has allowed the population of the city to mobilize itself quickly, organize protests, and construct road blockades.

Pablo Mamani, a sociologist who teaches at the Public University of El Alto, deconstructs the complex social infrastructure that was the backbone of the October revolt in his book, *Microgobiernos Barriales.* Mamani explains that the cultural practices of visiting neighbors regularly, sharing work efforts, and pooling money together for construction material for community projects—all customs based on traditions in rural communities and practiced in El Alto to this day—contribute to the creation of solidarity among residents.[7]

The depth of organization of El Alto's working poor is evident on every corner of the city. Many migrants to El Alto are employed as street vendors. As I navigated my way through the city in February, 2006 I spoke to various vendors who all said they belonged to a union. They were required to go to meetings and were not allowed to sell anything during strikes. As Felix Patsi, a sociologist who has extensively re-

searched community organizing in Bolivia, explained, "The market stalls
[in El Alto] are not private property, but rather, are managed by the syn-
dicates, the so-called unions, which is to say that the ownership is collective. The people obey the union because if they cannot sell or trade, they
cannot survive."[8]

The sense of collective identity that the union provides is also important to vendors who operate in an often isolated and economically
competitive atmosphere. I spoke with one proud and assertive vendor
who was wrapped in woolen shawls and surrounded by mounds of soda
and candy under a blue tarp. She explained her participation in the
union using the refrain of El Alto: "We all [belong] to a union. We have
to be unified, we're stronger that way. One person alone is not strong."
She told me that decisions to mobilize are made collectively, and that
during blockades and meetings the union takes attendance to make sure
that all members are present. Most street vendors belong to a union that
operates under the umbrella of the Regional Workers Center (COR). The
COR is primarily made up of labor groups, street vendors, unions, and
student groups. It acts as an instrument of social and political change,
articulating demands from its base and organizing mobilizations to pressure the government.[9]

Cohesiveness among the informal economy in El Alto is also due
to the fact that most workers are either self-employed or in a family-run
business. In his book *Dispersar El Poder*, Uruguayan writer and analyst,
Raúl Zibechi examines the roots of El Alto's capacity to rebel, current
networks of dispersed power, and where this movement might be headed next. According to Zibechi, there exists in the city an "autonomous
labor management" which is based on productivity not dependent on
the traditional hierarchical system of a boss-worker relationship. This informal family-organized business sector controls itself without a higher
power looking over it. Most workers in restaurants, sales, construction,
and manufacturing teach each other the work and manage their own
hours. The fact that most people run, or operate within, their own family
business contributes to the sense that citizens own the city and are self-
managing it.[10]

Another reason for the autonomy of *Alteños* is their distrust of
politicians. At the end of the 1980s and early 1990s, the political party
Conscience of the Nation (*Condepa*) held considerable power in El Alto,
leading the political opposition against traditional parties. It was led by
"Compadre" Carlos Palenque, a popular media personality, with a wide
reach of support throughout El Alto.[11] His network of contacts, friends,

and family constituted the base from which *Condepa* grew. He became
a voice for the repressed of the city and played an important role in refreshing its revolutionary spirit. Eventually *Condepa* fell victim to the
same corruption that it combated, using its ties with the community to
co-opt social leaders and maintain power through bribes and manipula-
tion.[12]

When Palenque died in 1997, *Condepa* crashed. The party could
not survive with out its central and charismatic figure. Community
and labor organizations filled the new political space. One major event
that marked this era in El Alto politics was the youth mobilization for
the creation of a university in El Alto. President Banzer gave in to the
demands in 2000, but much of the money for the university went to corrupt politicians in the city. The students organized, throwing out the
corrupt rector. This set a precedent in El Alto protest movements, showing that leaders could be thrown out with popular force.[13]

Two organizations that filled the political void left by *Condepa*,
and channeled the civic momentum generated by the student protests,
were the Federation of Neighborhood Councils (FEJUVE) and the Regional Workers Center (COR). Though these two groups don't officially
work together, the needs and demands of the population are often articulated through them. Their buildings are located right next to each other
in the city center and are run down, with peeling paint outside and cold,
unheated rooms inside.

Mamani explains in *Microgobiernos Barriales* that the neighborhood councils emerged during a period of peak migration to the city in
the 1980s, and were eventually converted into a network of micro-gov-
ernments, tied together through the umbrella of the FEJUVE. The individual neighborhood councils gather information from local community
members about people's needs and wants. Council leaders then either
administer the creation of services themselves, or go to state officials as
community representatives to demand change. As the population of El
Alto boomed, and the minimal existing services were strained even further, the councils gained responsibility for making such demands.[14]

The councils, of which there are nearly 600 within the eight dis-
tricts of the city, are perhaps the most important organizations for social
change in El Alto.[15] There are specific requirements for council participants: Leaders are selected every one or two years, and cannot be employed as merchants, bankers, transportation workers, or political party
leaders. They must have at least two years of residency in the neighborhood and at least one member from each family or household must at-

tend every meeting. Each FEJUVE neighborhood group has to have at least 200 members.[16]

One Sunday afternoon in El Alto, I headed to a plaza to attend a FEJUVE meeting. The gatherings occur twice a month in this neighborhood. A series of pot-hole ridden dirt roads led to the plaza, which included two small soccer fields—in use, when I arrived. The council president asked those playing soccer to leave, and then set up a microphone, table, and chairs as neighborhood representatives sat down in the bleachers. About a hundred people, including men and women of all ages, attended the event. As the meeting began, the president, secretary, and vice president took attendance and community members handed in their membership cards.

Each person at the meeting represents their street and all the families on it. I asked why so many participate in meetings, protests, and road blockades and what would happen if they did not. Meeting members told me that it's simply part of the way the community works. If, for example, one family does not participate in a campaign to get cheap public water or electricity for the neighborhood, then they aren't connected to the new system when it is won. For this reason—among others such as family and social pressure to participate—community activism is extensive.

In another part of El Alto, I met the sprightly president of the Alto La Portada FEJUVE, Eliadoro Castañeta Castillo, who immediately invited me out to see his barrio. The skyscrapers in the capital city below offered a stark contrast to the poverty in his neighborhood of eight hundred people. Many of the homes are crumbling brick structures with weak, tin roofs. We walked over a dirt road riddled with garbage, putrid puddles, and streams of residential waste water. "On Sunday we'll all get together to clean up the streets," Castillo noted.[17]

Nearly everything I saw in the neighborhood was resident-organized and constructed through his local FEJUVE. We strolled past the sports field, which was made by residents' labor, materials, and money. Neighbors also constructed a series of stone walls and pathways around homes which led down to the highway below. Castillo said his council has a meeting each month to decide what needs to be improved. Community members discuss who will do what work, and what organizations should be approached for funding.

In another feat of self-determinism, community members of Alto La Portada moved a road. Years ago, the government built a cobblestone street through the neighborhood. Unfortunately, it didn't lead to the

most trafficked area of the community. So, in 2005, the FEJUVE decided
to move the rock slabs. They rented a truck and hauled all of the stone
to a more densely populated area. Each household took care of the rocks
needed to fill the space in front of their home. For two months solid,
residents worked on evenings and weekends until the road was relocat-
ed. Through the neighborhood council, public gardens and grassy areas
are also constructed and maintained. Small streams have been built to
redirect water and prevent flooding. The self-constructed sports field
operates as a community gathering place where, among other events,
the FEJUVE meetings are held. Graffiti on a cement wall behind the
bleachers seemed fitting: "You can't always win. The important thing is
to participate."

It is a small leap from the tightly structured community organization of the FEJUVEs to the order of the protests and blockades.
Throughout the October revolt, communication between different
parts of El Alto helped sustain blockades and vigilance. Youth ran from
neighborhood to neighborhood, relaying messages. Organizers used cell
phones and radios to coordinate marches and establish security vigils.[18]
During the uprising, a system of shifts was implemented to help blockades continue, provide and distribute food, and take care of children
and the injured. This allowed some people to rest while others worked
or protested. For example, one El Alto neighborhood of 100 residents
took turns from 6 am to 3 pm, then another from 3 pm until midnight.
Beyond that, participation was voluntary. This let half the people rest,
while the others worked, sustaining long mobilizations and road blockades that are more difficult to suppress.[19] When police and military
removed certain blockades, others were constructed. Some blockades
were short, compact, and a few feet tall, while others were built for confrontations, or to totally block the passage of the road. Other blockades
were made out of blankets of rocks covering the road for hundreds of
feet, making them hard for security forces to clear.[20]

Regular collaborations among neighbors in the FEJUVE contributed significantly to such strategies in the 2003 Gas War mobilizations.
As Castillo explained, when they needed to hit the streets, "The solidarity was already there."

Before the city-wide uprising of October, 2003, two events electrified
the city into action. One was the conflict in Warisata on September 20th
that produced seven deaths, enraging the *altiplano*, and subsequently

its primary urban extension—El Alto. Another event that mobilized the city was the mayor's application of a tax increase referred to as *Maya* and *Paya*, Aymara for one and two. The FEJUVE led the charge against this increase, paving the way for larger demonstrations, which ousted a president and reversed a corporate policy.[21]

The organizational capacity of El Alto was put to use on October 8th, 2003 when diverse neighborhood councils, student, and labor groups coordinated a city-wide strike against the gas exportation plan.[22] Located on main highways that lead into the capital city of La Paz, El Alto is in a strategic position. When roads are blocked in El Alto, La Paz is essentially cut off from the rest of the country. Other key highways extend from El Alto to Lake Titicaca, Oruro, and Peru. When the strike began at 8:30 am, El Alto was completely shut down. The government sent security forces to the city to clear the roads, leading to confrontations with protestors that resulted in 16 injuries, some of them from bullet wounds. Five hundred miners arrived in El Alto that day from a march they had begun in Huanuni against President Sánchez de Lozada and the gas exportation plan.[23]

The Gas War was gaining momentum nationally, with El Alto leading the revolt. Indigenous groups in Oruro and Potosí marched toward La Paz in protest while 8,000 people demonstrated in Santa Cruz.[24] Protests turned deadly on October 11th when gas trucks attempted to go through El Alto to La Paz. Thousands of protestors, and the road blockades they constructed, prevented the trucks from passing, leading security forces to shoot tear gas and bullets into the demonstrating *Alteños*. In Villa Ballivan, the confrontation resulted in the death of Walter Huanca Choque, who was shot in the face by a soldier.[25]

Conflicts raged between protestors and security forces for the rest of the day. The El Alto air filled with tear gas, smoke from burning tires, chants, and bullets. Around 6:30 in the evening, the military and police, who were still accompanying the gas trucks, made another push through El Alto. Security forces shot bullets and tear gas canisters at blockaders while protestors responded with rocks, molotov cocktail bombs, and dynamite. The military and police caravan battled residents for two hours as they advanced toward La Paz. One bullet traveled four blocks away from the scene of the conflict, into the mouth and out of the head of five-year-old Alex Llusco Mollericona. As the news of his death swept throughout the city, people became even more furious. Protests against the repressive Sánchez de Lozada administration escalated and, in response, the military escalated its attack on El Alto. Soldiers circled the city in helicopters, shooting into crowds from above. Neighborhoods of former miners were hit particularly hard with bullets and tear gas. Various bridges were taken over by police and military forces while residents in other areas strengthened their road blockades.[26]

Some of the harshest repression against the El Alto mobilizations in the Gas War took place on Sunday morning, October 12th, when heavily armed military and police, escorting gasoline trucks, once again tried to pass through the blockades to La Paz, where gas shortages had brought the city to a standstill. El Alto residents maintained their blockades and refused to let the caravan pass. The confrontation began at 10 am, when police and military fired out of helicopters into crowds of unarmed people and homes. The death toll by the end of the day was 28.[27]

In the book, *Agonía y Rebelión Social*, Teofilo Balcazar explains that he and his wife had gone to visit her sister in Rio Seco, El Alto during the street protests. They were sitting in the living room, eating, when they started to hear the gunshots. His wife, Teodosia Mamani, suddenly fell to the ground. A bullet had come through the wall and killed her. She was four months pregnant. In the same area, Juana Valencia was laying on her bed resting. She reached up to close the window and was shot.[28]

The violence visited on *Alteños* was also visited on soldiers who refused to commit acts of violence. Nemesio Siancas Garcia, a soldier from Santa Cruz, was executed in Rio Seco in El Alto during this massacre. Residents in the area explain that Garcia refused to follow orders to shoot at the people in the neighborhood. In response, one of his superiors punched him in the face, knocking out his teeth, and then shot him in the head, killing him instantly. Other soldiers that were brought into El Alto from other parts of the country that refused to shoot at residents were tortured. Defectors elsewhere joined protestors; when one police station in El Alto was surrounded by demonstrators, the police waved white flags in surrender, then joined the mobilization.[29]

On October 13th, while military-escorted gas trucks continued attempts to break through to La Paz, some neighborhoods collected money to pay for medical treatment for the injured and coffins for the dead. The FEJUVE, COR, and other business unions in El Alto decided not to negotiate with the government after such massacres had taken place. *Alteños* not only demanded the resignation of the president, but also continued working to "kick the palace out of the government"—to throw all of the politicians out of power. The movement was spreading like wild fire. Protestors marched and maintained road blockades across the country. In Buenos Aires, Argentina, more than a thousand Bolivians protested the deaths in El Alto and demanded the resignation of Sánchez de Lozada.[30]

Still, the Bolivian president held on to power, making wilder accusations against protesters as the conflict raged on. In a public address on October 13th, he said he would not step down as president and, in doing so, succumb to "a huge subversive project from outside the nation, which is attempting to destroy Bolivian democracy." Afterward he said that the Peruvian Shining Path and Bolivian coca growers, trained by Colombian terrorist groups, were plotting against him. He also accused non-governmental organizations (NGOs) in Bolivia of funding these terrorist activities and declared that protestors were "narco-unionists that wish to carry out a coup in the nation." Sánchez de Lozada also referred to himself as "the little Dutch boy holding his finger in the hole in the dike of democracy." His comments proved him to be out of touch with the harsh reality facing Bolivia and misrepresenting the situation in order to justify his excessive use of force to quell unrest.[31]

The US government, in turn, brought out its vocabulary of doublespeak to stand up for this increasingly unpopular leader. In spite of widespread government repression of protesters, Richard Boucher, the US government spokesman, said in a press statement on October 13th, "The American people and their government support Bolivia's democratically elected president, Gonzalo Sánchez de Lozada, in his efforts to build a more prosperous and just future for all Bolivians. All of Bolivia's political leaders should publicly express their support for democratic and constitutional order."[32]

These comments sounded even weaker, however, when Vice President Carlos Mesa, stopped supporting President Sánchez de Lozada and demanded his resignation on October 13th, stating, "We cannot refuse to listen to the voice of the people. We need to create a constitutional succession in order to end the confrontations and violence that the Bolivian people are living in now."[33] Other leading political figures and longtime allies of the president also withdrew their support.[34]

In response to the fatal repression in El Alto, many residents of the city and neighboring communities marched into La Paz. El Alto journalist Julio Mamani described the rising tide of anger against the government:

> It transformed into a fury. After the massacres, people gathered together and left El Alto to march into La Paz spontaneously. Women were wearing black clothes for the dead. The men were

carrying sticks and Bolivian flags. It was a multitude of people marching into La Paz. During the march, more tanks arrived and the FEJUVE leaders told the people to go back to prevent more bloodshed. But people didn't listen to them, they kept marching past the FEJUVE leaders and eventually the tanks backed off. The march was so big, the street so full, that the military and tanks kept backing off, and they let people go into La Paz.[35]

On October 16th, marches from around the country arrived in La Paz demanding that Sánchez de Lozada resign and the gas exportation plan be cancelled. Due to their reputation as protagonists of Bolivian history, the arrival in La Paz of miners marching from Potosí and Oruro evoked fear and awe in the hearts of the city's residents. The miners' presence in the capital increased the conflict's symbolic proportions. The dynamite charges they tossed everywhere rallied protestors as much as they frightened the Sánchez de Lozada administration. Emilse Escobar Chavarría, a historian living in El Alto, said the miners' arrival hearkened back to their participation in the Revolution of 1952.[36] "There is a consciousness among people about the miners' struggle. They were always at the front lines during the past movements for nationalization of natural resources," she explained, "miners don't have a fear of death. This is because of their organizational strength, their history and their working conditions."[37]

On Friday, October 17th, hundreds of thousands of protestors from all walks of life converged in La Paz for one of the biggest demonstrations in the country's history.[38] By noon that day, unconfirmed reports circulated in the media that Sánchez de Lozada was going to resign. National protests were in full swing and few indications suggested the conflict would end abruptly. However, by 2 pm it had been confirmed by the media that Sánchez de Lozada was in fact going to resign. By five o'clock the celebration parties were starting. People across the country exhaled for the first time in a month. Protesters who had been marching and blockading each day were ecstatic. As I walked through Cochabamba after the announcement, people hauled blockades off the road and taxis wove around protest bonfires. In the plaza, where confrontations had taken place earlier that same day, thousands of people danced and played music, jumped up and down, and cheered. Though celebrations went on around the country, many of the friends and families of the 67 people killed in the conflict were still mourning.[39]

That night I gathered with some friends at a rowdy bar with a big television. On one side of the split screen was footage of Sánchez de Lozada's plane leaving the Santa Cruz airport to Miami. On the other side of the screen, a riotous congress cheered and threw papers into the air as the president's letter of resignation was read out loud. When Carlos Mesa came on to the screen, the bar grew silent. Mesa, who had pulled his support from Sánchez de Lozada earlier in the week, was now, as stipulated by Bolivia's constitution, taking the position of president.

Mesa gave a speech that Bolivians across the country listened to attentively. He set forth major principles for his presidency: a broad-based referendum on the exportation of the nation's gas, a full-fledged war to fight government corruption, justice regarding the atrocities that took place during the Gas War, and a solution to the country's land distribution problems. He stated that his government would not be able to meet all the demands of the protesting sectors, and asked that these groups be patient and collaborate with the new government. He knew that he was stepping onto a tightrope, which he might not be able to walk on without falling.

Unlike Sánchez de Lozada, Mesa at least appeared to care about the Bolivian people. It remained to be seen whether he would follow through with his promises, or was just trying to say the right things in order to appease the public. Outside of politics, he was known as a journalist, historian, and TV personality with a private fortune of about $1.5 million. After he officially took office, Mesa said, "I want to create a government for all Bolivians, for a great multiple and diverse country, where we can respect the equality of everyone. I am only going to be the president if I serve you [the country], because if you end up serving me you will kick me out."[40]

I spoke with Evo Morales about the new administration just after Mesa took office. "It is hard to say how long Mesa will last," he told me. "We have given him time and we understand that one month is not enough time to change a political model. He needs time, and we'll give him time. A lot will depend on some clear signs that he is trying to change the economic model and political system. A lot depends on him." The poverty and inequality in Bolivia continued to fuel fires of unrest throughout Mesa's first months in office, indicating that, as activist leader Oscar Olivera told me on a street corner the day Sánchez de Lozada left, "The Gas War wasn't the main victory; it was just one battle in a longer war."

Protesting sectors agreed to a ninety day truce to allow the new government time to produce results. They pledged to renew a campaign of blockades and demonstrations if Mesa did not meet demands, particularly regarding the gas nationalization issue. When I asked Felipe Quispe what would happen if Mesa didn't comply with protestors' demands, he replied by slicing his finger across his throat, "It'll be over for him. We'll kick him out. He's finished if he doesn't meet our demands in three months."

Sánchez de Lozada's departure opened up not just a series of new political opportunities and uncertainties, but it also exhibited the power of the Bolivian people. Like the Water War in Cochabamba, it pushed the boundaries of what people believed was possible through sustained mass mobilizations. It forged ties between social movements, bringing people together from varying economic sectors and labor groups. The autonomous labor and social organizations in El Alto, which sprung into action during October, embodied the spirit of this month of national outrage and resistance.[41] Much of the revolt, particularly in El Alto, happened without leaders or an organized structure. "In fact," writes Zibechi, "it could be argued that if unified, organized structures had existed, not as much social energy would have been unleashed. The key to this overwhelming grassroots mobilization is, without a doubt, the basic self-organization that fills every pore of the society and has made superfluous many forms of representation."[42]

The legitimacy and power of the Bolivian government was forever changed in those October days, when citizens united against bullets and the economic weapons of neoliberalism. "The army can enter the city, they can kill many people, but they cannot take the city," sociologist Pablo Mamani said in his office overlooking El Alto. "During the uprising, the state was broken, it stopped existing," his voice lowered to an emotional whisper as he swept his hands through the air, "it died in El Alto."

(Endnotes)

1 Unless otherwise indicated, all quotes from Pablo Mamani are from author interview in February, 2006.
2 Based on author interviews with journalist Julio Mamani February, 2006.
3 Kohl and Farthing, *Impasse*, 159-160.
4 Crabtree, *Perfiles de la Protesta*, 70, 79.
5 Ibid., 81.
6 Interviews with the author at Fejuve meeting, El Alto, (February, 2006).
7 Pablo Mamani, Microgobiernos Barriales, p.107-108, p.112
8 Raúl Zibechi, "El Alto: A World of Difference," *IRC Americas* (October 12, 2005), http://americas.irc-online.org/am/1622.
9 Interview with Julio Mamani.
10 See Raúl Zibechi, *Despersar El Poder: los movimientos como poderes antistatales*

(Buenos Aires: Tinta Limon, 2006), 67–71. Also see "Álvaro Garcia Linera, *Reproletarization. Nueva clase obrera y desarollo del capital industrial en Bolivia (1952-1998)*, (La Paz: Muela del Diablo, 1999), 118. Also see Zibechi, "El Alto: A World of Difference."

11 Crabtree, *Perfiles de la Protesta*, 82.

12 Zibechi, *Despersar El Poder*, 113, 117. and Zibechi, "El Alto: A World of Difference." Also see Rafael Archondo, *Compadres al micrófono* (La Paz: HISBOL, 1991). Also see Contratapa. Maro Quisbert, FEJUVE El Alto, 1990–1998, 69.

13 Kohl and Farthing, *Impasse*,161.

14 Pablo Mamani, *Microgobiernos Barriales*, (El Alto: Centro Andino de Estudios Estratégicos, 2005), 29–32.

15 Crabtree, *Perfiles de la Protesta*, 81.

16 Zibechi, "El Alto: A World of Difference."

17 Quotes from Castillo from author interview in July 2006.

18 Pablo Mamani, *Microgobiernos Barriales*, 124.

19 Zibechi, "El Alto: A World of Difference." Also Pablo Mamani Ramírez, *Geopolíticas indígenas* (El Alto: CADES, 2005), 76.

20 Information based on author interviews with Rosseline Ugarte and Emilse Escobar Chavarría. in February and July 2006.

21 Crabtree, *Perfiles de la Protesta*, 85.

22 Pablo Mamani, *Microgobiernos Barriales*, 118.

23 Edgar Ramos Andrade, *Agonia y Rebelion Social* (La Paz: Capítulo Boliviano de Derechos Humanos, Democracia y Desarrollo Plataforma Interamericana de Derechos Humanos, Democracia y Desarrollo Comunidad de Derechos Humanos, 2004), 117–119, 126–130.

24 Ibid.

25 Ibid.,130–132.

26 Miners were militant participants in the El Alto revolt and so were targeted by security forces. Ibid.

27 Benjamin Dangl and Kathryn Ledebur, "Bolivia: Thirty Killed in Gas War," *ZNet* (October 13, 2003), http://www.zmag.org/content/print_article.cfm?itemID=4342&sectionID=52.

28 Andrade, *Agonia y Rebelion Social*, 138–139.

29 Ibid., 141–144, 191–192.

30 Ibid., 141–148.

31 Benjamin Dangl, "Bolivian Government Falling Apart," *Z Magazine* (October 17, 2003), http://www.zmag.org/content/print_article.cfm?itemID=4365&sectionID=52.

32 Dangl, "Bolivian Government Falling Apart." and *El Diario* (October 14, 2003).

33 Ibid.

34 Dangl and Ledebur, "Bolivia: Thirty Killed in Gas War."

35 Author interview with Pablo Mamani.

36 For more information on this history, see Escobar Chavarría ed, *Nos hemos forjado así: Al rojo vivo y a puro golpe, Historias del Comité de Amas de Casa de Siglo XX*.

37 This quote is from an author interview with Emilse Escobar Chavarría. The miners' tactics worked: the president left the country shortly after their arrival.

38 Forrest Hylton, "Bolivia in Historical and Regional Context," *Counter Punch* (October 30, 2003), http://www.counterpunch.org/hylton10302003.html.

39 From author interviews with El Alto residents on Sánchez de Lozada's departure.

40 *El Diario* (October 21, 2003).

41 "El Alto emerged as the most militant and radical area in the country, replacing the coca growers who had spearheaded resistance in the 1990s." Kohl and Farthing, *Impasse*, 162.

42 Raúl Zibechi, "El Alto: A World of Difference."

Chapter Eight

Paradise Now: Street Theater, Hip-hop, and Women Creating

El Alto-based hip-hop artist Abraham Bojórquez raps
in the Wayna Tambo cultural center.
Photo Credit: Benjamin Dangl

"The street is my work without a boss, it is my home without a husband, it is my colorful ballroom"

—**Graffiti by Mujeres Creando**[1]

An audience dressed for winter settled into the theater's narrow wooden seats. The teenage actors, some barefoot, pounding drums, jumping up and down, with facial expressions changing rapidly, paraded on stage. After this thunderous introduction, other actors walked in, carrying notebooks and suitcases brimming with papers. Each spouted fragments of political speeches. They accused a man in a military suit of fascism, then swiftly hanged him on the many ropes swooping down from the ceiling.

Miners ran in, singing protest songs and chanting. Another monologue began about police killing innocent civilians. Debates took place between businessmen and protestors on the nationalization of mines. The play depicted revolts and counter-revolts throughout the country's ravaged history, ending with a dramatic exchange between a mother and her dead son. "Don't cry, Mom! I died bravely even though they gouged my eyes out and tore me apart. Don't cry!," cried out the ghost of the boy, who was tortured and killed by members of the dictatorship.

"Bolivia's history is one big tear," Vladimir Mamani Paco told me after the show was over. He is a member of *Teatro Trono* and one of the authors of the play. "It's a history of frustration, but also of glory."[2]

One might think this is heavy material for a group of young actors, yet such themes aren't distant from Bolivia's daily reality, particularly in El Alto where the actors live. State repression against civilian protestors is common in this poor city, and the question regarding whether or not to industrialize and nationalize Bolivian natural resources still divides the country and creates violence in the streets. At *Teatro Trono*, homeless children are the actors and the themes of the plays often confront Bolivia's harsh reality head-on.

Teatro Trono is one of many organizations in Bolivia blending art, music, unconventional activism, and the street to bring about social change. *Mujeres Creando* (Women Creating) is another such group. While *Trono* helps homeless children recuperate through the world of theater, *Mujeres Creando* offers a space for women to rebel and take refuge from an often chauvinistic, sexist, and repressive society. These organizations have developed their own communities, which are worlds unto themselves and offer examples of how society can change on a larg-

157

er level. Meanwhile, in a growing Bolivian hip-hop movement, artists use their music as an instrument of struggle, expressing through lyrics what street mobilizations cannot. While each group has its own history, methods, and messages, all three seek to use a nexus of politics and art to change society and fight for social justice.

The *Teatro Trono* building stands out in the flat city of El Alto. The seven story building confronts the sky in a posture of defiance not unlike a giant, many-windowed pirate ship. Its colors are strong and loud in a neighborhood of grey walls and orange bricks. A friend and I entered the monstrous building through a creaky door and climbed a winding staircase. We passed an exercise room, movie hall, offices, dormitories, ballet, and music rooms until finally hitting the roof, where the stairs opened up to a patio looking out over El Alto, La Paz and the snow-capped peaks of the Andes.

The building was bubbling with the activity of people dancing, singing, acting, and blowing into trumpets and flutes. The sound of hammers and saws mixed with the cheers of a practicing troupe of ac-tors. In one workshop, a man was building a puppet, while juggling lessons were taking place on the stage of the theater. In the basement, which also operates as a mining history museum, a group was filming a movie. It was a bustling environment, a cocktail of order and chaos.

Iván Nogales, the cheerful, fit director of *Teatro Trono*, lives on the sixth floor in an apartment full of antiques, books, tapestries, sculptures, and paintings. It is a bohemian dwelling, not luxurious, but colorful and full of life, art, and sunlight. While we talked, members of the theater darted in and out of the room with questions, papers to sign, and phone calls to answer.

Nogales, now middle-aged, started the theater company as a young actor in 1980. It was hard to organize events back then, he ex-plained, due to the constant government repression from the dicta-torship of Luís García Meza. "We were trying to reclaim democracy through theater and art," he said. However, the police would often arrive to shut down street performances, sending the actors sprinting away for safety. "Art was a tool to influence the public, but with a connection to the public. It was more efficient than large media. [Most TV and news-papers] don't reflect the excluded sectors," he explained. During the dic-tatorship, the focus of their work was always political. "We worked with people in hard situations, like homeless children and miners in Potosí."[3]

"In 1989 I did work with people who lived in the streets in El Alto," Nogales said. "We founded a group and worked together for years." Often this involved bringing homeless kids back to his home to live with him. His then small apartment had a stage that converted into beds at night. The group operated this way for seven years, and the close quarters strengthened the troupe's ability to cooperate and act together. They eventually expanded the operation by buying the house next door. This was the beginning of what is now *Teatro Trono*. In Spanish, the word 'trono' means something that breaks, falls down or crashes, but it also means 'throne.' "That's black humor," Nogales told me. "The actors would say, 'I'm broken; I'm from the streets.' But at the new theater they'd say, 'I am the king. I live in the throne.'"

Their book, *El Mañana es Hoy*, is made of stories of *Teatro Trono* told by the actors themselves. It traces the group's history, even as far back as the mining communities where some of them grew up before moving to El Alto. Their gripping accounts are full of love, humor, adversity, and poverty.[4] Claudio Urey writes of growing up in a mining family the year most of the mines were shut down. His father lost his job and his bosses gave him a suitcase full of money for severance pay. All the kids thought they were rich, but the inflation had made the mountain of bills worthless. At the time, some citizens even used money for wallpaper. The family packed up their belongings and headed to La Paz, where they began a new life. Claudio remembers his father coming home at night with a false smile after days of trying unsuccessfully to find work. "In a very short time, my father, the miner, revolutionary, and dreamer, became a builder of adobe to construct his own dream house, but he built it for other people who had a little bit of money." Urey's father was eventually forced to sell what was left of his mining equipment in order to support the family of six.

Before describing their arrival at *Teatro Trono*, others tell stories of living in the streets of El Alto. Chila, whose family's alcoholism forced him into homelessness at age nine, said the street was his house. There he united with his friends and shared food, spoils from robberies, and drugs. One day, Chila distracted an orange vendor by asking questions while his friend picked the woman's pocket. They split the loot in a nearby public bathroom. Other stories in the book tell of the prejudiced treatment the boys received while living in the streets. Their hunger and drug addiction drove them to rob friends and other homeless men and women. In his section, *Trono* member Angel Urey writes, "Beloved street, you have accompanied me day and night in my trouble and happiness, you are witness to thousands like me and those that surround me,

I know I'll never leave you because I still walk your avenues, streets, and alleys chasing a dream."[5]

Many of El Alto's homeless-boys-turned-*Trono*-actors spent time at *The Centro de Diagnostico y Terapia Varones*, a local reform school. The doctors there believed that they could solve the kids' problems through medical and psychiatric treatment. However, the facility looked and operated more like a prison than a rehabilitation center. The patients, ages 9–20, were beaten and forced to clean and work. Discipline and abuse was part of their daily treatment. Many children succeeded in escaping, some running away to the new *Teatro Trono*, run by Nogales. He didn't accept everyone who arrived on the doorstep, though, and kids who didn't take the work of acting and creating a show seriously enough were kicked out. Soon Nogales and his new actors organized street performances and began traveling around the countryside to perform. One young actor commented that traveling in the troupe and then returning to El Alto was like "coming back to earth after going to the moon." For many of the young actors, El Alto had been their only world. The cost of a bus ticket made it impossible for them to go anywhere else.[6]

"The pieces we did back then were very critical of the bureaucracy, the police and the government," Nogales recalled in his apartment. "We created another throne. The kids would say, 'we are the kings of fantasy and one day we will be bigger than the police.' And now look, we travel all over the world, we have a huge building." Eighty people currently work in the theater and many were busy preparing for a tour in Europe, where they would perform a play based on the Andean traditions linked to the coca leaf. "We have reconstructed a family [for the kids of the street]," he explained. "Now many of the children are art teachers here, or work as teachers in other cities." The troupe toured Europe for the last eight years and they used the money they raised to build the house. I asked him how the operation was financially possible: "It works through magic." In reality, the organization receives funding from various European arts organizations and *Trono*'s tours in Europe.[7]

Teatro Trono is unique among the other buildings in the neighborhood. Most of its windows are recycled and some doors are from retired city buses. Set crews buy used material at a nearby market for theater props and construction. Friends of the theater often drop off boards, nails, toilet seats, and windows—anything *Trono* might be able to use for their work or building. "All kinds of things arrive here," Nogales said, pointing to a window donated by a friend. "The design of the building is very unique. We made up styles and now people are copying us. We have influenced the architecture of El Alto." The basement is built like a mine, to operate as an exhibit of mining life. "This country was built on the lungs and backs of miners," Nogales said. They built the mine in the basement "so children can come and know this history, this ancestry."

Trono makes it a point to share what they have. Nogales has helped organize a community hostel in the neighborhood where locals can rent out rooms to tourists as well as share their culture, life, and history. He said he hopes increased tourism can help the economy of El Alto. *Trono* also has a traveling truck for their circus, which drives the troupe around the city and country. "This art could be a big part of social transformation," Nogales said. They want to expand their reach and impact even more by creating an entire village for artists. "Municipalities are asking me to come to their area to do this...They thought I was crazy when I said we would build this building. Now when I tell them we'll build the town, they say, 'Okay, I believe you.'"

In one of the building's busier rooms, I sat down with Raquel Romero, the coordinator of *Teatro Trono*. The office we sat in had a number of congratulatory letters on the wall from international visitors to the theater. Next door, a band practiced and the wail of trumpets and tubas shook the windows, making Romero raise her voice more than once while we spoke. She moved around the room with the ease of someone who had been dancing and acting her whole life. When I asked her about how she began her work, she winced at the word "work." It's not work, she said, smiling. "It's love. I fell in love with the *Trono*." She sees "art as an important vehicle to liberate the brain and the body. This is the *Trono* philosophy. We are talking about dreaming collectively." Each play is a collective creation, made by the group and is often written after it is acted out. She linked the focus on homeless children to the use of recycled material in their props, costumes and building. For her, this meant "reinvigorating and transforming" used or damaged material.[8]

Though the theater started out working with homeless children, *Trono* now works more on prevention, rather than rehabilitation. Outreach seeks to prevent children from becoming addicted to drugs, or ending up on the streets.[9] Nogales described his work as developing leaders for the future: "There is a vacuum of leadership among children and young people in this country, and we try to change this through theater."[10] Current plays put on by the troupe focus on the environment, sexuality, and youth rights.

One of *Trono*'s biggest challenges has been gaining the trust of El Alto residents. According to Romero, there is a popular idea in the

city that anything related to art is unproductive and linked to laziness
and drugs. It has taken time to prove otherwise. "It was a hard process
but eventually people understood this was a good thing," she said. The
murals, free street performances, and the relationship between actors'
parents and *Trono* have all helped develop community trust. The lessons
the children learn at *Trono* are also applied to other aspects of their life.
Raquel said, "We teach kids that art is not everything and that you have
to do your homework for school as well."

Besides preparing for an upcoming tour in Europe, Raquel named
ongoing community classes in dance, theater, circus, and ceramics as
current *Trono* activities. "We try to spread this into the streets. The kids
and teachers go to other neighborhoods, share the skills and teach in
schools." The *Trono* building is the center, but many activities happen in
the periphery and surrounding neighborhoods of El Alto.

In one *Trono* play called "The Meeting of the Water Gods," a busi-
nessman buys a river from local residents who later come to him for a
drink. One girl gives the man her earrings for a small cup of water which
has to be shared among the whole community. Such a scenario is familiar to El Alto residents who have dealt with high water costs, privatization, pollution, and water shortages.[11]

In another piece called "The International Market," actors learn
about how to make chocolate. In this play, an English-speaking business-
woman arrives on stage, smells the chocolate, and offers to buy it for one
peso a pound, only to sell it back to the villagers for ten pesos per pound.
Locals end up working in the woman's factory abroad. "This is the way
it happens in the international market," said an actor who, in the play,
refuses to work in the factory. "It's always the same."[12]

It is the focus of such plays and the methods of the theater company that draw other educational, artistic and social organizations to
collaborate with *Trono*. "Art is expansive. Everyone needs a bit of it,"
Romero said. Social workers arrive at the theater regularly to "be involved in this process of liberation." Romero raised her voice above the
ruckus of pounding drums to tell me about the group's participation in
the 2003 Gas War. "The movement at that time was so big that everyone
had to participate," she yelled. "It was a necessity and involved everyone.
We accompanied people in marches and played music. Sometimes we
led protests at the front with drummers."

Nogales also emphasized the group's ongoing relationship with
Bolivian social movements. "We have always been linked to social movements, miners, *cocaleros*, the FEJUVE and COR," he told me. "We have

a good relationship with these groups. During the 2003 protests, people loved our drumming so much that they demanded we keep coming back to join the marches." The lack of transportation meant the drummers marched all over El Alto and La Paz on foot.

After Sánchez de Lozada was thrown out in 2003, Nogales believed positive changes were possible in Bolivia, and he saw *Trono* as an instrument to bring about such changes. "We're working to understand that local problems have international significance," he told journalist Kari Lyderson. "International organizations like the IMF and World Bank defend the interests of transnational companies. In Bolivia this is very clear. The question is, how do we change this? The US has such immense power, it's not easy." He tries to bring about such change by helping actors, and the audience around the world, understand neoliberalism's impact on his country. "[*Trono* actors] are the echo of voices of the humble, poor people," he said. "This voice needs to be listened to."[13]

Vladimir Mamani Paco, 27 years old, walked into the *Trono* office and sat down to chat after Romero left. He started at *Trono* three years ago and calls himself one of the oldest students. He is currently one of the coordinators of a play dealing with Bolivian history, a job which he described as a collective learning experience. "I was involved in the process all along. Some studied the Chaco War, others studied the mining movements. We had meetings, study sessions and learned little by little. Slowly people eventually put it all together. All of this was done collectively without a director."

"I like what I do here," he said. "You fall in love with this place. The kids learn something and it helps them." The camaraderie is another reason he has stuck around. "If you don't have money to eat, someone helps out. It's a community."

We walked up a couple flights of stairs, past bathrooms with used doors from local buses and into a room that smelled like a high school gym class. Inside, kids were bouncing around the room and practicing their flutes. Laurena Chavez, 12, said she enjoys learning new music. "It's pretty. It makes you happy. It's relieving. With the music you can imagine a lot of things." Brian Lauravega, 13, said, "I learn a lot here so I can teach it to others." Jeremy Kevin Acarapi Garay, 13, the most outspoken and boisterous of the group, advertised his temperament with wildly spiked hair. At *Trono*, he said, "They make us do theater in front of people we have never met. They help us lose our fear."

In El Alto, it is not uncommon to see children the age of these *Trono* students sleeping in the streets. Occasionally passersby see a teenager passed out on the sidewalk, his clothes black with dirt and an empty bottle of glue in his hand. Throughout La Paz and El Alto kids beg in the streets at all hours of the day and night.

My interview with the *Trono* group was interrupted by a teacher who came in to ask them to play their most recent song to prepare for their upcoming trip to Europe. They stumbled through it once or twice before the lesson ended. Many of them had never been outside of El Alto. I asked Kevin if he was excited about the trip. "It'll be a great adventure," he said, a smile spreading across his face.

Down the steep hill which separates El Alto from La Paz is another hopeful organization that uses similar means to change the world. *Mujeres Creando* is an anarchist/feminist group based in La Paz. Though they are relatively small in size, the group's activities are known throughout the country. I first visited them at their center called *La Virgen de los Deseos* (The Virgin of Desires), which they often refer to simply as *La Virgen*. The building contains a restaurant, natural food store, pharmacy, bookstore, hostel, and classroom. It was lunchtime when I arrived and the place was packed with businessmen, teachers, students, tourists, and others who had been attracted by *La Virgen*'s cheap, healthy food.

Many of the people I met in La Paz—generally progressive thinking leftists—were critical (or frightened) of *Mujeres Creando* and responded to my questions with raised eyebrows or shaking heads. Their critiques rarely went beyond "crazy man-hating lesbians" or "too confrontational," comments that seemed to have more to do with the homophobia and sexism of the critics than with actual analysis of the collective's activities and ideologies. For many Bolivians, the openness with which the *Mujeres* address socially taboo issues of sexuality, women's rights, and domestic violence is too overt to be acceptable. What *Mujeres Creando* do, however, is create new theoretical parameters for the possibility of women's and men's participation in resistance and creative response to political and social injustice.

La Virgen is the manifestation of the group's earlier hopes for a "house with a fireplace," part of a long process of collective dreaming and cooperation. Now complete, the first floor walls are decorated with nearly life-size black and white antique photographs of indigenous women, between which the group's famous cursive graffiti announces the collective's principles. On the shelves behind the counter are texts unavailable in most Bolivian bookstores, dealing with social movements in Argentina, the negative impact of non-governmental organizations (NGOs) in Bolivia,[14] feminism, sex education, and anarchism. They have regular visitors from abroad. During my stay, journalists, photographers, and documentary filmmakers stopped by often to interview the collective members and to document their home, activities, and history.

In an article called "Escaping to Construct," one of the most well known members of group, María Galindo, explains that the *Virgen de los Deseos* is a house, but it is also a means to recuperate women's strategies against patriarchic and repressive systems in society. It's a space for collective disobedience and rebellion, she writes.[15] Their website declares that collective members "want to make our craziness contagious to the people who surround us and listen to us." They describe themselves as a group of "rebel women, indians and whites, lesbians and heterosexuals, old and young women, of the city and the countryside, believers and atheists, fat and thin, dark and light skinned all at once and different at the same time…We want to enjoy paradise here and now, so that our children can begin a new era of love, health, solidarity, respect, freedom, a lot of sweet poetry, chocolate cake, toys, books, tenderness, music… Our instruments of struggle and construction are creativity, disobedience to the patriarchic and *machista* system, the ethic of our actions and love."[16]

La Virgen is a resource for people of all walks of life. There are computers with internet access, classrooms, and a film screening room with over 300 videos about violence, homophobia, homosexuality, abortions, racism, and other issues. Book readings and discussions around political and social issues take place regularly, and other facilities, such as the bathrooms and showers, are available to workers, street vendors, and travelers. Within the center is a health clinic, which offers free medicine to people without health insurance. People suffering from domestic violence can find refuge in *La Virgen*, where they can get advice on how to get out of harmful relationships. Outside of the functions of their house, the *Mujeres Creando* participate in street activism and produce a lot of writing. One book, written by Julieta Paredes and María Galindo, is part of the sexual education proposal made by the collective, and is called "Sex, Pleasure and Sexuality." Within its chapters are informal but informational sections directed to readers of all ages about sex, motherhood, sexual abuse, prostitution, domestic abuse, incest, pleasure, abortion, and menstruation.[17] Through their writing and actions, the activists of *Mujeres Creando* manifest the kind of changes they want to see in the world.

Julieta Ojeda, a member of the *Mujeres Creando* collective, sat down with me in the storage room of their dining area to talk about how the group operates. She spoke of the group's philosophy that words and opinions must be followed with action. Members enact this philosophy through numerous meetings and discussion where they decide on not only their collective vision for the group, but also its financial and organizational issues. "Each group gives a percentage of what they earn to the space," Ojeda explained. The library, restaurant, natural food and medicine store, and the hostel are all run by smaller cooperatives, which contribute to the overall financial well-being of the house. The percentage that each group contributes depends on how much they make. Some work in these cooperatives as volunteers, others have salaries. "We have had many meetings to see what each person's capacity is. Some like cooking, others like the logistics of running things, dealing with the hostel, food or library...Because of our ideologies we don't organize hierarchically. Each person has to work a lot. It takes time, but it is satisfying." She said the biggest challenge within the group has been maintaining the solidarity between members and "re-learning" how to work cooperatively. "We're used to working in society for ourselves and no one else. People aren't used to sharing."[18]

If things are working smoothly now within *Mujeres Creando* it is largely because of their long experience as a collective. It's been a road full of challenges. "Mujeres Creando was born in 1992," Galindo told me. "Neoliberalism was booming in Bolivia. The social movements were still sleeping at the time." Galindo and Julieta Paredes had just returned to Bolivia from Italy, where they had been living in exile. They began to organize a space for university students, mothers with babies, women from the country and city, lesbians, Aymaras, and Quechuas. Like *La Virgen*, this group organized health classes, maintained a library on childcare, and ran a natural food store. It was then the group began articulating the kind of changes they were working toward to the society around them.[19]

They opened the *Centro Cultural Feminista Café Carcajada* (Cultural Feminist Center Cackle Café) for their activities. La Paz residents met the opening with a lot of hostility. "[T]he urban culture didn't understand the concept of a women's space," their recent book, *La Virgen de los Deseos*, explains. "When breaking with the language of the left, a strong explosion of creativity arrived and, little by little, each person developed her own forms to better express herself..." Despite the unfriendliness of some community members, they continued expanding their space for action, facing more anger and violence as time went on.

Racism, sexism, and homophobia are strong in Bolivia, and the group confronted them directly.[20]

Mujeres Creando tried to communicate to regular citizens, instead of just speaking to higher classes and political elites. They expressed these messages through graffiti, murals, dancing, and singing in street marches. They created a publication called *Mujer Publica* (Public Woman) which sold in major cities across the country.[21] Later, they organized seminars such as "Ninguna Mujer Nace Para Puta" (No Woman Is Born To Be A Whore) which dealt with prostitution and involved the participation of prostitutes from La Paz and Oruro. The focus of the seminar included a discussion of the business of prostitution, health concerns and the repression, dangers, and prejudice prostitutes face from society.[22]

After talking with Julieta Ojeda, I walked up the crowded streets to a museum in the Plaza Mendoza where *Mujeres Creando* had an exhibit about prostitution and violence against women. The exhibit was hugely popular and the room was packed most of the time. Graffiti covered the walls, and facts and statistics regarding violence against women were placed around the exhibit. One work was a bed with a quilt made of photos of a woman who was battered to death by her boyfriend while people at the bar just watched because "she was just a prostitute."

María Galindo sat between the bed and a table full of books and pamphlets that the group was selling. Part of the *Mujeres Creando* ethos is being visible, and Galindo makes sure that she doesn't blend in. Her hair was buzzed short on the sides, and was long on the top. She wore a red leather jacket, heavy makeup and eye shadow, and smoked steadily. When I told her I had just arrived in La Paz from Venezuela, she listened to my stories of the government and social programs there with an intense interest.[23]

The group's first action in the street was distinctive political graffiti. "The street is the most important political setting...So we took the street and made the graffiti that we continue to make in four cities in the country. With graffiti we try to mix different topics simultaneously."[24] Their philosophy started with the idea that "as women, we are mute" and that "graffiti is an instrument to conquer words." Their graffiti deals with neoliberalism, prostitution, women, and much more. "There isn't one [issue] that's more important than the other." Through this graffiti they created a means of directly communicating with society.

Their feminist graffiti often addresses vocabulary and stereotypes demeaning toward women. "I believe basically that much of the mute-ness of women is cemented in humiliating experiences." Galindo explained. "For example, the word '*puta*' [whore] is very important to us because it's one of those instrumental words with which [women] have been humiliated for hundreds of years. Or the word 'indian' or the word 'ugly' or 'fat.' They are words with which we have been humiliated. We are reclaiming these words."

She illustrated her point by naming some of the graffiti slogans the collective has invented, such as 'Long live the fat girls!' 'Long live the brown ones!' 'I want to be a woman without models to imitate.' "It's graffiti that the young girls love," Galindo said. "It leaves them content. At the same time, it is not an instrument of proselytism. It's not 'long live me!' or whatever. There is no proselytizing behind it. It's not a utilitarian vision. The graffiti only has a meaning solely for itself. It's not a campaign to obtain anything. Besides, we're anarchists." Their distinctive, cursive phrases, however, dare the city to reconsider gender stereotypes in a way that perhaps no other action could.

Mujeres Grafitiando (Women Graffiti-ing), a book the group produced includes hundreds of photos of their graffiti around the country, primarily in La Paz. On the cover is a photo of a woman putting her foot print on a public wall with blue paint. In the introduction, Galindo writes that the collective uses graffiti in part to "break with the political routine" and "break the silence of women." "The act of creating graffiti is something very serious," they write. "It's an action in which we put our body into the historical struggle to transform our society. We don't put a heroic body, or a militarized body, we put a vulnerable, sensible, sensual, creative, unarmed and non-violent body."[25]

Some of the graffiti included in the book reads:

"As much as you want me, I don't want to be yours."
"Although they call you crazy for fighting, resist, Woman."
"After making you dinner and making your bed, I no longer want to make love to you."
"Long live the fat women, long live the dark skinned women, I want to be a woman without models to imitate."
"You want me to be a virgin, you want me to be a saint, you have me pissed off."
"We want all of paradise, not 30% of a neoliberal hell."[26]
"A penis, any penis, is always miniature."
"The street is my work without a boss, it is my home without a husband, it is my colorful ballroom."[27]

Like the group's other activities, their graffiti is often met with hostility. At times, the *Mujeres* have found swastikas sprayed over the phrases, and "*Kill Feminists and Indians*" and "*Die Mestizo Indian Pigs*" graffitied over their slogans.

Galindo and other members of the group are very critical of the Bolivian left's authoritarianism, lack of self-criticism, and the ways in which political parties have co-opted various social movements. *Mujeres Creando* member Florentina Alegre said that one of the Bolivian social movements' main problems is the way in which the women's organizations always come behind those of the men, as supporters of their work. She says the Aymara world is closed to discussion about this and the women keep on working "without their own voice." According to Alegre, in these traditional organizations, all decisions are made by men while the women cook, clean, wash clothes and don't speak. Women are not taken into account as political actors and, if they are, it is in a role of supporting the men.[28]

Mujeres Creando has participated in major mobilizations in the country's recent history and has often found as much to critique about their comrades on the left as the elites of the right. In the 2003 Gas War, the *Mujeres* criticized the slogans protesters were using, particularly 'Sánchez de Lozada is a son of a whore.' "We launched a [graffiti] action that said that 'The life-loving whores declare that Sánchez de Lozada is no son of theirs,'" Galindo explained. "We went into the streets with this slogan. It was really nice, because it was funny, because a lot of people agreed."

The *Mujeres* also took more physical actions in order to be seen and heard. In the mobilizations during the Gas War, "the numerical quantity of women was also large," Galindo recalled, "but the possibility of them having a say was zero...So we decided to take the Public Advocate's office. Three of us began the strike; the president of the sex workers of La Paz—Florentina Alegre—a woman from the countryside, an indian, and me, a lesbian. So we took the Public Advocate's office and they came and seized us from the ministry of the government and removed us from the strike." They were violently evicted by the police, who took the women by the hair and dragged them down from the fifth floor and into the street.

This wasn't the first or last time the group had been violently repressed. In 1994, María Galindo, Julieta Paredes and Julieta Ojeda were invited to a party by French NGO workers. According to an account of the event in the book *Virgen de los Deseos*, the night turned out very differently than the expected solidarity party. When the three women refused to dance with certain men, and rejected an offer for group sex, they were attacked by about 15-20 people, including a Bolivian, three French women and French men. They were beaten for two hours until they lost consciousness and were dragged out into the street. The whole act was dismissed by the press, authorities, politicians, and police. According to *Mujeres Creando*, the story was buried because the women were feminists and lesbians. The French people who committed the crime returned to their country and were protected from judicial proceedings by the French Ambassador. The three women then went on a 15 day hunger strike in protest. However, the perpetrators never met justice.[29]

I asked Galindo about the roots of this sexism and repression in Bolivia. She said she didn't think Bolivia was different than anywhere else in the world, but that, for such a politically and socially active country, the lack of space for women's participation is startling. "I don't believe that Bolivia is more dramatic," she theorized, "What happens in Bolivia is there are a lot of very strong social movements, and there's a lot of rebellion, and there is a lot of organizational capacity at the social level. So I can't explain to you, how in a society in which there is this degree of social transformation, the women are so silenced... [I]f you go for a walk in the street, you will realize that this society is sustained by women. Whether the men are making political organizations or participating in what they want, it's at the expense of women who stay in the house, take care of the children, and struggle for survival." [30]

She described this environment as a product of contemporary colonialism. "The conquistadors captured the original authorities, legitimized them and gave them some privileges and they mutually conspired" to create an alliance that subjugated women. "The woman's only social value is her reproductive function. Here in this country if a woman is not a mother, she's a dog. You're nothing. But at the same time, a woman who is a mother doesn't have the right to demand a responsible father. All that remains of the father is the last name. Period." *Mujeres Creando* suggests one way to change this in their proposal for "maternal filiation," that children should take their mothers' last names instead of their father's. This name change "reclaims the place of the mothers, where women change from being objects of reproduction to subjects of maternity, as well as reclaiming the daughters' place in the family, which all statistics show us is not valued in comparison to their brothers."[31] It is

this kind of radical creative thinking that makes the collective the vision-
ary, and yet grounded force for social change that it is.

One Bolivian woman I met on a bus to Cochabamba broke out in
tears while she told me about her abusive husband, whom she had left
years ago. Once, he beat her unconscious, sending her to the hospital.
She woke up one month later with disabilities that still plague her. I
thought of this woman while learning more about *Mujeres Creando*. I
knew stories like the one I heard on that bus are common throughout
Bolivia and the rest of the world. Despite criticism of *Mujeres Creando*,
La Virgen was nearly always packed with people at all hours of the day
and night. The crowds that come through their door are a testament to
their ultimate success. Beloved or hated, the *Mujeres* have an integral
role in providing Bolivians with a cultural reference that pushes the limits of their gender stereotypes toward a more just society.

While the *Mujeres Creando* use their styles of living, street activism,
writing and graffiti as tools for social change, a growing hip-hop movement in Bolivia utilizes lyrics and beats in a new "instrument of struggle." Drawing from the challenges and culture of El Alto, many young
musicians and activists are turning to hip-hop to express themselves and
fight a battle outside of street protests and political elections.

At 13,000 feet, the hip-hop movement in El Alto, Bolivia is probably the highest in the world. The music being created by a generation
of young, politically conscious *Alteños* blends ancient Andean folk styles
and new hip-hop beats with lyrics about revolution and social change.
As the sun set over the nearby snow-capped mountains, I sat down with
Abraham Bojórquez, a well known El Alto hip-hop artist and former soldier who had participated in Bolivia's IMF-related conflict in February,
2003. We opened up a bag of coca leaves and began to talk about what
he calls a new "instrument of struggle."[32]

We met at *Wayna Tambo*, a radio station, cultural center, and
unofficial base of the city's hip-hop scene. Bojórquez pulled a leaf out
of the bag to chew and said, "We want to preserve our culture through
our music. With hip-hop, we're always looking back to our indigenous
ancestors—the Aymaras, Quechuas, Guaraní." He works with other hip-
hop artists in El Alto to show "the reality of what is happening in our
country." Bojorquez sees hip-hop as a political voice for young Bolivians.
"Through our lyrics we criticize the bad politicians that take advantage

of us. With this style of hip-hop, we're an instrument of struggle, an instrument of the people."

Bojórquez, 23-years-old, belongs to a group of rappers in El Alto whose share the name of *Wayna Rap* (Wayna means young in Aymara). Under the umbrella of Wayna Rap are smaller bands like *Insane Race, Ukamau y Ke, Clandestine Race,* and others. They often get together in freestyle events, where different singers take turns at the mic, rapping.

Some songs are completely in the indigenous Aymara language, while others include a mixture of Spanish, English, Quechua, and Portuguese. This fusion of languages is an integral part of the group's philosophy and adds to their appeal in El Alto, where a large section of the population speaks Aymara. "The door is open to everyone...This is our proposal for how to change society," Bojórquez said. Though they collaborate with a wide variety of people, "we don't just sing things like 'I'm feeling bad, my girlfriend just left me and now I am going to get drunk.' It's more about trying to solve problems in society." The social and political themes in the music come from the city's reality. The death and conflicts in the 2003 Gas War ravaged El Alto, and many of these songs reflect that anger.

A song that Abraham wrote in his own group, *Ukamau y Ke,* deals with the October, 2003 mobilizations in El Alto against the gas exportation plan and president Sánchez de Lozada. In the song, "we speak about how bullets are being shot at the people and how we can't put up with this because the people are reclaiming their rights." This song starts out with a recording of President Sánchez de Lozada announcing his refusal to resign. His voice is ominous, gruff, and peppered with an unmistakable US English accent: "*Yo no voy a renunciar. Yo no voy a renunciar*" (I will not resign). The sounds of street clashes in the song become louder. The roar of machine guns and helicopters come and go until the beat and lyrics begin.

"We are mobilized, arming street barricades. We are mobilized without noticing that we are killing between brothers," begins the MC. Another singer comes in, rapping about the "corrupt governments...with closed eyes that don't look at the reality in the society. Many people are ending up in poverty and delinquency, which is why they demand justice..." The song goes on to call Sánchez de Lozada a traitor and assassin. The MCs demand his head, along with that of Carlos Mesa. The music fuses with a testimony from a weeping woman whose family member was shot by soldiers. The lyrics kick back in, "We hear over there that there are dead: 80 citizens, five police, and a mass of people gravely injured. We're in a situation worse than war, killing each other, without a solution."

In many of Bojórquez's songs, Andean flutes and drums mesh with the beat. This aspect, along with the indigenous language, sets the music apart from standard hip-hop. The topics covered are also specific to Bolovia. In one song, rappers grapple with issues such as street violence and homelessness in El Alto. The song laments the "children living in the street, orphans of mothers and fathers and the violence that grows every day. The lack of work, all of these things," Bojórquez explained. "We try to show the true reality of what is happening in the country, not hide it."

One of the most moving experiences Bojórquez said he's had within his musical career came when he was invited to perform at the office of the FEJUVE of El Alto. He was nervous at first because the place was full of older people, and his music is directed toward a younger audience. After the first song, people clapped weakly. "Then we sang in Aymara and people became very emotional, started crying. This was a very happy event for us. It made us think that what we are doing isn't in vain, that it can make an impact on people."

When Bojórquez and I met months later, it was clear that El Alto's hip-hop movement was growing. More people were calling him up for pointers on their music or for help with CD recordings. Others were starting their own groups and showing up at *Wayna Tambo* for concerts. "Today this music is arriving to many young people who identify with the songs and lyrics," Bojórquez said. "In El Alto there is a lot of poverty and in the lyrics we talk about this. People identify with it." The title of his next CD is "Instrument of Struggle", referring to his musical philosophy. "More than anything our music is a form of protest, but with proposals. We unite, we organize. We look for unity, not division. We want to open the eyes of people with closed eyes...The music is a part of life."

He recently helped initiate hip-hop classes for prisoners between the ages of 16 and 18 in San Pedro, a large prison in La Paz. The idea started when Bojórquez and others did a concert there. The reception was so enthusiastic that they worked to organize a hip-hop class in June, 2006. Through the classes, Bojórquez said they are trying to "show the jail's reality from the inside." He described the jail as another, complete city within La Paz, but a "dead city" without hope. "This is where the hip-hop comes in, so that people don't feel like all is lost." At the end of the program, the group will put on a performance and record an album. Based on the success of the class, Bojórquez expects the program to continue into the future.

"They are telling a history that reaches people and can prevent other youth from making the same mistakes," he said. "A lot of them regret what they did and they talk about it in their songs." He offered lyrics by Cesar as an example:

"*Yo soy preso en San Pedro*/I am a prisoner in San Pedro
Estoy esperando la puta paciencia de mi abogado/I am waiting on the fucking patience of my lawyer
Lo que el me ha dicho ya me olvidado/What he has told me I already forgot
Por tomar el camino más corto/ By taking the short cut
Yo mismo me fregado/I messed myself up"

Waiting for a bus to a hip-hop concert at *Wayna Tambo*, I ran into some of Bojórquez's fellow rappers, Grover Canaviri Huallpa and Dennis Quispe Issa. Both worked jobs and studied at the same time, leaving little room for writing lyrics and listening to music. It was cold and the bus was late, so we went inside and talked. Like others going to the concert, they were wore modern hip-hop clothing. The camouflage and baseball caps, the baggy pants, it was all very familiar. But it wasn't just the clothing style that these two felt a connection with. "I identify a lot with the hip-hop groups in the US that speak of violence and discrimination," Huallpa said. "My mother only studied to 5th grade. She has suffered discrimination. We used to all be out in the streets."[33]

Huallpa started listening to rap in the mid-1990s, and started writing his own lyrics a few years later. "Before *Wayna Tambo* there were pirated radios, secret places where we gathered because our parents didn't accept it." Both admitted their parents didn't understand their lifestyle as rappers. "They think we are just copying the US," Issa said. "People on the street discriminate against us for the way we talk, walk, and dress." However, they both agreed that this kind of hip-hop was growing in El Alto, in part because of the experience of the Gas War. "October, 2003 was a huge change for us musically," Issa explained, referring to the mobilizations, "It had a big impact on El Alto."

Below El Alto, in La Paz, another hip-hop movement is thriving. Sdenka Suxo Cadena, a 27-year-old hip-hop artist and marketing major in college, has been a part of the scene for over ten years. When I met her at the home of *Mujeres Creando,* Cuban salsa was playing on the radio. Her hair was in pigtails and she smiled and laughed while talking about her work.

She started rapping in 1996 when she was in high school. "I started doing it because I didn't like society's system—the classism, materialism, the elite. This didn't make people happy." After hanging out with different hip-hop groups in La Paz and El Alto, she decided to start a women's hip-hop group in 2000. "I didn't like to be controlled by a boy, or be someone else's *lady*. Other women didn't either. So we started our own group called the *Nueva Flavah* and had our own meetings and events."[34]

Each Thursday the *hip-hoperas* (women hip-hop artists) organized a gathering of men and women from different areas of the city to perform hip-hop, break dance and exchange styles. "We wanted to share hip-hop without caring about our differences," Cadena explained. They did, however, have some rules: "We didn't let people in that just talked about gangs, violence, drugs, and guns." Her music deals with such topics as Latin American unification, chauvinism, AIDS, race, women's issues, and nationalism. She described politics as important, "but for real change to happen, people have to change themselves."

When I met her, Cadena was about to open a center for hip-hop activities and recording. "Some kids need help editing music and recording. We help them get their message out," she said. One of the events the group now organizes is a CD exchange, in which artists can bring in their own disks and trade or buy one of Cadena's for less than a dollar.

Cadena believes hip-hop is becoming more popular in Bolivia because anyone can produce the music, regardless of whether or not they know how to play an instrument. "It's popular in poor neighborhoods where people might not have a guitar. All you need is a pen and paper. You don't need money. You can do it anywhere. People largely identify with it in marginalized neighborhoods, where people don't have access to music lessons or instruments." She also sees hip-hop growing along with the current political changes all around Latin America: "It's part of this regional protest movement."

I had an opportunity to see this movement in action at a hip-hop concert one cold June night in a neighborhood outside La Paz. Our bus zipped up into the hills like a roller coaster, weaving up steep streets past angry dogs, glowing corner stores, a woman shaking laundry out the window, and soccer games under street lamps. The route was a cavernous labyrinth that never seemed to end. We almost crashed twice and had to ask for directions three times. Eventually the city spread out below in a vast collection of blue, white, yellow, and orange lights, oozing and bubbling with life. Beyond the lights were the Andes Mountains in complete darkness. The stars were barely visible, belittled by the constellations of the city.

The concert took place at a large room in a school building. A banner hung outside the door, where young people in rap regalia were hanging out and smoking. Tilted baseball caps and baggy pants and shirts, with US sports logos, were the norm. I handed over the 12 cents for my ticket while my friend and I were frisked for alcohol: it was a dry event. Inside, the room was packed with people standing, seated, and all bopping to the music. On a balcony above the crowd the performers swung microphones, shook their fists in the air, and rapped tirelessly. To me, the event was a cross between a high school dance and a beat poetry reading. Many of the young people were sipping on clandestine bottles of booze, making out, and slicking back their hair. The sound quality of the speakers was poor, but the enthusiasm was high, and the audience clapped and cheered at every opportunity. Most raps mixed Spanish and Aymara, with three words making regular appearances: coca, revolution, and *Pachamama*.

The room was a convergence of cultures. The rapping mixed Andean phrases and symbols thousands of years old with themes and rhymes fresh out of MTV music videos. Some rappers spoke of blunts and guns in one breath and their president the next. Bojórquez wore a red baseball cap from a US team, but his coat had indigenous designs on it with the name of his band in Aymara written across the front. I recognized some of the beats from US music, but the flutes, drums, and rhythms were all Bolivian. The finale was a performance by a young kid who couldn't have been more than ten years old. He proceeded to swing his cap, move his feet and moon dance exactly like Michael Jackson. The crowd went wild. The artists were adeptly fusing nations, music, histories, and dance into their new Bolivian counterculture.

This hip-hop movement combats corporate globalization, political corruption, and state repression not just with blockades and protests, but with music, parties, and cultural preservation. When the blockades are hauled off the streets, they keep singing. This movement, along with *Teatro Trono* and *Mujeres Creando,* has started to build the world that these artistic activists want without changing presidents or corporate policies.

These groups complement traditional social and labor movements in Bolivia by thinking outside the box of typical activism, fusing art, theater, and music to amplify and communicate messages that many other groups grapple with as well. *Teatro Trono* not only uses theater to communicate social and political messages, but its acting troup in itself is changing the world through its incorporation of homeless and at-risk children. The analysis and critiques of Bolivian society from *Mujeres Creando*, and the refuge they have created at *La Virgen de los Deseos*, open new spaces for debate and living that perhaps would not exist otherwise. With the hip-hop movement, the hope and fire of street rebellions has been sustained and made portable through a new kind of rap that fuses indigenous culture with modern day politics and globalization in a way that few other groups are doing in Bolivia. These artists reach for their visions by working together to create their paradise collectively.

(Endnotes)

1 From Sdenka Huaranca and María Galindo, *Mujeres Grafitando*, (La Paz: Ediciones Mujeres Creando Creación colectiva, 1999).

2 For more information on *Teatro Trono*'s projects and their umbrella organization, Comunidad de Productores en Artes (COMPA), see http://www.compatrono.com/.

3 Unless otherwise indicated, all quotes from Iván Nogales are from author interview in July, 2006.

4 Iván Nogales Bazán, Angel P. Urey Miranda, Juan Santa Cornejo, and Claudio Urey Miranda, *El Mañana es Hoy: Teatro Trono: Teatro con Niños y Adolescentes de la calle* (Cochabamba: Fundación Arnoldo Schwimmer, 1998).

5 Nogales et al., *El Mañana es Hoy*.

6 Ibid.

7 Organizations that have contributed financially to *Trono* in the past include, Caritas Nederland, Stichting Kinderpostzegels Netherlands (SKN), and Terre des Hommes, Ashoka. Alfonso Gumucio Dagron, *Making Waves, Stories of Participatory Communication for Social Change: COMPA* (New York: The Rockefeller Foundation, 2001). Available online at: http://www.comminit.com/strategicthinking/pdsmakingwaves/sld-2593.html.

8 All quotes from Raquel Romero are from interview with author in July, 2006.

9 Kari Lydersen, "Live from the Streets of Bolivia: Teatro Trono," *Americas.org*, http://www.americas.org/item_14928.

10 Dagron, *Making Waves*.

11 Tulbert, "Just a Little Drop of Water: How a community based theater in Bolivia addresses the problem of water privatization," *Community Arts* (May, 2005), http://www.communityarts.net/readingroom/archivefiles/2004/05/just_a_little_d.php

12 Lydersen, "Live from the Streets."

13 Kari Lydersen, "A Tradition of Struggle, Why did Bolivians take to the streets?," *Americas.org* (October 24, 2003), http://www.americas.org/item_54.

14 *Mujeres Creando* are very critical of foreign NGOs operating in Bolivia. For further discussion and information on this, see Mujeres Creando, *La Virgen de los Deseos* (Buenos Aires: Tinta Limon, 2005). Also see Silvia Rivera, *Allyus y proyectos de desarollo en el norte de Potosí* (La Paz: Ediciones Aruwiyiri, 1992), and James Petras, *Social Movements and State Power: Argentina, Brazil, Bolivia*

and Ecuador (London: Pluto Press 2005).
15 María Galindo, "Huyendo para Construir," *Mujeres Creando*, http://mujerescreando.org.
16 See Mujeres Creando "Quienes Somos," Mujeres Creando, http://mujerescreando.com/quienes_somos.htm.
17 Julieta Paredes and María Galindo, *Sexo, Placer y Sexualidad*. (La Paz: Mujeres Creando, Undated).
18 All quotes from Julieta Ojeda are from interview with author in February, 2006.
19 Helen Álvarez ;"Utopía: Cabalgadura que nosh ace gigantes en miniature, Una historia de Mujeres Creando," ed. Julieta Ojeda in *La Virgen de los Deseos*, 36–40.
20 Mujeres Creando, "Mujer, confia en el sonido de tu propia voz," in *La Virgen de los Deseos*, 41.
21 Ibid. 42–23.
22 See Mujeres Creando, "Putas," *Mujeres Creando*, http://mujerescreando.org.
23 Many activists in Bolivia were interested in hearing of the Chávez government in Venezuela. Many of these interviews were conducted just after Evo Morales had been elected in Bolivia, so many people who were used to fighting in the streets as part of Bolivian social movements were now grappling with the fact that a possible ally was going to take office. For others, the example of Venezuela was very interesting in comparison to possibilities for Bolivia led by Morales.
24 Unless otherwise indicated, all quotes from María Galindo are from an interview with the author in February, 2006.
25 From María Galindo "Ponemos El Cuerpo," *Mujeres Grafiteando*, 5.
26 This refers to the quota in the Ley de Convocatoria (convoking the Constitutional Assembly) that 30 percent of the assembly people must be female.
27 See Mujeres Creando, *Mujeres Grafiteando*.
28 Julieta Ojeda, Rosario Adrián, Sdenka Huaranca, María Galindo, Florentina Alegre, Maritsa Nina y Gabí, "Por un política concreta, Conversación del Colectivo Situaciones con Mujeres Creando," in *La Virgen de los Deseos*, 171–172.
29 Mujeres Creando, "Es hora de pasar de la nausea al vómito," in *La Virgen de los Deseos*, 45–47.
30 For more information on the participation of women in the Bolivian informal economy, see Silvia Rivera, *Bircholas, Trabajo de mujeres: explotación capitalista y oppression colonial entre las migrantes aymaras de La Paz y El Alto* (La Paz: Editorial Mama Huaco, 1996).
31 María Galindo "Evo Morales and the Phallic Decolonization of the Bolivian State," trans. April Howard, *Upside Down World* (September 6, 2006), http://upsidedownworld.org/main/content/view/417/31/.
32 All quotes from Abraham Bojórquez are from interview with author in February and July, 2006.
33 All quotes from Grover Canaviri Huallpa and Dennis Quispe Issa are from interview with author in July, 2006.
34 All quotes from Sdenka Suxo Cadena are from interview with author in July, 2006.

Chapter Nine

Continent on a Tightrope

Thousands celebrate the inauguration of Tabaré
Vázquez in Montevideo, Uruguay.
                              Photo Credit: Benjamin Dangl

—Carlos Mesa[1]

In the cool dawn of Buenos Aires, Argentina pedestrians inhaled their first cigarettes of the day. Fresh produce, newspapers, and shop goods were hauled onto damp sidewalks as the daily chorus of car horns began. I bought a cup of coffee and waited ten minutes to cross the street. The traffic seemed to know something I didn't. "Road blockades," the man next to me quipped between a yawn and a stretch. "The traffic is moving like this to get through before the route is cut off." Before I could ask what he meant, the sea of taxis and buses came to a halt, and drivers leaned into their horns and cursed. I sucked down the remainder of the coffee just before the tear gas set in.

Down the street, people were waving signs and chanting in front of burning tires. Black smoke choked the air, mixing with the tear gas. Police, taxi drivers, and protestors converged in that smoky axis, battling with clubs, fists, and incessant horns. I ducked into a bar to escape the tear gas, ordered another coffee, and asked what was going on. A man behind the counter with a towel slung over his shoulder waved his hand in the air in exasperation, "They don't have jobs, so they block roads." It wasn't the last blockade or protest I would see in the city. Demands in later mobilizations included better working conditions in subways, and speedier justice against those implicated in the country's dictatorships. My eyes slowly stopped burning as I spoke with a few men at the bar who looked like they had been there all night. "The whole continent is blockaded," one of them mumbled, pointing to the television.

I looked up to the screen and sure enough, there were the familiar chants and marches from the *altiplano* in Bolivia. The images of tear gas-shooting cops in both countries seemed to mesh into one street conflict. People on the TV screen also rubbed their eyes and shook fists in the air. I even noticed a line of traffic behind the burning tires in El Alto, similar to the one outside the bar. For a moment, I felt as though I was in two countries at once. Outside, a group of angry Argentines was demanding work and better wages. The crowd in Bolivia was protesting against high water prices.

As Bolivia's Carlos Mesa began the difficult task of presiding over a divided country, the rest of Latin America was going through similarly tumultuous changes. Labor unions and social movements were increasing their collaborative efforts in various countries. Progressive political parties were gaining ground as responses to economic crises brought about by neoliberalism. Venezuelan president Hugo Chávez was using oil profits to fund projects in education, health care, and media. In Argentina, social uproar continued in the wake of the 2001-2002 economic crash. Other countries were gearing up for presidential elections where left-of-center leaders were expected to win. The new Latin American direction had a participatory, socialistic flavor to it with an emphasis on empowering poor sectors and weakening the influence of Washington and international corporations.

The Bolivian conflict over the price and availability of water, reported on the café's television, would prove to be part of a larger movement which would grow to include renewed demands for the nationalization of gas reserves. As Bolivian social movements diversified tactics and gained momentum, the Mesa administration would eventually be brought to its knees. Like the man at the bar said, the whole continent was rebelling. Once again, Bolivia was at the forefront of this regional uprising.

The January, 2005 conflict over water in El Alto was the culmination of years of discontent with corporate control of the city's water. After 1997, when the World Bank made the privatization of water a condition for loans to Bolivia, water systems in Cochabamba, El Alto, and La Paz were privatized. *Aguas de Illimani*, a private consortium owned by the French water company Suez, was given control of El Alto's water and subsequently increased rates by 35 percent. The price for a new water and sewage hookup rose to $445, the equivalent of six months of the national minimum wage. Because the company did not expand its reach to the surrounding areas of El Alto, more than 200,000 people were left without access to this vital resource.[2]

Residents in El Alto never asked for their water to be privatized in the first place. The government, eager to gain the approval of the World Bank, negotiated the contract secretly behind closed doors. Many in El Alto didn't know of the deal until they received bills with the increased fees. Eight years after dealing with the exorbitant rates and poor infrastructure, citizens in El Alto organized a general strike on January 11th, 2005.[3] As in Cochabamba's Water War, the culprit was a multinational corporation, one of the largest water management companies in the world,[4] and infamous for prioritizing high profits over functionality and access.[5]

Suez's operations in El Alto were far from transparent. The company raised connection fees, but not regular tariffs. El Alto water specialist

Susan Spronk wrote that, "since new customers only find out about the fees when they arrive at *Aguas de Illimani*'s office, it is more difficult to organize a protest about the costs of new connections than a tariff hike where comparing water bills becomes an important organizing tool."[6] The contract with *Aguas de Illimani* also prohibited the use of alternative water systems such as the numerous wells built autonomously by poor residents who were either off the company's connection grid or could not afford the monthly fees.[7]

Scattered protests took place against the water company since its arrival in 1997. These became more affective and better organized under the leadership of the FEJUVE.[8] The January strike, organized by the FEJUVE and the COR, lasted for 72 hours. Rainy weather didn't stop enormous marches against the company from being organized in El Alto and La Paz.[9] Protesters demanded that *Aguas de Illimani* leave the city and be replaced by a public-run water system. The residents' tactics worked. Responding to pressure from strikers and protestors, Mesa issued a decree on January 13th declaring that water and sewage systems in El Alto would go back into the state's hands.[10]

The 2000 Water War in Cochabamba was on people's minds during the El Alto movement against *Aguas de Illimani*. Yet the two revolts were quite different. Cochabamba-based sociologist Carlos Crespo explained that whereas the *Coordinadora* emerged out of residents' collective needs and action, the FEJUVE in El Alto already existed and had a long history of grassroots organization. Therefore, when citizens were confronted by water privatization problems, they had a pre-existing structure in place and experience grappling with similar problems related to electricity, road maintenance, and garbage collection.[11] In El Alto, the fight was against a company that had been operating there for years. In Cochabamba, as soon as the fees and contracts were implemented, people responded and took to the streets. "There's a chronic shortage of water in Cochabamba. So whatever happens, the people respond very quickly," Crespo said.[12]

I paid close attention to these events from Buenos Aires. Argentina, however, was having its own social problems closely linked to basic services and wages. Since the economic collapse of the country in 2002, many Argentines had developed their own alternatives to neoliberal policies, from barter systems to worker-run factories.[13] One example of this resistance took place during the first week of February, just after El Alto's Water War.

Hundreds of thousands of citizens use the Metrovias subway in Buenos Aires each day. So when subway workers went on strike, it created quite a stir. Since November, 2004, the workers had been demanding pay increases of 53 percent and better working conditions. After months of waiting for company executives to meet their demands, workers decided to strike.[14] From the 5th–10th of February, workers blocked all subway stops throughout the city. Many were on guard for 24-hour shifts, while others were accompanied by their entire families and slept on the concrete floors of the waiting areas. There were fights between Metrovias workers and angry citizens who didn't support the strike. Enraged commuters broke glass cases surrounding ticket counters throughout the city.

Like many Argentine citizens, Metrovias workers were struggling to survive on a meager salary. Meanwhile, the company's vice-president, Alberto Verra, received 86 times the annual income of most workers. "I make about 300 pesos per month," one Metrovias worker on strike explained. "That's about $100 US dollars. It's simply not enough for my family to survive on!" Metrovias, which is a US-owned company, had not performed general maintenance of the system since 2001 and employees complained of unhealthy working conditions, horrible air quality, and faulty equipment. Though the price of tickets had risen over the years, the salaries and the maintenance basically remained the same.

Due to the subway strike, buses were abnormally packed and bus lines remained on the sidewalks long into the evening. "Thousands of working people are forced to arrive late to their jobs, and so they lose money. This loss can be huge for people who depend on every cent to survive," one kiosk worker in the city's center explained. In a poll conducted by *Clarín*, a large Argentine newspaper, 67.6 percent of 26,434 people polled said they were against the subway strike and thought it was excessive. 32.4 percent of those polled supported it.

To consolidate forces and decide on tactics, a conference among the city's major unions took place in the worker-run cooperative Hotel Bauen. At the front of the conference hall, a sign read *"Si Gana el Subte, Ganamos Todos"* (If the subway workers win, we all win). There was sentiment at the meeting that, with the country's eyes on the Metrovias workers, it was a time to make the most of the strike's clout. Representatives from organizations from student groups to telephone worker unions were in attendance. Many proposed a city-wide strike demanding higher wages in general. Others suggested more street protests and road blockades.

The Metrovias strike was one step in a long fight for workers' rights in the country. However, leaders decided that collective action between unions for massive change should be put on hold. The end of the conflict came on February 10th, 2005, when Metrovias workers accepted an offer from the company for a pay increase of 44 percent. Improvements on the working conditions of the subway were still being discussed when the strike ended. Yet for many of the workers, the wage increase was a victory and served as an inspirational example to other workers in the city.

While such labor and social movements gained steam regionally, some leftists were leaving the streets and entering government palaces through elections. One such group was Uruguay's *Frente Amplio* (Broad Front) party and their leader, Tabaré Vázquez.

On March 1st, 2005, the night Tabaré Vázquez was inaugurated President of Uruguay, a sea of people, flags, and drum brigades surged through the streets of Montevideo. Fireworks pounded the air and car horns shrieked. The city bubbled with a cathartic happiness. In Uruguay, 15 percent of the population is unemployed and economic activity staggers along at a level 20 percent below what it was in 1990.[15] The country has the highest proportion of people aged over 60 in Latin America; 15 percent—most of them young—have left the country in search of work. Given the decreasing population, it was no surprise when I saw a government-sponsored ad in the main plaza with a picture of a pregnant woman on it: the government wanted Uruguayans to multiply.

In the face of these difficulties, voters in the October 31st, 2004 presidential election evidently thought twice before voting for business as usual. The new *Frente Amplio* government pledged massive reforms in healthcare and education. It promised to reactivate sugar production, provide credit to farmers, raise the salaries of rural workers, and implement an emergency strategy to deal with unemployment. The kidnappings and torture carried out by the military dictatorship in the 1970s were also scheduled to be investigated.

"Vázquez's victory is a powerful change for Uruguay," asserted Martin Bension, a history teacher in Montevideo. "Now the people will have more opportunities to participate in the government. Right from the foundation of the *Frente Amplio*, decades ago, there has been popular participation in it. The *Frente* makes people feel more connected, so more people become involved."

"A lot of people died and went to jail in the seventies to win what the *Frente Amplio* has today. The Vázquez administration knows this and will have to keep it in mind," Bension said. "Besides improvements in Uruguay, the nations of Latin America should unite—just as Venezuelan President Hugo Chávez is trying to do—in spite of our soccer rivalries! We can unify because of our common histories. We've all been colonized and controlled by foreign powers. These common characteristics can unite us." Shortly after taking office, Vázquez reopened relations with Cuba and signed trade deals with Venezuela, Bolivia, Argentina, and Brazil.

Bands played in the streets and people waved flags, pounded drums and drank the liquor stores dry to celebrate the inauguration. When the parties were over, much of this enthusiasm was channeled into "base committees" of the *Frente Amplio,* groups located around the city and countryside. Oscar Gandolo, a painter, has been active in his committee for five years. "The economy was going from bad to worse," he recalled. "I had to do something. We have meetings every week where we get together and decide what we think the Government needs to do, and cover issues that the government misses." A couple of days after the presidential inauguration, the mood at a base committee in Montevideo was upbeat. The setting was typical of other party offices around Montevideo: a cluttered meeting room with books and political pamphlets stacked along tables, a picture of Che Guevara painted on the wall, and campaign posters plastered everywhere. People filed into the room, joking and patting each other on the back.

Eventually participants sat down and introduced themselves. They were carpenters, school teachers, plumbers, students, electricians, unemployed people, and musicians. Some had been members of the party for decades, and others were showing up for the first time. They planned a cultural event with artists and musicians from Uruguay and Cuba. Then, after lengthy discussions, they elected a secretary, representative, and treasurer. Security in the neighborhood and the condition of one of the main roads were the next topics of discussion. Toward the end of the meeting, a long-standing member of the base committee spoke to the group: "For those who just arrived for the first time, we ask for your participation. It doesn't matter if you don't know anything about politics. You'll learn while you're here. With this new government in office, the responsibility of the people is greater than ever before."

To prevent the Vázquez government from bowing to the International Monetary Fund and corporate power, popular participation would be crucial. The new administration's feet would have to be held to the flames to avoid the shift to the right. Yet, in the glory of the moment, optimism reigned.[16]

While Uruguayans were drunk on hope in what many believed was the dawn of a new era, Bolivians struggled with the challenges of their own new government. The question of how best to use Bolivia's gas re-emerged as an electrifying issue for the country's social movements in 2005. Mesa presided over a restless country with many unmet needs. An estimated 800 protests took place during his time in office. On March 4th, just days after Vázquez was inaugurated in Uruguay, the Bolivian parliament passed a controversial law that maintained gas royalties at 18 percent, a far cry from the 50 percent royalties many protestors had been demanding.

"It would be very easy for me to say, 'Yes, we will nationalize through expropriation,' and I would probably be the most popular man alive. But I don't govern for popularity. I govern for the responsibility of the state," said President Mesa.[17] In response, groups of unions, farmers, civil society organizations, and students mobilized once again for gas nationalization. Through both independent and coordinated efforts, protesters marched and blockaded vital highways as they had so many times before.[18]

On July 18th, 2004, Mesa organized a referendum on gas industrialization and exportation. Voters chose "yes" or "no" to five questions including whether to repeal Sánchez de Lozada's gas exportation plan, increase revenue with a new plan, use the gas as a strategic way to gain access to the sea from Chile, and use most of the profits from the exportation plan for the development of schools, hospitals, roads, and jobs. The referendum did not include the nationalization of gas as an option. Many voters failed to understand the convoluted wording of the questions, which were not only pointed toward a "yes" vote, but also left open opportunities for continued corporate exploitation.[19]

Some citizens refused to vote while others wrote "nationalization" on the ballots or handed them in blank. Various social and labor groups boycotted Mesa's move while union and indigenous leaders Jamie Solares and Felipe Quispe led blockades and protests against the referendum. Evo Morales, on the other hand, supported the vote. Some viewed

Morales' endorsement as a strategy to gain urban middle class support for a presidential bid in the next election.[20] After the polls closed it was announced that seventy-five percent of the voters had voted "yes" to all five questions. Yet for months, gridlock in congress and pressure from foreign investors and protesting groups postponed any major decisions on the gas issue. Conflicts persisted around the country.

Eight months after the referendum, on March 6th, 2005, Mesa announced that protests, strikes, and blockades had made the country "ungovernable" and he offered his resignation, threatening to hand power over to the arch-conservative president of the parliament, Hormando Vaca Diez. Due to his ties to foreign investors and the main right-wing party in government, Vaca Diez was highly unpopular with Bolivian leftists and was expected to respond more violently to protests than Mesa. Mesa hoped the gesture, which many called a plea for sympathy, would force social movements to back off. Yet not only was Mesa's resignation rejected by congress, the announcement backfired. Diverse protest groups came together to re-launch a past defensive front known as the People's General Staff. They called for continued strikes and demanded that governmental royalties from the sale of the gas be raised to a minimum of 50 percent.[21]

Later that month, 100,000 protesters, primarily from El Alto, rallied outside parliament demanding Mesa's resignation. The movement grew as other sectors joined the El Alto protesters. The La Paz teachers' union called a strike, peasant unions across the country organized road blockades, and the National Congress of the Miners' Union marched to La Paz. The MAS party organized a demonstration from the city of Cochabamba to La Paz, a distance of 190 kilometers.[22] Not all protest groups shared the same long-term goals. Evo Morales maintained that Bolivia should receive 50 percent of the royalties from the sale of the gas, a demand previously supported by protesters but which by this point was viewed by many as too moderate.[23] Still, short term demands for nationalization were enough to unite sectors for the time being.

In response, on March 15th, the Bolivian Congress passed a law that imposed a new 32 percent tax on gas production on top of the existing royalties of 18 percent.[24] The bill still had to pass through Senate prior to reaching Mesa, who could have vetoed it. Under this new law, the state would receive $500–600 million in annual revenue. These figures were higher than the $150 million collected at the time, but lower than the $750 million many protest groups were demanding. The move set off another round of marches, strikes, and road blockades.[25] Protests continued into May, when in El Alto a combustible gas plant was taken siege by protestors demanding nationalization.[26] On May 24th, tens of thousands of protesters who had descended into La Paz from El Alto were met with rubber bullets and tear gas, leaving six protestors injured. Road blockades were set up on main roads across the country, shutting down routes to La Paz, the nearby international airport, and roads to Peru and Chile.[27]

One of the more controversial actions during this time was carried out by the anarchist/feminist group *Mujeres Creando*. In order to address the racism in La Paz against indigenous protestors from rural areas, collective members organized an action focusing on women from rural areas who had marched into La Paz demanding gas nationalization. When these women arrived in the city's main plaza they were booed and hissed at. Members of *Mujeres Creando* received the women by washing their feet. "Their feet are hot, they are super-tired, but at the same time physically, visually, it's an act of rebellion against racism," collective member María Galindo explained. "All of the racism comes from the city. [We did it] because it was refreshing, pleasant, and an act that didn't need words, explanations or discourse, nothing. Very simple. And it was a simplicity that anyone could understand. But as for the men, we didn't offer, nor did we agree to wash their feet. Even though they were tired. Even though they had marched. We didn't do it because it was a gesture from one woman to another." The action lasted for about two hours. "When we left, a group of *campesino* [men] circled us and publicly beat us for at least 40 minutes."[28]

"I believe that we [*Mujeres Creando*] irritate our own social movements," Galindo said. "[W]e have been operating for many years, and I believe that that time this beating was like an act as if to say, 'Look, we are fed up with you. We can't kill you, but we can beat you publicly in the street.'" When the activists were washing the marchers' feet, the media did not pay any attention. But when the beating began, all the cameras were on *Mujeres Creando*.

At the same time, marches, strikes, and blockades were gaining momentum across the country. Some of the most violent confrontations between police and protestors took place in La Paz. Christian Parenti reported from the streets during this conflict, explaining that for days La Paz was under siege, with road blockades on major highways obstructing the arrival of supplies and transportation. "For the third day running, tens of thousands of protesters—peasants, teachers, miners, shopkeepers, factory workers, and unemployed people—have marched on La Paz," he wrote, "[Protestors] descended en masse from the altiplano, above the capital. Joining them are 800 miners. In heavy jackets, fedoras, bowlers, and wool hats, their faces lined and buffed by years of wind and cold, the Aymara columns march fast and hard, carrying sticks, pipes, shepherds' whips, and wiphalas, the rainbow-colored banner of indigenous self-determination."[29]

On June 2nd, in a last ditch effort to quell demonstrations, Mesa announced plans to rewrite the constitution in a national assembly. With such an assembly, he hoped to offer marginalized indigenous people a larger voice in the government. Yet the move still had to be approved by congress.[30] Protesters were not satisfied with Mesa's plan, as it didn't offer an immediate response to their demands for nationalization of the country's gas. Many groups pledged to continue road blockades and marches until the gas was nationalized and plans for the constitutional assembly were concrete.[31]

Mobilizations reached a peak on June 6th, when hundreds of thousands of protestors descended into La Paz. Miners exploded dynamite in the streets in what was the largest demonstration since October, 2003.[32] That same day Mesa again offered his resignation to congress. "This is as far as I can go," he stated in a televised address. He asked Bolivians for forgiveness if he shared responsibility for the profound political crisis that was gripping the nation. His resignation was not a key demand of protest groups. For many Bolivians, the issue wasn't who was president; it was who was in control of the nation's gas.[33]

On June 7th and 8th, gas pipelines near Cochabamba, which normally sent 20,000 barrels of gas per day to Chile, were shut down by protestors. Almost 100 hunger strikes were organized around the country for gas nationalization.[34] On June 9th, politicians went to Sucre to agree on a solution for the crisis. The relocation from La Paz was intended to bring the debate to an area without protests—but the movement followed them. Tens of thousands of people traveled to Sucre from all over the country, flooding the central plaza to demand nationalization and prevent Vaca Diez from replacing Mesa.[35] That same day, a protester was killed by police fire in Sucre. Congress had no choice but to accept Mesa's resignation this time. Hormando Vaca Diez and Mario Cossio, the two in line to become president after Mesa, declined to accept the presidency, in part out of pressure from protesting sectors. The position went to Bolivian Supreme Court justice Eduardo Rodriguez. President Rodriguez announced that elections would take place within the year.[36]

The 2005 Gas War was very different from the one that took place in 2003. The demands in 2003 centered in part on the resignation of Sánchez de Lozada, while Mesa enjoyed relatively broad popularity, even among protest groups. There was a willingness among social movements to cooperate with his government that did not exist in 2003. Another difference was Mesa's restraint in dealing with protestors. This contributed to his popularity and also did not galvanize protests and discontent in the way the 2003 repression did. The mobilizations in May and June were effective in part because of the experience in recent revolts, such as the 2003 Gas War and the 2005 protests against *Aguas de Illimani.*[37]

The conflicts regarding water and gas under Mesa were representative of a regional movement. The backlash to neoliberalism was gaining strength in Latin America. Social movements and political parties had won new ground in the fight against corporate exploitation and Washington's economic policies. A dominant characteristic of this leftist shift was the demand to use natural resources to the benefit of the people. The fight against high water costs in El Alto and the movement for the nationalization of Bolivia's gas expressed the need to regain access to basic resources and services. The electoral victory of Tabaré Vázquez in Uruguay and the struggles of workers in Buenos Aires were part of this regional uprising to prioritize the needs of families, workers, students, and regular citizens over corporate greed. How these movements would grapple with the challenges posed by electoral victories in each respective country was still an unknown. In Bolivia, the relationship between the country's social movements and the government would soon be put to the test with the electoral victory of Evo Morales.

(Endnotes)

1 Benjamin Dangl, "Bolivia on a Tightrope," *Upside Down World* (June 8, 2005), http://upsidedownworld.org/main/content/view/101/31/.
2 Jim Shultz, "The Second Water War in Bolivia," *ZNet* (December 19, 2004), http://www.zmag.org/content/print_article.cfm?itemID=6893&sectionID=1.
3 Susan Spronk, "International Solidarity for the Struggle for Water Justice in El Alto, Bolivia" ZNet (May 10, 2005), http://www.zmag.org/content/print_article.cfm?itemID=7827&sectionID=52.
4 For more information, see Suez website: http://www.suez.com/metiers/english/environnement/index.php.
5 Stop Suez website: http://www.stopsuez.org/page.aspx. The company's track record in Buenos Aires had been disastrous. From 1993–1998, Suez had only made 54 percent of the connections it promised to make. This was because of a lack of investment on the part of the company in new infrastructure. Cited in Spronk: David Hall and Emmanuel Lobina, "Pipe Dreams: The failure of

the private sector to invest in water services in developing countries," *World Development Movement* (March, 2006), http://www.wdm.org.uk/resources/briefings/aid/pipedreamsfullreport.pdf.

6 Susan Spronk, "Another Hole in the Boat: Suez's 'Private Corruption' in Bolivia," *New Socialist* (July 27, 2006), http://www.newsocialist.org/index.php?id=929.

7 This is exactly the kind of arrangement Bechtel had in Cochabamba. Communal water systems and wells were outlawed there as well. See "Comenzó la Guerra del Agua en El Alto," *Indymedia Qollasuyu Ivi Iyambae Bolivia* (November 11, 2004), http://www.bolivia.indymedia.org/es/2004/11/13381.shtml. Also see Comisión para la Gestión Integral del Agua en Bolivia (CGIAB), http://www.aguabolivia.org/.

8 Spronk, "Another Hole." Also see Fundación Solón at http://www.funsolon.org/., and Public Citizen at http://www.citizen.org/.

9 Jeffrey R. Webber, "Left-Indigenous Struggles in Bolivia: Searching for Revolutionary Democracy," *Monthly Review* vol. 57 no. 4 (September, 2005), http://www.monthlyreview.org/0905webber.htm

10 The conflict with Suez in El Alto is still unresolved, see: Zane Grant and Kat Shuffler, "Bolivia's Second Water War," *Z Magazine* (March, 2005), http://www.thirdworldtraveler.com/Water/Bolivia_SecondWaterWar.html.

11 This is from an author interview with sociologist Carlos Crespo. All other views expressed by Crespo in this chapter are from author interview, February, 2006.

12 For more information on the history of social movements in El Alto, see chapter seven.

13 For more information, See Mristella Svampa and Sebastián Pereyra, *Entre La Ruta y El Barrio: La experiencia de las organizaciones piqueteros*, (Buenos Aires: Editorial Biblos, 2003)., and Raúl Zibechi, *Genealiogía de la Revuelta, Argentina: la sociedad en movimiento* (Montevideo-La Plata-Buenos Aires: Nordan-Letra Libre, 2003)., Marina Sitrin, *Horizontalism* (Oakland: AK Press, 2006).

14 For more information on the 2005 Argentine subway strike, see: Dangl, "Argentine Subway Strikers Win Wage Increase," *Upside Down World* (February 12, 2005), http://upsidedownworld.org/main/content/view/18/32/.

15 For more information on the Uruguayan inauguration, see Dangl, "Feet to the Flames," *Upside Down World* (March 24, 2005), http://upsidedownworld.org/main/content/view/69/48/.

16 Brazilian President Lula was a large disappointment to his followers, who hoped for radical change with his administration and instead only got more of the same. Since taking office, Vázquez has gone down a similar path of moderation, repeating the mistakes of his neoliberal predecessors. For more information, see Matthew Beagle, "Uruguay's Tabaré Vazquez: Pink Tide or Political Voice of the Center?" *COHA* (March 4, 2006), http://www.coha.org/2006/03/04/uruguay%E2%80%99s-tabare-vazquez-pink-tide-or-political-voice-of-the-center/.

17 Ramon Sanchez, "The gas referendum in Bolivia—a dirty trick," *In Defense of Marxism* (July 19, 2004), http://www.marxist.com/Latinam/bolivia_referendum0704.html.

18 Dangl, "Bolivia on a Tightrope."

19 Ibid.

20 Ibid.

21 At this time, with the exception of the FEJUVE of El Alto, some groups did not trust MAS, Morales and other leaders involved in the pact. Ibid.

22 Ibid.

23 For analysis on the MAS approach during the 2005 Gas War, see Forrest Hylton,

"Bolivia: The Agony of Stalemate" *CounterPunch* (May 5, 2005), http://www.counterpunch.org/hylton06022005.html.

24 US Treasury Department's Assistant Secretary of International Affairs, Randal Quarles has said that if the new gas law were to go into effect, it would be a "sure thing that the first measure would be the suspension of investments, at minimum while Bolivia continues this uncertainty." Quarles also suggested that the law might influence the amount of financial support that organizations such as the International Monetary Fund and the World Bank offer to the Bolivian government. This kind of blackmailing was typical of neoliberal proponents. Jeffrey R. Webber, "Bolivia Back to the Streets?," *ZNet* (May 9, 2005), http://www.zmag.org/content/showarticle.cfm?ItemID=7817.

25 Dangl, "Bolivia on a Tightrope,," and Federico Fuentes, "BOLIVIA: A nation holds its breath," *Green Left Weekly* (March 23, 2005), http://www.greenleft.org.au/back/2005/620/620p19.htm.

26 Mamani, *Geopolíticas Indígenas*, 99., and from author interview with Abraham Bojórquez.

27 Dangl, "Bolivia on a Tightrope."

28 All quotes and information from María Galindo are from an interview by the author.

29 Christian Parenti, "Bolivia's Battle of Wills," *The Nation* (June 16, 2005), http://www.thenation.com/doc/20050704/parenti.

30 Dangl, "Bolivia on a Tightrope."

31 Ibid.

32 Forrest Hylton and Sinclair Thompson, "The Chequered Rainbow," *New Left Review* 35 (Sept–Oct, 2005), http://www.newleftreview.net/NLR26903.shtml.

33 Dangl, "Bolivia on a Tightrope."

34 Hylton and Thompson, "The Chequered Rainbow."

35 Author interview with Abraham Bojórquez, and see Hylton and Thompson, "The Chequered Rainbow."

36 Dangl, "Bolivia on a Tightrope."

37 From author interview with Gregorio Cayllante and Julio Mamani in February, 2006.

Chapter Ten

Bolivian Moment: The Morales Administration

Cocalero union leader Berto Bautizado talks about the hopes and challenges facing Bolivia under the Evo Morales administration.

Photo Credit: Benjamin Dangl

"If the 19ᵗʰ century belonged to Europe and the 20ᵗʰ century to the United States, the 21ˢᵗ century will belong to America, to Latin America."

—Evo Morales[1]

Just before his official inauguration as president on January 22ⁿᵈ, 2006, Evo Morales participated in a traditional ceremony in Tiwanaku, a pre-Incan ruin. Barefoot and dressed in a red poncho, he received a gold and silver staff from Aymaran leaders as a symbol of his new power and responsibility. Five hundred years had passed since this ritual transfer of power last took place in Bolivia. The traditional act gained the attention of the world and the fascination of the international media. His radical rhetoric and informal attire—he wore a sweater to meet with the King of Spain—made him a new rebellious icon in the eyes of the world.

For many Bolivians, Morales' presidential victory meant a window of opportunity for historic change. Morales' popularity was born and buoyed by neoliberalism's harmful effects on the country, and Bolivians hoped he would go far in his fight against such policies. However, as many newly elected officials find out, promising to enact changes demanded by most sectors of society is one thing, and carrying them out in office is another. The first several months of the Morales presidency have demonstrated that hope and rhetoric can carry the day for only so long, and that the transition from the streets to the government palace is a rougher road than candidacy. On more than one occasion, the Morales administration has found itself between a rock and hard place. On one side are the demands from a country beset by countless problems. On the other side is the harsh reality that to reverse problems 500 years in the making is no easy feat.

The successes of street mobilizations carved the way to the heated 2005 presidential race between different visions of the future of Bolivia. Recent conflicts were on the forefront of the campaigns, and Morales represented the possibility of hope and change more than any other candidate. He promised to nationalize gas reserves, work as an ally to coca producers, redistribute land to poor farmers, reject US-backed free trade policies, and convoke an assembly to rewrite the constitution. At a campaign rally in La Paz, Morales announced the imminent death of neoliberalism in Bolivia. Elvira, a mother of four, embodied this Quixotic moment in Bolivian history with the comment: "I want Evo to change everything that is wrong with this country."[2]

In Morales' favor was the other main contender, former president Jorge Quiroga. Quiroga was educated in Texas, worked as an IBM executive and, as president, believed in using troops and violence to combat protests. The unofficial favorite of the US embassy, Quiroga was expected to use a hard-line approach on coca eradication, continue with the privatization plan for the country's gas, and work with the US to set up a free trade agreement with Bolivia. There were eight candidates in the race, and Morales led in most polls all the way up to Election Day. The Bolivian constitution requires that the winner receive more than 50 percent of the votes in order to secure the presidency, a margin which recent presidents have had to create through multi-party alliances. In the case of no absolute majority, congress decides between the top two contenders.

The first time I met Morales was during a rally after a Gas War protest in Cochabamba. A long room at the headquarters for the Six Federations of the coca growers of the Chapare was packed with people listening to speeches about gas nationalization. After the event ended, supporters showered Morales with hugs, handshakes, and words of encouragement. At one point a little girl no more than six years old ran up to him and hugged his leg, saying, "I love you, Evo! I love you, Evo!" Her parents looked on proudly.

The scene was less glorious later when I interviewed Morales in the MAS headquarters in Cochabamba in 2003. At the entrance to the building, I found a man sewing together a *Wiphala* flag while another ate his breakfast out of a mug. I inquired about Morales and they pointed up the stairs. The building housed administrative offices, and impromptu bunk rooms used by *cocaleros* who slept on blankets on the floor while they were away from home for a march or a meeting. The leader was sitting at his desk drinking orange juice and going through the morning newspapers. Campaign posters, many of himself smiling with coca leaves around his neck, plastered the walls, along with *Wiphala* flags, and large windows looked out over the plaza below. I sat down in one of the several chairs lined up in a row in front of his desk.

We talked about various things, the most pressing being the possible pressure he would receive from Washington and international corporations if elected president of Bolivia.[3] His reply was confident. "After more than 500 years, we, the Quechuas and Aymaras, are still the rightful owners of this land. We, the indigenous people, after 500 years of resistance, are retaking power. This retaking of power is oriented toward the recovery of our own riches, our own natural resources—such as the hydrocarbons. This affects the interests of the transnational corporations and the interests of the neoliberal system." His phone rang repeatedly throughout the interview, and he casually lifted the receiver and set it on his desk, leaving the caller to listen to his promises and predictions.

At this point in time, Morales himself was part of the social movements that he would later have to face. "I am convinced that the power of the people is increasing and strengthening," he said. "This power is changing presidents, economic models, and politics. We are convinced that capitalism is the enemy of the earth, of humanity, and of culture. The US government does not understand our way of life and our philosophy, but we will defend our proposals, our way of life, and our demands with the participation of the Bolivian people." After his election, Morales has continued to use the rhetoric of a people-powered movement to describe his administration.

In another interview, in the midst of his 2005 presidential campaign, he captured the hope of the day with the expansive prediction that "If the 19th century belonged to Europe and the 20th century to the United States, the 21st century will belong to America, to Latin America."[4] Such hope was manifest on December 18th, 2005—Election Day—when approximately 80 percent of the voting population showed up at the polls. The prospect of a Morales victory motivated Manual Cruz Quispe, an 82-year-old El Alto resident, whose son pushed him to the polling station in a wheel barrow. Just seconds after voting, he passed away.[5]

"I hope xenophobia will be extinguished," Morales said after casting his ballot in front of hundreds of residents in Villa 14 de Septiembre in the Chapare. "We only want to live well...The poor don't want to be rich, they just want equality." He was dressed with typical informality, in a short sleeved shirt and jeans, and earlier had eaten fish and boiled yuka for breakfast along with locals and journalists. After Morales voted, a local in a cowboy hat rushed through the town on a horse, waving the *Wiphala* flag, a symbol that had become commonplace at most MAS events. At a later press conference, Morales was surrounded by celebratory men and women with cheeks stuffed with coca leaves.[6]

He surprised the world with a landslide victory, gaining the necessary majority to prevent the decision from going to congress. Euphoria swept through the country and to supporters throughout the world. However, the delicate nature of creating the kind of change that MAS had promised soon became the focus of attention. No matter what the MAS leaders did, they were likely to upset corporate investors, social movements, or both. If Morales followed through on campaign promises, he would face enormous pressure from the Bush administration, corporations, and international lenders. If he chose a more moderate path, Bolivia's social movements were likely to organize the type of protests and strikes that ousted two presidents in two years. "The [54 percent by which Morales won] isn't a blank check; it's a loan," said political analyst Helena Argirakis. "The social movements' support of Morales will always be conditional," added her colleague Fernando García.[7]

Ministers and cabinet members in the Morales administration represented a break with the past. Instead of choosing more experienced politicians and adherents to neoliberalism, Morales chose allies from his years as a union organizer. Ministries from trade and mining to land and hydrocarbons were put under the management of leftist social organizers, intellectuals, and workers. A Ministry of Water was created with the El Alto FEJUVE's Abel Mamani as Minister. The title of Minister of Justice was assigned to Casimira Rodriguez, a longtime organizer of domestic workers, and the Vice President himself is a well-known academic and sociologist who was briefly jailed for his participation in an armed guerrilla group.

While these symbolic appointments created consternation in the right and appreciation in the left, not all social movements were starry-eyed, and all knew they would have to continue to participate in order to enforce change. Oscar Olivera, a leader in Cochabamba's Water War against Bechtel in 2000, warned "Now it will be more difficult for people to mobilize...If 'Tuto' [Quiroga] was in power he would clearly be 'the enemy'. If Evo fails, it will be a failure for the social movements. The gains of six years of struggles will be lost."[8]

Days after Morales took office, La Paz was full of hope and action. Most taxi drivers had MAS stickers on their cars, and campaign posters were still plastered around the city. I didn't meet a single person that didn't vote for Morales. Numerous meetings took place among unions, activists, social organizations, and intellectuals who were planning ways to make the most of what they saw as a great opportunity for change.

One meeting on trade issues in La Paz involved a number of union and *campesino* organizations. "Just because Morales is in the government doesn't mean that everything will be fine," warned trade activist Pablo Solon. There was a general feeling in the air that it was the time to pressure the government to make sure Morales did not fail, that this hope was not crushed by a lack of participation from the Bolivian people. The phrase "things won't change overnight" echoed through many meetings. Nonetheless, expectations seemed limitless.

Dionicia Aduviri has worked every day as a street vendor in La Paz for six years. During the 2003 Gas War, she participated in street mobilizations as part of her street vending union. Her take on the Morales victory was straightforward: "We have been slaves so that the rich could get richer, but now we have hope that things will improve for the first time in Bolivian history."

Much of this symbolic hope came to a head with the "nationalization" of Bolivia's gas. Nationalization had been a continued demand in protests around the country and on May 1ˢᵗ, 2005, Morales announced that the gas would be put into the hands of the state to benefit the majority of the country. "The time has come, the awaited day, a historic day on which Bolivia retakes absolute control of its natural resources," Morales proclaimed in a speech from the San Alberto petroleum field, while wearing a white helmet from the state-owned oil and gas company, *Yacimientos Petroliferos Fiscales Bolivianos* (YPFB). A nearby banner read, "Nationalized: Property of the Bolivian people." On the day of the announcement thousands converged to celebrate the nationalization in La Paz's central Plaza Murillo, and the military was dispatched around the country in a show reminiscent of the Revolution of 1952. Though the policy and the celebrations were more theater than action, they made a significant impact on public opinion.

Far from an all-out expropriation of the industry, the decree simply gave the state more power over the gas and oil business and aimed to generate more income for the government through increased prices, taxes, and royalties. The decree bumped up Bolivia's share of profits coming from two major gas fields, San Alberto and San Antonio, from roughly 50 percent to 82 percent. These fields, which represent 70 percent of Bolivia's natural gas, are owned and operated by Brazil's Petrobras, Spain and Argentina's Repsol, and France's Total. Smaller fields were to continue with a pre-existing tax arrangement, which allotted 50 percent to the government.[9]

The decree announced a brisk timeline for changes. Within 60 days of the announcement, YPFB was supposed to control oil and gas production, exploration, and distribution. Within 180 days, foreign companies were obliged to sign renegotiated contracts giving more control to the state. If they refused to renegotiate, they would be forced to leave the country. While the law did not call for the total expropriation of foreign assets, it did involve the mandatory sale of most assets in the oil and gas industry to the government. According to the decree, the state would seize the assets of those companies that refused to renegotiate contracts.[10]

Under the new decree, the government is able to set the base prices of gas, which then affect the taxes and royalties the state receives. In order to assert more control over the industry, the decree stated that the government is to recover 51 percent of shares from five companies that were carved out of the privatization of YPFB in 1996, when many of the current contracts were drawn up. These shares will be bought or negotiated.

In the flurry of excitement and hope that greeted the Morales administration, The Center for Studies of Labor and Agrarian Development (CEDLA) maintained its cool, honest analysis. Soon after the elections, I talked to Carlos Arze, the organization's director, who admitted that the MAS government and CEDLA are not each other's biggest fans. The organization's analysts have made it their business to prove that the emperor has no clothes by producing clearly written reports about the less-than-glorious details behind government actions. They hold classes and seminars around the country and meet frequently with labor and social organizations. When I met with Arze, he immediately launched into a condemnation of the Morales gas nationalization decree, comparing it to the 2005 Mesa administration proposal that led to the President's ouster. "This is not nationalization," he told me in his office overlooking La Paz. "Nationalization is expropriation."[11]

Though the decree establishes that YPFB receive a majority of share holdings, in reality, the state company remains only a business colleague, and one with a disadvantage in terms of capital. In order to be a powerful partner with the big companies, YPFB has to buy shares, but it doesn't have any money to do so. However, the shares can be bought with gas—so again, under this agreement, the gas will go to international companies, not the state. However, the "nationalization" plan does stipulate that gas distribution be improved, with lower prices for Bolivians, a key protest demand.

"If this MAS reform looks like revolution, what will the right do?" Arze asked. "Morales has so much power, but at the same time he's weak, he's not radical. The right doesn't sleep, and they have the money and experience of managing the state."

On October 29th, 2006 Morales and officials in YFPB signed contracts with the ten biggest gas and oil companies operating in Bolivia, successfully meeting the 180 day deadline set out in the Nationalization Decree. The new deals touch upon gas and oil industry development and exploration. Morales said that in four years the renegotiated contracts will generate $4 billion in yearly government revenue, which will be used to develop the poor country.[12]

Besides the protest call for gas nationalization, Bolivian social movements have for decades been demanding that a constituent assembly be organized to rewrite the constitution. From 1826 to 2004, Bolivia has had 16 constitutions and six reforms. The first constitution, drafted by Simón Bolívar himself in 1825, promised to be the "world's most liberal constitution." However, even the most liberal of constitutions is ineffective if its dictates are not enforced, which has been the case throughout Bolivian history.[13]

Calls for a new constitution as a tool to create a more egalitarian society re-emerged most recently in the 1990s when indigenous groups in the east of Bolivia demanded a constituent assembly to open new space for their political participation in decision-making at the government level. According to the Andean Information Network, indigenous organizations advocating a *constituyente* "sought greater participation in the political decisions regarding the use and distribution of land and natural resources, the allocation of state resources, and national development policies."[14] In fact, these demands correspond to many of the un-applied rights and guarantees made by previous constitutions.

On March 6th, 2006, under Morales, Congress approved a law to convoke the constitutional assembly. The *"Ley de Convocatoria"* asserts that the government itself cannot intervene in the process and that when the constitution is rewritten by the assembly, it must be approved by at least 2/3 in a nationwide referendum. If this new constitution is rejected in the referendum, the old one will continue to be used instead. The law set the date for the election of *asambleístas* (representatives chosen to re-write the constitution) on July 2nd of the same year and gave the assembly the power to write a new constitution. It stipulated that the assembly's activities be known to the public and set the time of the assembly to a maximum of one year. According to the law, at least 30 percent of those elected to the assembly were to be women.[15]

The constituent assembly was conceived of as *by* and *for* the people and MAS was careful to present it that way throughout the presidential election. As the July 2nd Election Day approached, however, more criticisms emerged about the organization of the electoral race and the formation of the assembly. Though the MAS policies and candidates for the assembly had support, many Bolivians complained that the way in which the elections and assembly were organized excluded the country's social movements. As Jim Shultz wrote, in order to qualify to run a candidate in the election, "Unions, indigenous groups, and other social movements had to hit the streets and gather 15,000 signatures each—complete with fingerprints and identification card numbers—in a few weeks."[16] As a result, many powerful social and labor organizations outside of political parties were blocked from participating in the election. However, MAS militants were quick to point out that many social and labor groups are operating within the party: of the 50 MAS *asambleístas* from La Paz, 18 are leaders of labor and social organizations. Many of the MAS politicians belong to unions, indigenous groups, and neighborhood councils, and some are leaders of coca farmer, miner, and student organizations.

To the defense of the MAS, this organization was simply following the timeline and rules set by the Law of Convocation of the constituent assembly. This compromised law was written in tandem with conservative parties who had as much interest as MAS in keeping social movements out and party politics in. However, both sides would find that the grey areas that allowed the parties to pass the law quickly led to a product that fell somewhat short of creating a smooth road to the assembly. Furthermore, the assembly election took place along with an unspecific referendum on departmental autonomy. The referendum, coupled with the assembly election to pacify conservative factions in the eastern departments, asked citizens to vote yes or no on "autonomy," the transfer of power to their departmental government rather than the central government. Strangely, a definition of the powers that autonomy would entail was not a part of the referendum. It is likely autonomy will signify more power within the province to manage the economy, taxes, education, gas, and other natural resources without the omnipresence of the central government in La Paz. The MAS describes autonomy as a way for business leaders in the east to continue exploiting natural resources and pushing neoliberal policies.

A few days before the July 2nd election was to take place, the MAS party closed its campaign in the main plaza in La Paz. Music, lofty speeches, and cold wind marked the rally against autonomy and for the MAS representatives to the constituent assembly. A banner hung behind the main stage with the words "Bolivia changes its history: democratic and cultural revolution." Below this phrase a hand clutched a pencil colored like the Bolivian flag. A giant portrait of a smiling Evo Morales framed by an indigenous flag hung next to the stage.

As the event began, with Andean music and speeches about coca leaves and radical change, the plaza filled with people carrying banners against autonomy and for a MAS victory. One sign simply said, "Autonomy—destruction of Bolivia." The crowd was decidedly pro-MAS. "We have had enough exploitation in this country," a woman next to me said. She was confident MAS was going to win in La Paz. "The transnational companies have taken everything. I'll vote for MAS because we need change, it's long overdue."

The gathering was a convergence of revolutionary fervor and elements of daily life in La Paz. Large advertisements for a lottery company, construction materials, and car oil were plastered on buildings behind the stage. Vendors selling shish-kabobs, steaks, and potatoes lined up along the streets; their grills sputtered with flames and spewed smoke throughout the crowd. A young girl walked past selling cigarettes and candy. At one point I counted more child vendors than adults. In Bolivia, child labor is rampant. The presence of these kids in the crowd made the event's speeches of development and new opportunities sound ironic. Fireworks cracked feebly in the air while a cameraman from the TV program *Telesur* asked a shoeshine boy to back up a bit so he could get a better shot.

The audience grew to include over 15,000 people. A man on stage dressed in a Bolivian flag jumped around in between sets from Andean folk and rock bands. Images of Che Guevara bobbed on placards in the crowd as the moderator on stage yelled, "Vote for MAS. Vote for a new Bolivia!" A number of candidates to the assembly sat on stage, buried in flower necklaces and confetti, and nodding their heads on cue. Eleven-year-old Arturo Rojas stepped up to the microphone and gave a rousing speech that could have come from the mouth of a 40-year-old man. "A thousand times no to the exploitation of our country!" he shouted, and "The people are in power to construct a new country!" At the end of his speech the moderator shook his fist in the air and asked the audience if they wanted coca. Thousands responded with cheers and bags of the green leaf were tossed into the crowd.

On Election Day the voting areas were full of life. Kids played among the ballot boxes, kicking soccer balls and chasing pigeons. Traffic was limited to government and election official vehicles. As a result, the streets were quiet and full of pedestrians instead of traffic jams.

Most voting areas, set up in schoolyards with soccer goals and basketball courts, had the air of informal family picnics. Games went on among neighbors while the voting happened. Outside the booths people grilled steaks and sausages.

Not all voters were caught up in the splendor of the MAS. Dora Araya Castro, a retired woman, spoke with me on the sidewalk as people meandered in the empty streets toward their voting places. She wore a green shawl and gloves and peered through eyes surrounded by vast wrinkles. Each moment before speaking she looked around to make sure no one was listening: she was afraid to be chastised for being so supportive of right-wing parties. Shaking her finger at me while she talked, she said it was "a shame that I have the same last name as that bastard Fidel Castro." According to her, the Morales government was "full of terrorists. I never voted for this *campesino* president Evo. He doesn't even know how to speak. The US should cut all ties and stop financial aid to Bolivia."

The many proposals and critiques of the way the assembly was organized illustrated the vast diversity of Bolivia. "Long live the deserters, the so-called cowards and all youth who object to the use of weapons," the feminist group *Mujeres Creando* wrote, explaining that the assembly should get rid of Bolivia's obligatory military service. Their assembly proposals were against the power the church had within education and the fact that women had to use their husband's last name. They also protested the lack of direct participation of social movements in the assembly: "Every political party is a weapon loaded with blood, machismo, and corruption," they wrote.[17]

Few people were surprised when the election results were announced on the evening of July 2nd. MAS won 135 seats in the assembly while right-wing PODEMOS won 60, and *Unidad Nacional* won 11. However, the MAS didn't get all they had hoped for; 2/3 of the seats (170 out of 255) were needed to control the assembly. In the referendum on autonomy for provinces, the NO to autonomy won 54 percent and the YES won 46 percent nationally. Departments that voted for autonomy were the eastern "half-moon" of Santa Cruz, Beni, Pando, and Tarija. Those that voted against the referendum were La Paz, Oruro, Potosí, Cochabamba, and Chuquisaca. When the results came in, huge marches and rallies in Santa Cruz celebrated their victory for autonomy.

As time went on, the months of whole-hearted optimism following the Morales victory dispersed into a series of questions and conflicts. The constituent assembly entered a gridlock in arguments over voting procedures. The president of YFPB resigned amidst corruption charges. The Minister of Hydrocarbons quit out of anger with the Morales administration's bow to pressure from Brazil's Petrobras company during gas contract negotiations. Though, under Morales, coca areas are generally less militarized and markets for the leaf are expanding, Law 1008 continued to criminalize the innocent, leading to violence in coca fields and protests in jails.

When attending a meeting at the United Nations in New York City in September, 2006, Morales held up a coca leaf and spoke of the importance of this natural resource in his country and advocated for its legalization in the eyes of the UN. The defiant move caught the world's attention but, back home in Bolivia, Morales' own coca policies had met with as much failure as success.

The Morales administration is continuing and expanding cooperative eradication efforts that were initiated in the Chapare in October, 2004 under former President Carlos Mesa. Cooperative eradication goes on between security forces and coca farmers and has created a much more peaceful environment than previous years when violent, forced eradication was the norm. Under Morales, this approach is going beyond the work of previous governments, and increasing the pacific nature of coca crop control. At the same time, the legal coca market is expanding and a hardline approach to drug trafficking continues. As Morales and others on his coca policy team come directly from coca union leadership, they have the support they need from the Six Federations union to enact coca policies that are peaceful and productive.[18]

Mesa's 2004 coca policy allows each family to grow one *cato* (1,600 square meters) of coca. Coca produced beyond those parameters is eradicated. This one *cato* of coca brings in around $70–$110 per month. Cooperative eradication and the production of one *cato* per family in the Chapare has been met with success. In the Yungas, however, forced eradication has continued as farmers there refuse to sufficiently cooperate in coca eradication beyond their *cato*.[19]

Many Bolivians took Morales' understanding of the reality of coca production and the history of violent militarization and eradication for granted. However, Morales' focus on the Chapare coca growers and his continuation of forced military eradication elsewhere has perplexed those who assumed coca policy would dramatically improve under Morales.

In one conflict on September 29th, 2006, in an isolated area near Carrasco National Park in the Yungas de Vandiola, near the Chapare, two coca farmers were killed in eradication efforts.[20] Morales, a longtime defender of the rights of *cocaleros*, approved the security forces' action. The coca growers, Ramber Guzmán Zambrana and Celestino Ricaldis, were killed by Bolivian police and military eradication forces, the *Fuerzas de Tarea Conjunta*. The land and the farmers that worked it operate outside the Six Federations in the Chapare, the standard organization used for negotiation with the government, and a group of which Morales is the current president.[21]

Coca grower representative Nicanor Churata said the area in dispute is a traditional growing area.[22] On the other hand, the government said that according to an agreement signed with Carlos Mesa, coca growing is illegal in national parks.[23] The area where the conflict took place is far from any roads and is only accessible by foot or helicopter. In this case, coca is one of the few crops that could stand the rigorous transport to markets. However, the isolated location led Ministers of Defense, Walker San Miguel and Alicia Muñoz, to say that the farmers' crops go to illegal production for the use of cocaine, as no other markets are accessible in the area.[24] They also said the farmers were armed by foreign narco-traffickers. This is rhetoric similar to that used by government officials from the previous administrations when defending excessive use of force against coca farmers. "This is not a problem of narcotrafficking," the Andean Information Network's Kathryn Ledebur said of the conflict, "this is a problem of subsistence farmers trying to survive."[25]

Another roadblock toward the revolutionary change that MAS promised occured in the mining town of Huanuni from October 5th–6th, 2006. A conflict broke out between poor miners over access to extensive tin mines, resulting in 16 deaths and dozens of injuries. The battle was between unionized, salaried workers, who receive a steady pay check and some minimal benefits and another group referred to as cooperativists. Cooperativists are paid based on the amount and quality of ore they are able to mine on any given day, and then sell to state and private companies.[26]

During the conflict, miners battled with dynamite and rolled tires filled with the explosive toward each other. A critical moment took place in the afternoon on October 5th, when a stick of dynamite landed in a dynamite storage building, setting off a chain reaction among thirty-nine other buildings. The explosions, which miner Salustiano Zurita said were "like an atomic bomb," left 100 families without homes and killed two women. Quintín Calle and his eight sons spent that night searching through the rubble for his wife. The following morning he came down the hill with the news that he had found his wife. In reality, he had found parts of her hair and skin, a piece of her skirt, and a section of her spinal column.[27]

Though conservative sectors point to the events in Huanuni as a failure of the Morales government, in reality the conflict stems from economic policies of past administrations. The majority of the disputed Posokoni deposit in Huanuni was sold to the English company Allied Deals PLC as the Empresa Minera Huanuni (EMH) in 2000, under the government of Hugo Banzer, for $501,123 and the promise to invest $10,250,000 in the first two years of business. When Allied Deals went bankrupt in 2001, the company owed the public mining corporation COMIBOL approximately $95 million. Subsequent conflicts stemmed from the private cooperatives that sought to buy Allied Deals, and COMIBOL leaders demanded at least the company's territory, if not the payment of its debt. Though the Morales administration failed before and after the conflict to negotiate an agreement between the sectors, the crisis has its roots in poverty, neoliberalism, and privatization.[28]

One possible solution to the ongoing mining crisis is the nationalization of the mines. However, on October 31st, Morales admitted that "the state doesn't have the economic resources to achieve mining nationalization" and any moves in that direction would be postponed until 2007.[29] It remains to be seen whether or not the Morales government will be able to rise above the rubble of Huanuni, reversing this curse of wealth.

While blood flowed in Huanuni, human rights groups were working for the closure of another conflict. The movement to bring Sánchez de Lozada to justice for the deaths during the Gas War and Black February of 2003 has gained momentum under the Morales administration. At the time of this writing, Sánchez de Lozada is free in the US. The *Comité Impulsor del Juicio de Responsabilidades*, a Bolivian human rights group, is working to judge him in Bolivian courts.[30]

Meanwhile, the right-wing business elite in Santa Cruz, led by the PODEMOS right-wing political party and the *Comité Cívico*, grow stronger. These leaders have money, the media in their back pocket, and the pitfalls of the Morales administration to give them just the ammo they needed to fight a dirty war of words on their terms. Perhaps the biggest concrete challenges to the Morales administration have come

from Santa Cruz, an economic powerhouse that supports 45 percent of
Bolivia's economy. The department is home to many businesses, landowners, and politicians that are leading the charge against Morales and
any social organizations that lie in their path toward neoliberal success.

Though it is known around the country as a shiny, rich city, poor
working class communities are spread across the capital of Santa Cruz,
in between high rises, malls, and well kept plazas. One carpenter, 37-
year-old Mario Colque, had migrated to Santa Cruz from Potosí to find
work. He rubbed his calloused hands together while speaking of the racism he has been met with in the city as an outsider. "There is no heart
here. You have to be begging on the ground in order for someone to toss
you a coin—if they feel like it—if they don't they'll kick you instead."

One hotel manager—who asked that his name not be used here—
typified the kind of anger that Colque has come up against. Though he
was born in Tarija, Bolivia, the hotel manager had spent time in the US
and spoke perfect English. He referred to Vice President Garcia Linera
as a "queer," said the Morales administration as full of inept "indians"
and didn't believe the MAS would last longer than a year in power. "The
same people that put Morales in the government will take him out," was
his prophecy.

It was the hotel manager who explained where I could find the
Comité Cívico Pro-Santa Cruz, an organization closely linked to the
department's businesses and right-wing politicians which spearheaded
the autonomy movement. The headquarters are located in one of the
wealthiest parts of the city. Inside the infamous building were photos of
the autonomy movement's victory rallies, awards, and framed slogans
such as "If you don't have anything to do, don't do it here: dignified
work." The journalists that stopped by were friendly with those in the
Comité, some even making dates and plans to meet for drinks and a
family barbeque.

In the press conference room, which had a sickly olive green car-
pet and reeked of men's cologne, the *Comité*'s mustachioed president,
German Antelo, spoke into a dozen TV cameras about how the MAS
was trying to divide the country with blockades and protests, pressuring
the Bolivian people into supporting their government. Antelo said his
organization was for legality and democracy, not the dictatorial ways of
the MAS. His smooth, well formulated speech thinly veiled the anger
he almost let boil over when speaking of his own righteousness. "We
don't use scare tactics," he explained, saying the *Comité* consisted of hard

working Bolivian people. The journalists nodded their heads and turned off their cameras on cue.

The other powerful group in Santa Cruz is the political party PODEMOS. Senator Jorge Aguilera repeated the stance of the *Comité* against the MAS and suggested that perhaps Evo and Linera are following the path that they are with the startling assertion that "they don't have families and so don't value human life." Ruben Cuellar Diario, the constituent assembly leader for PODEMOS, spoke about MAS's desire to keep power centralized, instead of supporting autonomy. He said Morales believes that "poverty shared is better."

If PODEMOS and the *Comité Cívico Pro-Santa Cruz* are the mouths and faces of the Santa Cruz business elite and autonomy movement, the youth organization, *Unión Juvenil Crucenista*, is the group's brass knuckles. Whereas PODEMOS and the *Comité* go after the left in rhetoric and economic policies, the *Unión Juvenile* has been known to beat and whip *campesinos* marching for gas nationalization, throw rocks at students organizing against autonomy, toss molotov cocktails at the state television station, and brutally assault members of the landless movement struggling against land monopolies.[31] The *Unión* is a younger, less polished version of the *Comité*. Though leaders claim to be independent of the *Comité*, their headquarters are located right behind the *Comité*'s building, and many youth members go on to join the *Comité*.

I sat down with two of its leaders in an office with comfortable sofas and photos of past leaders. Though the air conditioning was on, they left the door opened, a move I could only interpret, in poor Bolivia, as a sign of opulence and waste. Wilberto Zurita, the vice president of the *Unión Juvenile*, sat next to me. He had new jeans, slicked back hair, a nice watch, sideburns, and a cell phone, which rang regularly throughout our conversation. He studied civil engineering and now works in the construction industry. His collegue, Alfredo Saucedo, is in the *Unión*'s public relations department. He studies law and wants to get into politics. Both are 31 years old, four years from a forced retirement from the *Unión*, and from becoming part of the "old guard."

I asked about some of the complaints of violence on the part of the *Unión*. Though they said those were rumors planted by the left, they did admit they were willing to take up arms to defend Santa Cruz from what they saw as a *kolla*—a derogatory term, generally used among Santa Cruz elite, to refer to *campesino* or indigenous people from the west—invasion. They saw the Morales administration as a threat, which powered their desire for autonomy. "When we have to defend our culture by force, we will," Saucedo said. "The defense of liberty is more important than life...Here in this department people will do anything to defend liberty." When asked if a military coup against Morales might be necessary, both said no, yet Zurita seemed particularly nervous about the question, shaking his knee up and down in response. They openly criticized *campesinos* who "just in order to save money, didn't bathe or change their clothes regularly." They said *cambas*—who they described as lighter-skinned, wealthy Santa Cruz city dwellers and large land owners—were friendlier and cleaner than *kollas*.

Both Zurita and Saucedo had helped spearhead the movement for autonomy and felt disconnected from the Bolivian culture outside of Santa Cruz. Saucedo admitted he doesn't "want to have anything to do with *Pachamama* and all that. We don't even know what *Pachamama* is." Even so, they seemed to understand that the same racism they exhibited was dividing Santa Cruz. "We are probably at the beginning of where you were in the US before the civil rights movement with whites and blacks," Saucedo said. When I asked about the meaning of the cross on *Unión Juvenil's* banner, Zurita told me, "It's not a Nazi symbol." I told him that I hadn't asked if it was a Nazi symbol. They were already on the defensive. "We aren't racist," he said.

Silvestre Saisari was one of the people directly affected by the violence unleashed by right-wing groups such as the *Unión Juvenile*. He was attacked by the group when giving a press conference about landowners' repression against landless farmers.[32] I met him in Santa Cruz shortly after he started his job as the President of the Comission for Land and Territory for Bolivia's Landless Movement (MST) in Santa Cruz. Saisari said the MST has been at the forefront of the groups proposing changes to the land distribution legislation, the INRA Law, in an "agrarian revolution" under MAS. Their proposed reforms focus on the effective distribution of unused land to landless farmers. On November 28th, 2006, various landless farmer, *campesino* and worker organizations arrived in La Paz after marching from around the country to demand such changes to the INRA Law. In response, that same day, the Senate—minus boycotting opposition party members—passed the reforms.[33]

Other land distribution advances have been made under the MAS administration. Outside the city of Santa Cruz, 16,000 hectares of land have been given to 626 families, along with credits with low interest. The area has been re-named *Pueblos Unidos* (United People), and despite the difficult access to the community and the lack of basic services, the land is giving some farmers the chance to feed themselves. However, the landowners in Santa Cruz have moved against such progress by hiring thugs and members of the *Unión Juvenil Crucenista* to harass and destroy such landless settlements.[34]

Though the MST is autonomous from political parties, Saisari described his organization's relationship with the MAS as positive. He saw the MAS electoral victory as an opportunity that should be utilized by social movements. His organization has access to the government, and offers advice and proposals to the administration in ways that never existed with previous governments. "We feel listened to," he told me. The following day, he was to travel to a meeting between Bolivian social movements and the Morales administration. Saisari said that it was important to support the government policies that are good for them, and offer criticism and advice when necessary. "Our democracy depends on us as social movements," he said.

Adolfo Chávez, the president of the Bolivian Confederation of Indigenous Peoples (CIDOB), also spoke positively of the relationship between the MAS government and his organization. In his office in a poor neighborhood in Santa Cruz, he said the participation of social movements in their support, advice, and critiques will guarantee that the Morales government succeeds: "Previous administrations believed they were the ultimate authority. It was hard to get a meeting with them. Presidents never spoke with social organizations this way."

Though Morales had allies like Saisari and Chávez in Santa Cruz when the president paid a surprise visit to the city, it was clear that his enemies were stronger than ever. He arrived with armed escorts to an official event celebrating the anniversary of Santa Cruz. I crammed into the back of the room where the event was held, along with other sweating journalists, and watched the city's rich and powerful enter the room. The guests of honor—the prefect, mayor, and other dignitaries—sat in front of a large painting depicting indigenous slaves kneeling down to Spanish conquistadors in armor and fancy clothing. Just as I noticed this painting, Morales walked into this room of rich white people. Instead of bowing down, like in the painting, this indigenous man was their President. Morales wore a leather jacket with colorful embroidery on it. Unlike every other man in the room, besides the journalists, he did not have a tie on. Tensions were high, the air was hot. People stood up when he entered the room, but did not clap.

214 THE PRICE OF FIRE

In Morales' speech, he talked of "how to help Bolivia's abandoned people" and that loving one's country did not mean privatizing the resources of that country. "To love one's country is to reclaim those resources. We want to help the country with these riches." He said he was the president because he was honest, not corrupt, and presented himself as a leader for the poor, not the rich. Throughout most of his speech, the Santa Cruz leaders talked and joked amongst themselves in clear disregard.

After the event, a small group of anti-MAS and pro-autonomy protesters gathered in the front of the building. Many waved their department's flag and chanted "Evo is a son of a bitch," "Evo is a Fidel Castro of shit," and "Evo is shit in our land." One of the leaders of the Santa Cruz group said, "Even my indigenous maid supports autonomy!" The press flocked from the elite's cocktail party to the noisy crowd in the street. Soon the TV cameras outnumbered the people and an inevitable fight broke out between a MAS supporter and a livid *autonomista*. Police ended the conflict with clouds of mace. When Morales' caravan finally did leave, it was attacked by the angry mob and an equally persistent horde of TV journalists. The protestors pounded their fists on his jeep, and thumped sticks and clubs on the windows as it sped away. A torrent of insults chased him out of town.

A twenty-five hour bus ride away from Santa Cruz, another fight over the destiny of Bolivia was taking place in the constituent assembly. The assembly is officially based in the century-old, five-story *Teatro Gran Mariscal*, an ornate theater in Sucre, the country's constitutional capital. Some commentators have pointed out that the stage is an appropriate location for the assembly, due to the hot air and theatrics that have occurred there. So far, events have included fistfights and one fall into the orchestra pit, which left MAS *asambleísta* Roman Loayza in a coma for several days. The building has a beautiful facade, but all of the important comings and goings take place through a back door where journalists regularly mob for scraps of information or updates. A handful of newspaper and cigarette stalls dot the sidewalks outside. The city is at a high altitude, and a cool wind blows through its narrow colonial streets.

Most *asambleístas* I spoke with agreed, at least verbally, to the idea that they must work toward consensus, and that the assembly should be used to end corruption, reclaim natural resources, redistribute land, and create a plurinational state.[35] The event had been riddled with conflicts, some verbal, and some physical. Some in the MAS said

PODEMOS used every opportunity to stall the assembly from making progress, in order to limit the gathering's potential and slow the progress of the MAS agenda.

When I arrived, the assembly members had been fighting for weeks over voting rules. The MAS was pushing for 51 percent vote approval to pass changes to the constitution, even though the *Ley de Convocatoria* mandated a 2/3 majority. However, since MAS did not gain a 2/3 majority of *asambleistas*, they were pushing for an absolute majority. This would allow them to make the changes they wanted without depending on the right-wing parties for their approval. PODEMOS, on the other hand, was arguing for the 2/3 assembly vote approval for changes, which would allow their party to block any MAS proposals. Weeks later, a mixed voting system was approved, with some issues to be decided by absolute majority, and others by 2/3 majority.

Willy Padilla Monterde is an *asambleista* for the *Concertación Nacional* party. He had dark, well combed hair and seemed to pride himself on his Hollywood smile. In a calm, priestly tone of voice, he expressed his desire for peace. "We don't want to return to the bitter times of 2003," he said. "If the constituent assembly doesn't do its job, this is a possibility." Outside the theater, in the streets of Sucre, children were begging and shining shoes on nearly every block. In the main plaza, 13-year-old Juan Carlos had been working as a shoeshiner for over two years. He wore a dirty yellow baseball cap and was hopeful about the assembly: "It is for us, for the youth and for the poor, not the old and rich."

Many of the *asambleistas* were based in a converted convent just blocks from the theater. Fervent MAS *asambleista* Mirian Cadima told me, in her party's shared office, that "PODEMOS doesn't want change, they are happy with the way things are." She spoke of the day MAS leader Roman Loayza fell into the orchestra pit during a general upheaval. There was mayhem in the theater, but according to Cadima, the conflict was initiated when PODEMOS *asambleistas* booed, hissed, and pounded bottles on tables in protest against the assembly President, Silvia Lazarte of the MAS party. "They yelled, 'dictator' and ran to attack President Lazarte," Cadima recalled. "MAS people rose up to defend her and Roman stood up to ask people to calm down, and that's when he fell."

María Luis Canedo, a teacher and *asambleista* with the MAS, sat next to Cadima and said the biggest issue in the assembly for her was the demand for a "plurinational" state, "It has to do with representation. All indigenous cultures in Bolivia should have representation, no more exclusion in the government, leaving the MAS out." She said the government should include more indigenous and rural representatives, not just the rich from the city. "Representation needs to be direct," she said. As a move toward such representation, both women met regularly with their bases in their home communities.

After this meeting, I was waiting outside the back door of the theater for the arrival of the president of the assembly when a demonstration of indigenous groups marched past to support the MAS and their demand for a majority vote approval in the assembly. The participants, many of whom had traveled all the way from the Chapare, waved *Wiphala* flags and signs with such messages as, "Leaders of the Cochabamba tropics ask that they respect absolute majority. We won't permit that the minority commands the assembly." Many marched with cheeks bulging with coca leaves. When the demonstration arrived at Sucre's main plaza, the leaders gave a press conference to a small group of journalists and cameramen. Some spoke about the need for the majority of Bolivia to be represented in the assembly. One man from the Chapare said, "We want to make sure the new constitution is for everyone." As Mauricio Arias of Potosí explained to me, many were there as representatives from their organizations to monitor the assembly.

Across the country, the constituent assembly is viewed as a way to remedy Bolivia's many social, political, and economic problems in one year-long meeting. However, the extent to which conflicts have broken out just over the voting procedures suggests that issues such as land, coca, and natural resource nationalization will produce similar debilitating fights between voting blocks. Carmen Carrasco, the coordinator of a bi-weekly forum in Sucre, which holds debates on assembly issues, predicted that, "the level of conflicts in the assembly will go up and down like a wave, sometimes calm, sometimes turbulent, depending on the topic of discussion."

Regionally, some political analysts are hopeful that the road that leaders such as Morales have taken in Latin America are indications that neoliberalism may have met its match. Not only is regional integration building between progressive Latin American governments, but the entire balance of power is shifting away from Washington and multinational corporations and into the hands of Latin American social movements and left of center governments. Many of the region's new leaders were themselves persecuted in past dictatorships and have pledged to investigate such crimes and prevent them from happening again. Others have cut off their ties to US military institutions such as the School of the Americas. Meanwhile, the interconnectedness of social movements around the world is increasing through the internet and global encounters such the World Social Forum.[36]

The IMF and Washington are waning in their influence in Latin America, breaking down the vicious cycle of debt and militarization that have paralyzed the region. What Mark Weisbrot of the Center for Economic and Policy Research calls the "cartel of creditors" that shaped the political policies of Latin American governments is losing ground in the region. Various governments in Latin America are refusing to work with these institutions, in part because of their disastrous track record.[37] After nearly 20 years of adhering to IMF policy, the Bolivian government, with Morales at the helm, let its last agreement with the IMF expire. Yet the Bolivian government is dependent on credit and aid from other wealthy countries, and so far none has threatened to cut off aid if Morales' policies don't change. This is a change from the past, when the US or other countries could strangle a country by cutting off aid. This is no longer likely to happen in Latin America primarily because international lenders such as the IMF have been, in part, replaced by Venezuela.[38]

When Argentina paid off its final debt of $9.8 billion to the IMF, Venezuela pitched in $2.5 billion. Venezuela also bought $300 million worth of bonds from Ecuador and is providing discounted oil to Caribbean countries. When Colombia was about to cut off $170 million in soybean imports due to its participation in a free trade deal with the US, Venezuela bought the soybeans from Bolivia instead, also offering a $100 million loan for land reform and other projects. Weisbrot explained, "Venezuela's lending and aid programs, unlike that of the international financial institutions or the G-7 governments, do not have economic policy conditions attached to them." Unless oil prices drop suddenly, this trend is likely to increase for some time. According to Weisbrot, "a tipping point has been reached, and there will be no turning back of the clock."[39]

Countries in Latin America are also looking to Asia instead of the US for investments. According to political analyst Noam Chomsky, "Venezuela, the leading oil exporter in the hemisphere, has forged probably the closest relations with China of any Latin American country, and is planning to sell increasing amounts of oil to China as part of its effort to reduce dependence on the openly hostile US government."[40] This new shift in power relations gives Latin American governments breathing room to enact policies without Washington or IMF pressure.

Meanwhile, in Bolivia, social movements have the capacity to hold the government's feet to the flames, preventing the application of harmful neoliberal policies. According to Uruguayan social analyst, Raúl Zibechi, Bolivian social movements are perhaps the strongest in the region. He poses the question of the day for Bolivia: "What will happen to this enormous historical and social force? ... It is necessary to decolonize the Bolivian state. If MAS makes progress in this process, it will obtain a very important legitimacy on the continent and will be an inescapable point of reference for the indigenous people who are, in fact, the most active sector in the movements."[41]

I asked Zibechi if the social movements were losing in this regional leftist shift. "They have won, not lost," he explained:

> It is good that there are progressive and leftist governments for many reasons. They don't repress, they engage in a dialogue, sometimes they listen and other times they take the same course as the movements. They certainly don't do everything that the movements demand, but you have to take into account that the state can't make the profound social changes mobilized societies need to. Profound changes are not laws or decrees, they don't consist of what land or gas happens to pass from one set of hands to another. It is something much more deep, and the best example we have is the role of the women in the world. They changed the world without having power, without structural reforms, but by changing their place, their self-esteem, their capacity, and their potential instead. And that does not have a reverse gear. Now the women are not going to return to their houses to clean their spouses' clothes, but gas could be re-privatized if the forces above it change.

While this grassroots power has the potential to transform Bolivian society, other elements keep open the possibilities for profound change. Bolivia's vast wealth underground, such as gas and mineral resources, could be used to rehabilitate the economy. The Morales administration's ties with other like-minded governments in the region can help the impoverished country set its own course without bowing to pressure from Washington, international lenders and corporations. According to Weisbrot, this involves setting up "alternatives to the NAFTA [North American Free Trade Agreement] model. For that to work, countries have to cooperate and not think of things in purely nationalist terms. There has to be a willingness to make sacrifices, and be willing to cooperate for the benefit of the group of countries." He believes that some kind of regional integration can be spurred through Mercosur, a trade bloc among Latin American countries, to "help get these countries development strategies that would exclude the US market." That way, if the US tried to impose free trade policies on the region, "Mercosur could provide an alternative where trade is to be mutually beneficial in member countries." He believes that if the region keeps going in the direction it is, with less dependence on the US and the IMF, and more policies directed at benefiting the poor, then in 25 years, Latin America will be much stronger economically and poverty will be reduced.[42]

Trade agreements such as NAFTA have exacerbated economic inequalities between member countries, favoring corporations and US markets while destroying economies, worker rights, and the environment in Latin America.[43] Bolivia recently became a part of a People's Trade Agreement (PTA), a progressive alternative to standard free trade agreements. It is based on collaborations between countries, increased public ownership of the economy, and sustainable trade relationships, rather than exploitative practices standard in other agreements—such as NAFTA and the FTAA. In April, 2006, Venezuela, Cuba, and Bolivia signed a PTA in a move toward creating a "Bolivarian Alternative for the Americas," a sustainable trade project to eliminate poverty throughout the region. In the PTA, Venezuela eliminated tariffs and opened its state buyers to Bolivian producers, policies which are not usually applied to Bolivia's smaller economy. Through the PTA, both Venezuela and Cuba will send doctors and technicians to Bolivia, as well as provide health care and college scholarships for Bolivians.[44]

The PTA gives states more power over economic decisions and regulates the economy to help the poorest sectors of society instead of corporations. The agreement highlights the role of agriculture, stating that "People have the right to determine their agricultural and food policies and to protect national agricultural production from being inundated with food from abroad." The standards of free trade policies—privatization of natural resources and public services, while corporate investors receive incentives and protections—are absent from the agreement. The PTA emphasizes supporting smaller economies, rather than exploiting them.[45]

Neoliberalism has dug its own grave in Latin America, and new alternatives, both in the street and the state, are evolving in its place. Social movement victories in conflicts over access to basic resources, such as land, coca, water, and gas have opened new windows of possibility for change. The recent elections of left of center leaders throughout Latin

America is a sign that regional economic integration is an attainable goal. However, if these new leaders and economic alliances fail to reverse destructive policies, social movements know what they want and how to make themselves heard.

Others are not waiting for modified policies or new decrees. Community organizations in El Alto, landless farmers in Santa Cruz, factory workers in Buenos Aires and other movements across Latin America wield a power to organize and create an alternative social fabric that is in many cases stronger than the state. Their autonomy is based on the fact that fire should have no price and access to natural resources and basic necessities is a right, not a privilege. Instead of marching for change, their march is the change.

(Endnotes)

1   America Vera-Zavala, "Evo Morales Has Plans for Bolivia," *In These Times* (December 18, 2005), http://www.inthesetimes.com/site/main/article/2438/
2   John Hunt "High Hopes in Bolivia as Election Day Approaches," *Upside Down World* (December15, 2005), http://upsidedownworld.org/main/content/view/146/31/.
3   For full interview, Dangl, "An Interview with Evo Morales: Legalizing the Colonization of the Americas," CounterPunch (December 2, 2003), http://www.counterpunch.org/dangl12022003.html.
4   America Vera-Zavala, "Evo Morales Has Plans for Bolivia."
5   John Hunt, "Anxiety and Optimism in the Dawn of a New Bolivia," *Upside Down World* (December 26, 2005), http://upsidedownworld.org/main/content/view/153/31/.
6   John Hunt, "Evo Morales Elected Bolivian President in Landslide Victory," *Upside Down World* (December 18, 2005), http://upsidedownworld.org/main/content/view/147/31/.
7   Mark Engler and Benjamin Dangl, "Bolivia and the Progressive Mandate in Latin America: What will Evo Morales learn from leftist governments in Argentina, Brazil, and Venezuela?," *Z Magazine* vol. 19 no. 3 (March, 2006), http://zmagsite.zmag.org/Mar2006/dangl0306.html.
8   John Hunt, "Anxiety and Optimism."
9   Dangl, "The Wealth Undergound."
10 Ibid.
11 Information from author interview with Carlos Arze in July, 2006.
12 At the time of this writing the details of the gas deals are still unclear, but are likely to follow the analysis of CEDLA. These renegotiated gas and oil contracts were ratified by the Bolivian Senate on November 28th, 2006. Also see Gretchen Gordon "Bolivia and Foreign Oil Companies Sign New Contracts," *The Democracy* Center (November 01, 2006), http://www.democracyctr.org/blog/2006/11/bolivia-and-foreign-oil-companies-sign.html.
13 Kohl and Farthing, *Impasse*, 41.
14 "A New Constitution for Bolivia: the History and Structure of the Constitutional Assembly," *The Andean Information Network*, (June 28, 2006), http://ain-bolivia.org/index.php?option=com_content&task=view&id=19&Itemid=32.

15 Ibid.
16 Jim Shultz, "The Constituent Assembly—Lite," *The Democracy Center* (June 11, 2006), http://www.democracyctr.org/blog/2006/06/constituent-assembly-lite.html.
17 Galindo, "The Phallic decolonization."
18 The government of Venezuela is assisting Bolivia with funds to develop the coca industry for coca flour, coca tea and other products. India, Cuba and Venezuela are prospective buyers for new products.
19 "Crisis or Opportunity? Bolivian Drug Control Policy and the U.S. Response," *Andean Information Network / Washington Office on Latin America* (June 28, 2006), http://www.wola.org/publications/AIN-WOLA%20Drug%20Poli cy%20Memo%20FINAL%20brief.pdf.
20 April Howard, "Bolivia: Coca growers killed in action approved by Evo Morales," *Upside Down World* (October 3, 2006), http://upsidedownworld.org/main/content/view/450/1/.
21 Ibid.
22 "Dirigencia cocalera dice que no inició el enfrentamiento," *La Prensa* (September 30, 2006),
23 Roberto Navia, "Evo propone a campesinos pagar impuesto por el cato de coca,"*EL DEBER* (October 3, 2006).
24 "El gobierno propicia el diálogo dentro de la la ley para solucionar conflicto en Parque Nacional Carrasco," *Agencia Boliviana de Información* (ABI) (October 1, 2006).
25 Howard, "Bolivia: Coca growers killed." The Six Federations union leaders, whose crops are not affected by eradication in national parks, met with Morales about the conflict. Union leader Asterio Romero said the organization would continue to "support the politics of the fight against narcotrafficking and the control of the government of our friend Evo Morales over coca plantations...We will not permit more plantations in national parks and we will add ourselves to the eradication efforts made by the army and the police." " Sindicatos bolivianos deciden sumarse a erradicación de coca," *Reuters America Latina* (October 2, 2006).
26 April Howard and Benjamín Dangl "Tin War in Bolivia: Conflict Between Miners Leaves 17 Dead," *Upside Down World* (October 11, 2006), http://upsidedownworld.org/main/content/view/455/1/.
27 For all sources, Howard and Dangl, "Tin War in Bolivia."
28 Ibid.
29 Hal Weitzman, "Bolivia backs away from mines takeover," *The Financial Times Limited* (November 1, 2006), http://www.ft.com/cms/s/fd723518-69ce-11db-952e-0000779e2340.html.
30 For more information, go to Comité impulsor del juicio a Gonzalo Sánchez de Lozada website, http://juiciogoniya.free.fr/ and The Bolivia Solidarity Network website http://boliviasolidarity.org/.
31 See Raquel Balcázar, *YUQUISES, LO QUE LA PRENSA BURGUESA NUNCA MOSTRARÁ* (Santa Cruz, Bolivia, Videourgente, 2005)., Raquel Balcázar, *REPRESIÓN FASCISTA EN SANTA CRUZ* (Santa Cruz, Bolivia, Videourgente, 2006)., Raquel Balcázar, *AUTONOMÍA PARA LOS RICOS, REVOLUCIÓN PARA LOS POBRES*, Videourgente, 2006).
32 Ibid.
33 For more information on the passage of these changes to the INRA Law, and the likely implications of the reforms, see the "Bolivian Congress Passes Agrarian Reform Legislation in Spite of Heightened Regional Tensions," Andean Information Network (December 1st, 2006). For more information on the INRA

Law and land issues in Bolivia, see "Bolivia's Agrarian Reform Initiative: An Effort to Keep Historical Promises," Andean Information Network (June 28, 2006), http://ain-bolivia.org/index.php?option=com_content&task=view&id=22&Itemid=27.

34   Balcázar, *AUTONOMÍA PARA LOS RICOS.*

35   Julio Aliaga L. et. al., Asemblea Constituyente y pueblos originarios (Alexandria: Jach'a Uru Indigenous Organization, 2006)., *Nueva constituci ón plurinacional,* (La Paz: Confederación Sindical Única de Trabajadores Campesinos de Bolivia (CSUTCB), 2006).

36   Previous movements for hope in the 1960s and on were crushed by military dictatorships backed by the US, which is why what is happening now is so unique: there is hope for change without coups. In Venezuela, the US worked for a coup in 2002 but they failed because of popular support in the streets. For more, see Chomsky and Dwyer, "Latin American Integration,"

37   Mark Weisbrot, "Latin America: The End of An Era," *International Journal of Health Services* vol. 36 no. 4 (2006), http://www.cepr.net/columns/weisbrot/2006_06_end_of_era.htm.

38   Weisbrot, "Latin America."

39   Ibid.

40   Ibid.

41   Noam Chomsky, "The Crumbling Empire,Latin America and Asia are Breaking Free of Washington's Grip," *Infoshop News* (March 15, 2006), http://www.infoshop.org/inews/article.php?story=20060315141547380.

42   Author email interview with Zibechi in July, 2006.

43   Author phone interview with Weisbrot in September, 2006.

44   Green, *The Silent Revolution*, 143-145., Also see "FTAA and Workers' Rights and Jobs," *Public Citizen,* http://www.citizen.org/trade/ftaa/workers/., and "FTAA Overview," *Public Citizen,* http://www.citizenstrade.org/ftaaexplained.php.

45   Jason Tockman, "Bolivia Advocates Alternative Vision for Trade and Integration," *Upside Down World* (July 11, 2006), http://upsidedownworld.org/main/content/view/355/31/.

46   Ibid.

ABOUT THE AUTHOR:

BENJAMIN DANGL has worked as an independent journalist throughout Latin America, writing for publications such as *Z Magazine, The Nation,* and *The Progressive*. He edits *Toward Freedom* (www.TowardFreedom.com), a progressive perspective on world events, and *Upside Down World* (www.upsidedownworld.org), an online magazine uncovering activism and politics in Latin America. He won a 2007 Project Censored Award for his coverage of U.S. military operations in Paraguay.

Contact him at: Ben@upsidedownworld.org

FRIENDS OF AK PRESS

Help sustain our vital project!

AK Press is a worker-run collective that publishes and distributes radical books, audio/visual media, and other material. We're small: a dozen individuals who work long hours for short money, because we believe in what we do. We're anarchists, which is reflected both in the books we publish and in the way we organize our business: without bosses.

AK Press publishes the finest books, CDs, and DVDs from the anarchist and radical traditions—currently about 18 to 20 per year. Joining The Friends of AK Press is a way in which you can directly help us to keep the wheels rolling and these important projects coming.

As ever, money is tight as we do not rely on outside funding. We need your help to make and keep these crucial materials available. Friends pay a minimum (of course we have no objection to larger sums!) of $20/£15 per month, for a minimum three month period. Money received goes directly into our publishing funds. In return, Friends automatically receive (for the duration of their membership), as they appear, one FREE copy of EVERY new AK Press title. Secondly, they are also entitled to a 10% discount on EVERYTHING featured in the AK Press distribution catalog—or on our website—on ANY and EVERY order. We also have a program where individuals or groups can sponsor a whole book.

PLEASE CONTACT US FOR MORE DETAILS:

AK Press
674-A 23rd Street
Oakland, CA 94612
akpress@akpress.org
www.akpress.org

AK Press
PO Box 12766
Edinburgh, Scotland EH8, 9YE
ak@akedin.demon.co.uk
www.akuk.com

ALSO AVAILABLE FROM AK PRESS

BOOKS

DWIGHT ABBOTT – I Cried, You Didn't Listen

MARTHA ACKELSBERG – Free Women of Spain

KATHY ACKER – Pussycat Fever

MICHAEL ALBERT – Moving Forward: Program for a Participatory Economy

JOEL ANDREAS – Addicted to War: Why the U.S. Can't Kick Militarism

JOEL ANDREAS – Adicto a la Guerra: Por que EEUU no Puede LIbrarse del Militarismo

PAUL AVRICH – Anarchist Voices

PAUL AVRICH – The Modern School Movement: Anarchism and Education in the United States

PAUL AVRICH – Russian Anarchists

DAN BERGER – Outlaws of America

ALEXANDER BERKMAN – What is Anarchism?

ALEXANDER BERKMAN – The Blast: The Complete Collection

STEVE BEST & ANTHONY J. NOCELLA II – Igniting A Revolution: Voices in Defense of Mother Earth

HAKIM BEY – Immediatism

JANET BIEHL & PETER STAUDENMAIER – Ecofascism: Lessons From The German Experience

BIOTIC BAKING BRIGADE – Pie Any Means Necessary: The Biotic Baking Brigade Cookbook

JACK BLACK – You Can't Win

MURRAY BOOKCHIN – Anarchism, Marxism, and the Future of the Left

MURRAY BOOKCHIN – Ecology of Freedom

MURRAY BOOKCHIN – Post-Scarcity Anarchism

MURRAY BOOKCHIN – Social Anarchism or Lifestyle Anarchism: An Unbridge-able Chasm

MURRAY BOOKCHIN – Spanish Anarchists: The Heroic Years 1868–1936, The

MURRAY BOOKCHIN – To Remember Spain: The Anarchist and Syndicalist Revolution of 1936

MURRAY BOOKCHIN – Which Way for the Ecology Movement?

MAURICE BRINTON – For Workers' Power

DANNY BURNS – Poll Tax Rebellion

MAT CALLAHAN – The Trouble With Music

CHRIS CARLSSON – Critical Mass: Bicycling's Defiant Celebration

JAMES CARR – Bad

NOAM CHOMSKY – At War With Asia

NOAM CHOMSKY – Chomsky on Anarchism

NOAM CHOMSKY – Language and Politics

NOAM CHOMSKY – Radical Priorities

WARD CHURCHILL – On the Justice of Roosting Chickens

WARD CHURCHILL – Pacifism as Pathology

WARD CHURCHILL – Since Predator Came

HARRY CLEAVER – Reading Capital Politically

ALEXANDER COCKBURN & JEFFREY ST. CLAIR (ed.) – Dime's Worth of Difference

ALEXANDER COCKBURN & JEFFREY ST. CLAIR – End Times

ALEXANDER COCKBURN & JEFFREY ST. CLAIR (ed.) – Politics of Anti-Semitism, The

ALEXANDER COCKBURN & JEFFREY ST. CLAIR (ed.) – Serpents in the

Garden
DANIEL & GABRIEL COHN-BENDIT – Obsolete Communism: The Left-Wing Alternative
EG SMITH COLLECTIVE – Animal Ingredients A–Z (3rd edition)
VOLTAIRINE de CLEYRE –Voltarine de Cleyre Reader
HUNTER CUTTING & MAKANI THEMBA-NIXON – Talking the Walk: A Communications Guide for Racial Justice
HOWARD EHRLICH – Reinventing Anarchy, Again
SIMON FORD – Realization and Suppression of the Situationist International: An Annotated Bibliography 1972–1992
BENJAMIN FRANKS – Rebel Alliances
YVES FREMION & VOLNY – Orgasms of History: 3000 Years of Spontaneous Revolt
EMMA GOLDMAN –Vision on Fire
BERNARD GOLDSTEIN – Five Years in the Warsaw Ghetto
DAVID GRAEBER & STEVPHEN SHUKAITIS – Constituent Imagination
DANIEL GUÉRIN – No Gods, No Masters
AGUSTIN GUILLAMON – Friends Of Durruti Group, 1937–1939, The
ANN HANSEN – Direct Action: Memoirs Of An Urban Guerilla
WILLIAM HERRICK – Jumping the Line: The Adventures and Misadventures of an American Radical
FRED HO – Legacy to Liberation: Politics & Culture of Revolutionary Asian/Pacific America
STEWART HOME – Neoism, Plagiarism & Praxis
STEWART HOME – Neoist Manifestos / The Art Strike Papers
STEWART HOME – No Pity
STEWART HOME – Red London
GEORGY KATSIAFICAS – The Subversion of Politics
KATHY KELLY – Other Lands Have Dreams: From Baghdad to Pekin Prison
JAMES KELMAN – Some Recent Attacks: Essays Cultural And Political
KEN KNABB – Complete Cinematic Works of Guy Debord
KATYA KOMISARUK – Beat the Heat: How to Handle Encounters With Law Enforcement
MACPHEE & ERIK REULAND – Realizing the Impossible
RICARDO FLORES MAGÓN – Dreams of Freedom: A Ricardo Flores Magón Reader
NESTOR MAKHNO – Struggle Against The State & Other Essays, The
G.A. MATIASZ – End Time
CHERIE MATRIX – Tales From the Clit
ALBERT MELTZER – Anarchism: Arguments For & Against
ALBERT MELTZER – I Couldn't Paint Golden Angels
RAY MURPHY – Siege Of Gresham
NORMAN NAWROCKI – Rebel Moon
MICHAEL NEUMANN – The Case Against Israel
HENRY NORMAL – Map of Heaven, A
HENRY NORMAL – Dream Ticket
HENRY NORMAL – Fifteenth of February
HENRY NORMAL – Third Person
FIONBARRA O'DOCHARTAIGH – Ulster's White Negroes: From Civil Rights To Insurrection
DAN O'MAHONY – Four Letter World
CRAIG O'HARA – Philosophy Of Punk, The

ANTON PANNEKOEK – Workers' Councils
ABEL PAZ – Durruti in the Spanish Revolution
BEN REITMAN – Sister of the Road: The Autobiography of Boxcar Bertha
PENNY RIMBAUD – Diamond Signature, The
PENNY RIMBAUD – Shibboleth: My Revolting Life
RUDOLF ROCKER – Anarcho-Syndicalism
RUDOLF ROCKER – London Years, The
RAMOR RYAN – Clandestines
RON SAKOLSKY & STEPHEN DUNIFER – Seizing the Airwaves: A Free Radio Handbook
ROY SAN FILIPPO – New World In Our Hearts: 8 Years of Writings from the Love and Rage Revolutionary Anarchist Federation, A
MARINA SITRIN – Horizontalism: Voices of Popular Power in Argentina
ALEXANDRE SKIRDA – Facing the Enemy: A History Of Anarchist Organisation From Proudhon To May 1968
ALEXANDRE SKIRDA – Nestor Makhno – Anarchy's Cossack
VALERIE SOLANAS – Scum Manifesto
CJ STONE – Housing Benefit Hill & Other Places
ANTONIO TELLEZ – Sabate: Guerilla Extraordinary
MICHAEL TOBIAS – Rage and Reason
TOM VAGUE – Anarchy in the UK: The Angry Brigade
TOM VAGUE – Great British Mistake, The
TOM VAGUE – Televisionaries
JAN VALTIN – Out of the Night
RAOUL VANEIGEM – Cavalier History Of Surrealism, A
FRANCOIS EUGENE VIDOCQ – Memoirs of Vidocq: Master of Crime
MARK J WHITE – Idol Killing, An
JOHN YATES – Controlled Flight Into Terrain
JOHN YATES – September Commando
BENJAMIN ZEPHANIAH – Little Book of Vegan Poems
BENJAMIN ZEPHANIAH – School's Out
HELLO – 2/15: The Day The World Said NO To War
DARK STAR COLLECTIVE – Beneath the Paving Stones: Situationists and the Beach, May 68
DARK STAR COLLECTIVE – Quiet Rumours: An Anarcha-Feminist Reader
ANONYMOUS – Test Card F
CLASS WAR FEDERATION – Unfinished Business: The Politics of Class War

CDS

THE EX – 1936: The Spanish Revolution
MUMIA ABU JAMAL   175 Progress Drive
MUMIA ABU JAMAL – All Things Censored Vol.1
MUMIA ABU JAMAL – Spoken Word
FREEDOM ARCHIVES – Chile: Promise of Freedom
FREEDOM ARCHIVES – Prisons on Fire: George Jackson, Attica & Black Liberation
FREEDOM ARCHIVES – Robert F. Williams: Self Respect, Self Defense, & Self Determination
JUDI BARI – Who Bombed Judi Bari?
JELLO BIAFRA – Become the Media
JELLO BIAFRA – Beyond The Valley of the Gift Police
JELLO BIAFRA – High Priest of Harmful

JELLO BIAFRA – I Blow Minds For A Living
JELLO BIAFRA – If Evolution Is Outlawed
JELLO BIAFRA – In the Grip of Official Treason
JELLO BIAFRA – Machine Gun In The Clown's Hand
JELLO BIAFRA – No More Cocoons
NOAM CHOMSKY – American Addiction, An
NOAM CHOMSKY – Case Studies in Hypocrisy
NOAM CHOMSKY – Emerging Framework of World Power
NOAM CHOMSKY – Free Market Fantasies
NOAM CHOMSKY – Imperial Presidency, The
NOAM CHOMSKY – New War On Terrorism: Fact And Fiction
NOAM CHOMSKY – Propaganda and Control of the Public Mind
NOAM CHOMSKY – Prospects for Democracy
NOAM CHOMSKY/CHUMBAWAMBA – For A Free Humanity: For Anarchy
WARD CHURCHILL – Doing Time: The Politics of Imprisonment
WARD CHURCHILL – In A Pig's Eye
WARD CHURCHILL – Life in Occupied America
WARD CHURCHILL – Pacifism and Pathology in the American Left
ALEXANDER COCKBURN – Beating the Devil
ANGELA DAVIS – Prison Industrial Complex, The
NORMAN FINKELSTEIN – An Issue of Justice
ROBERT FISK – War, Journalism, and the Middle East
JAMES KELMAN – Seven Stories
TOM LEONARD – Nora's Place and Other Poems 1965–99
CASEY NEILL – Memory Against Forgetting
CHRISTIAN PARENTI – Taking Liberties
UTAH PHILLIPS – I've Got To know
UTAH PHILLIPS – Starlight on the Rails CD box set
DAVID ROVICS – Behind the Barricades: Best of David Rovics
ARUNDHATI ROY – Come September
VARIOUS – Better Read Than Dead
VARIOUS – Less Rock, More Talk
VARIOUS – Mob Action Against the State: Collected Speeches from the Bay Area
Anarchist Bookfair
VARIOUS – Monkeywrenching the New World Order
VARIOUS – Return of the Read Menace
HOWARD ZINN – Artists In A Time of War
HOWARD ZINN – Heroes and Martyrs: Emma Goldman, Sacco & Vanzetti, and
the Revolutionary Struggle
HOWARD ZINN – People's History of the United States: A Lecture at Reed College, A
HOWARD ZINN – People's History Project
HOWARD ZINN – Stories Hollywood Never Tells

DVDS
NOAM CHOMSKY – Distorted Morality
NOAM CHOMSKY – Imperial Grand Strategy
STEVEN FISCHLER & JOEL SUCHER – Anarchism in America
ROZ PAYNE – What We Want, What We Believe
ARUNDHATI ROY – Instant Mix Imperial Democracy
HOWARD ZINN – Readings from Voices of a People's History

Advance praise for: *The Price of Fire*

"With lively narrative and unpretentious but intelligent analysis, Dangl presents a compelling critique of our backwards global system wherein nations as rich in natural resources as Bolivia are also the poorest. But *The Price of Fire* is not yet another bleak 'tell-all' account of globalization, its pages are filled with stories of resistance, struggle and, above all, hope."
Teo Ballvé—editor of the *NACLA Report on the Americas* and co-editor of *Dispatches from Latin America: On the Frontlines Against Neoliberalism*

"Ben Dangl takes the reader on an unforgettable and inspiring journey through Bolivia and neighboring countries, providing a window on the revolutionary struggles of the poor and dispossessed and particularly on the resurgence of indigenous resistance and leadership."
Roxanne Dunbar-Ortiz, author of *Blood on the Border: A Memoir of the Contra War*

"Most Americans know nothing of Bolivia, an ignorance that only plays into the hands of empire. Ben Dangl's book is both informative and inspiring, a cure for the apathy that grows from that ignorance. A must read for those already interested in solidarity with Latin America and indigenous people."
Tom Hayden, author of *The Zapatista Reader* and *Street Wars*, among other works

"Ben Dangl has found himself under the skin of the Bolivian freedom struggle: he accurately represents its constraints, its opportunities and its hopes. On your feet, Bolivia! We're ready to march with you."
Vijay Prashad, author of *The Darker Nations: A People's History of the Third World*

"Ben Dangl's *The Price of Fire* documents how the people of Bolivia, along with their comrades in other Latin American countries, are waging a global war against terror—against the terror of not having enough food to eat, the terror of watching children descend into mines to emerge old and wasted, and the terror of Bechtel and the IMF. With great empathy and lucid prose, Dangl captures the exemplary courage that has put Latin America in the vanguard of the new internationalism and has made it one of the few bright spots on an otherwise dismal global landscape."
Greg Grandin, author of *Empire's Workshop: Latin America, the United States, and the Rise of the New Imperialism*

"*The Price of Fire* by Ben Dangl informs, outrages, and builds hope. People's movements for societal betterment in South America are an inspiration for human rights activists worldwide and Dangl gives us a full serving of encouragement and hope. He documents how historical imperialism, dominated by US corporate/government capital interests, is being successfully challenged by indigenous activists. *Price of Fire* is the story of cultural resistance from the street to international geo-political alliances. I highly recommend this book for working people, students, and radical democrats to hear the voices of South American people and their chronicle of grassroots democratic empowerment.
Peter Phillips, Professor of Sociology, Sonoma State University, Director Project Censored, and co-editor with Dennis Loo of *Impeach the President: The Case Against Bush and Cheney*